PS 2638 .P436 2003
Peeples, Scott.
The afterlife of Edgar Allan
 Poe

DATE DUE

The Afterlife of Edgar Allan Poe

Studies in American Literature and Culture:
Literary Criticism in Perspective

About *Literary Criticism in Perspective*

Books in the series *Literary Criticism in Perspective* trace literary scholarship and criticism on major and neglected writers alike, or on a single major work, a group of writers, a literary school or movement. In so doing the authors — authorities on the topic in question who are also well-versed in the principles and history of literary criticism — address a readership consisting of scholars, students of literature at the graduate and undergraduate level, and the general reader. One of the primary purposes of the series is to illuminate the nature of literary criticism itself, to gauge the influence of social and historic currents on aesthetic judgments once thought objective and normative.

The Afterlife of Edgar Allan Poe

Scott Peeples

CAMDEN HOUSE

First published 2004
by Camden House

Camden House is an imprint of Boydell & Brewer Inc.
668 Mt. Hope Avenue, Rochester, NY 14620, USA
and of Boydell & Brewer Limited
PO Box 9, Woodbridge, Suffolk IP12 3DF, UK

ISBN: 1–57113–218–X

Library of Congress Cataloging-in-Publication Data

Peeples, Scott.
    The afterlife of Edgar Allan Poe / Scott Peeples
        p. cm. — (Studies in American literature and culture. Literary criti-
cism in perspective)
Includes bibliographical references and index.
ISBN 1–57113–218–X (Hardcover: acid-free paper)
    1. Poe, Edgar Allan, 1809–1849 — Criticism and interpretation —
History.   2. Fantasy literature, American — History and criticism —
Theory, etc.   I. Title. II. Series

PS2638.P436 2003
818'.309 — dc22

                                                           2003017325

A catalogue record for this title is available from the British Library.

This publication is printed on acid-free paper.
Printed in the United States of America.

In memory of my parents

Contents

Preface

TO DISCUSS POE'S AFTERLIFE is really to discuss his after*lives*, since he takes so many forms in literary criticism and other media. That's true of any famous, dead author, but the multiplicity of after*lives* is particularly pronounced in Poe's case, partly because he is quite possibly America's most famous literary figure. The films, the countless illustrated editions and adaptations of his work, the NFL team named after his best-known poem, the tributes of mystery writers and rock musicians, the annual newspaper articles about the mysterious visitor to his grave or the latest theory of his death all keep Poe in the public eye. Even so, the Poe of 1900 differs somewhat from the Poe of 1950 or the Poe of 2003, and the Poe of American International horror films differs from the Poe who is alluded to in the novels of Paul Auster and Don DeLillo. There is a similar variety of Poes in literary criticism: the romantic Southern outcast, the patron saint of the French symbolists, the hack, the test case for Freudian psychoanalysis, the proto-deconstructionist, the racist, the anti-racist, and so on. For over 150 years, critics have been arguing not so much about who Poe was but about what "Poe" is — that is to say, how to interpret this enormous jumble of biographical and historical documents as well as poems, fictions, essays and reviews, how to give coherence to a mass of often contradictory and incomplete texts.

This book is not another attempt to provide that coherence, but rather a description of the most influential and widely debated ways of seeing Poe, a general survey of Poe studies from Griswold's obituary to the year 2002. Like any survey, it is incomplete: my goal was to represent large trends through representative works of criticism and, in the last chapter, plays, fiction, films, and graphic art. I have tried to be more of a storyteller than a bibliographer, often leaving things out in order to make the story coherent but trying earnestly to provide reliable narration. For instance, I say almost nothing in the following chapters about the heroic editorial and bibliographic work of Thomas Ollive Mabbott and Burton R. Pollin, but their contributions to the field are enormous. I have similarly neglected the large body of work focusing on Poe's literary sources and relationships with other writers, an area of research that has produced landmark studies such as Perry Miller's *The Raven and the Whale* (1956), Sidney P. Moss's *Poe's Literary Battles* (1963), and Michael Allen's *Poe and the British Magazine Tradition* (1969). I also acknowledge that I have focused almost exclusively on Anglophone and Francophone Poe criticism, mainly to make the project manageable.

I have tried, then, to write an accessible introduction to Poe studies and a history of a major author's reception, providing in the process a broad overview of twentieth-century critical trends. The critical traditions that I've organized these chapters around obviously overlap in time, but I have tried to provide a sense of chronology nonetheless. Chapter 1 traces Poe's reputation in the United States from his death in 1849 to the 1910s, when psychoanalytic readings began to appear. Chapter 2 focuses on those readings, ranging from Lorine Pruette's vaguely Freudian analysis of Poe in 1920 to Jacques Lacan's seminar on "The Purloined Letter" and the responses it generated. From the 1930s to the 1960s, formalist readings of Poe competed with psychoanalytic interpretations even as the two "schools" shared a number of assumptions and techniques. Chapter 3 starts with the sometimes hostile response to Poe by American New Critics before surveying some of the most influential formalist and philosophical readings of the mid-twentieth century and the deconstructive approaches to Poe of the 1970s and 1980s. Chapter 4 traces the countertradition of historical and sociological scholarship on Poe, particularly analyses focused on race and gender, which became more prevalent and more sophisticated in the 1980s and 1990s. Finally, in chapter 5 I describe Poe's changing image in American popular culture, focusing on melodramatic plays written early in the century, horror films and comic books, detective fiction, and avant-garde fiction and film.

I remember when I took my first course in literary criticism in the late 1980s getting the impression that "schools" of criticism were the academic equivalents of political parties, or possibly street gangs. You chose your club, swore allegiance, and at best peacefully coexisted with rival groups. Sometimes a new faction would rise to power and another would fall, but there was very little mixing, and it was a wonder that, say, a deconstructionist could bear to sit at the same conference table as a

Marxist. I don't mean to discount the vehemence of methodological debates, nor am I attempting to position myself above or outside the politics of theory and interpretation. I merely want to suggest that Poe scholarship, especially that of the last ten or fifteen years, is much more fluid than critical categories suggest, and the best new readings of texts draw on various critical traditions. So while I have organized the middle three chapters of this book around critical traditions, that process — deciding where to put what — has made me more aware that those traditions do not create anything like strict categories.

Thus the argument that runs through the story told in this book (particularly the first four chapters) is that the enterprise of understanding "Poe" is best understood not in terms of fixed, eternal schools or methodologies but rather in terms of historical evolution. Broadly speaking, we start with an obsessive search for the "real" biographical Poe, a search that begins with the Ludwig obituary in 1849, continues through the early Freudian readings of the 1920s and 1930s, and resurfaces in the debate concerning Poe's personal racism (as well as in twentieth-century popular culture). From there, we move on to psychological readings whose aim is to explain traits of human consciousness generally rather than Poe's personality, as well as humanist new criticism that also focuses on Poe's insights into human behavior and values generally. Even as more recent critics demonstrate the limitations of any universalizing claims about human consciousness and values, showing how differently literary works register when read in the historical contexts of antebellum America and when read by women, they build on the formalists' and psychoanalytic readers' habits of textual explication, of making coherent that which only seemed inscrutable. Again, there are certainly irreconcilable differences to be found between readings, but they are just as likely, if not more likely, to occur between writers from similar theoretical backgrounds as they are between writers of different schools. More often, new arguments build on, without flatly contradicting, old ones, and a reader can best appreciate a challenging new essay on, say, "William Wilson" in light of what it's challenging, but simultaneously absorbing — that is, in light of the critical history.

While I have not assumed that readers will bring any knowledge of literary theory or criticism to this book, I do expect that anyone interested in my topic is already familiar with Poe's major writings. While I do

remind readers of details from the stories that become points of contention among literary critics, to provide summaries of stories and poems
would be awkward and digressive in a book that is ultimately not about
Poe but about how people interpret Poe. Besides, there is no substitute
for reading or rereading "The Fall of the House of Usher" or "The
Purloined Letter."

I would like to acknowledge the assistance I received in this project
from research grants provided by the College of Charleston, as well as the
encouragement of my colleagues and students. The College of Charleston
Library's interlibrary loan staff, especially Michael Phillips, Astra Gleason,
and Eliza Glaze, managed to get virtually every book and article I needed
over the past four years. Richard Kopley made a number of helpful sug-
gestions to the manuscript, and Simon Lewis helped me work through
several rough spots. Jim Walker and Jim Hardin at Camden House were
unfailingly patient and encouraging. *Biography: An Interdisciplinary Quarterly* granted permission for my reuse of material that appeared there in a
1995 article, and Mike Keith graciously allowed me to use his collage for
the book jacket. Finally, my wife Nancy and my son Alex have supported
this project every day; my deepest gratitude is to them.

S. P.
June 2003
Charleston, SC

1: The Man That Was Used Up: Poe's Place in American Literature, 1849–1909

Edgar Allan Poe is dead.
He died in Baltimore the day before yesterday.
This announcement will startle many,
but few will be grieved by it.

THESE INFAMOUS WORDS, written by the Rev. Rufus Wilmot Griswold and published in the *New York Tribune* on October 9, 1849, two days after Poe's death, mark the beginning of Poe's afterlife. The *Baltimore Sun* had reported Poe's death a day earlier, and had also cast doubt on how fondly Poe would be remembered, declaring that this news "will cause poignant regret among all who admire genius, and have sympathy for the frailties too often attending it" (A. H. Quinn 644). Similarly, the *New York Journal of Commerce* on October 9 hoped that recollection of everything about him other than his "great ability" would be "lost now, and buried with him in the grave" (Walker, *Critical* 303).[1] But it was Griswold, the Poe-lover's arch villain, who deserves credit for assuring that Poe would have an afterlife worth writing a book about. The flat declamation of Ludwig's opening sentences, more like the opening lines of a hard-boiled detective novel than an obituary, evokes the unsentimental message, but he loosens up his prose style to explain why few will be grieved:

> The poet was known, personally or by reputation, in all this country;
> he had readers in England, and in several of the states of Continental
> Europe; but he had few or no friends; and the regrets of his death will
> be suggested principally by the consideration that in him literary art lost
> one of its most brilliant and erratic stars. (Walker, *Critical* 294)

Here Ludwig sets the terms of debate over Poe's reputation that dominated nineteenth-century commentary on him, and that persist to this day: that Poe was known in America but actually read in Europe; that he was brilliant but erratic and (deservedly) friendless. One hundred years after "Ludwig," European critics would still wonder why Poe was not read with more sympathy by American critics, and American critics would ask why he was so revered in France.[2]

Throughout the second half of the nineteenth century, the period this chapter examines, even the most hostile critics and biographers never denied Poe's brilliance or genius; instead, they denied that he possessed the human sympathy that would make his work live — a man who had no friends could not inspire real emotion through his writing, or as James Russell Lowell had famously put it the year before Poe's death, "The heart somehow seems all squeezed out by the mind" (142). Meanwhile, Poe partisans produced scrap after scrap of evidence that he *did* have friends, that he was devoted to his wife and his mother-in-law, that he was more often sober than drunk, more often honorable than devious.

From his cold announcement of Poe's death Griswold proceeded to a largely erroneous account of Poe's life, based partly on false information given to him by Poe, and then to a general character assassination, describing Poe as dishonest, choleric, conceited, crudely ambitious, and cynical. A few of Poe's friends and admirers, most notably Nathaniel Parker Willis, one of the most popular American writers at mid-century, defended him in print, and a series of testimonials to Poe's character — most of them favorable — appeared over the next several months, as the Ludwig article was widely reprinted and the first volumes of Poe's collected works were issued. Susan Archer Talley, Henry Beck Hirst, Lambert Wilmer, and John Neal, all writers who had known Poe, and magazine mogul and onetime Poe employer George Rex Graham came to his defense, either by excusing his bad behavior or recalling instances of good behavior. Meanwhile, Lewis Gaylord Clark, longtime editor of the *Knickerbocker* magazine and one of Poe's bitterest enemies, backed up Ludwig's assessment of Poe as a brilliant writer but a disreputable human being, and C. F. Briggs, who was briefly Poe's partner as coeditor and proprietor of the *Broadway Journal,* argued that Poe's associates were trying to hide his personal failings. Other commentators sought some kind of middle ground, but their efforts ultimately reinforced Griswold's portrait. For instance, John R. Thompson, writing in the *Southern Literary Messenger,* paid tribute to Poe's fearless literary criticism by declaring, "Now that he is gone, the vast multitude of blockheads may breathe again" (Walker, *Critical* 326), but also echoed Ludwig's claim that Poe was virtually friendless: "The untimely death of Mr. Poe occasioned a very general feeling of regret, although little genuine sorrow was called forth by it, out of the narrow circle of his relatives" (328). George Ripley paid tribute to Poe's genius, but after discussing his character concluded that "[t]he effect of his writings is like breathing the air of a charnel house" (334). John Daniel, clearly in awe of Poe, nonetheless claimed that his genius was so powerful that Poe could not rein it in, causing him to live and write desperately: "The majority of his prose writings are the children of want and dyspepsia, of printer's devils and blue devils" (357).

Thus, the great Poe biographer Arthur Hobson Quinn reasonably asserted that "[t]he damage [Griswold's] article did to Poe's reputation is incalculable" (647). The Ludwig obituary in itself probably would not have continued to generate controversy for the rest of the century; however, Griswold was handed an opportunity to expand and greatly extend the distribution of his defamation when Poe's mother-in-law, Maria Clemm, arranged for him to collect and edit Poe's works, even assigning him the legal publication rights. The first volume of Griswold's edition, published in January of 1850, contained only Willis's response to the Ludwig article and a biographical essay by Lowell, originally published in 1845 but heavily revised, as Quinn points out, to reflect less favorably on Poe, and Volume 2 contained no introductory essays.[3] Griswold added his own memoir to Volume 3, published in September of 1850, in which he expanded his attack on Poe's character.

Killis Campbell in 1919 and Quinn in 1941 provided thorough reviews of Griswold's lies, forgeries, and distortions. Both suggest that the clear-cut lies are on the whole less harmful than the exaggerations, assumptions, and negative spin Griswold put on the materials he had to work with, including personal memories and rumors as well as documents. For example, on the basis of letters and testimony from people who were there, it is clear that in 1848, the year after his wife's death, Poe was engaged to the poet Sarah Helen Whitman, that her mother disapproved, and that the engagement was called off after Poe broke a pledge to stay sober.[4] Griswold, however, invents a conversation between Poe and "an acquaintance in New York" in which Poe is congratulated on his upcoming marriage, to which he replies, "It is a mistake: I am not going to be married." In Griswold's version, Poe "left town the same evening, and the next day was reeling through the streets of the city which was the lady's home [Providence], and in the evening — that should have been the evening before the bridal — in his drunkenness he committed at her house such outrages as made necessary a summons of the police." In addition to fabrications of this kind, Griswold forged parts of letters from Poe to reflect well on himself, and his general statements about Poe's character are incredibly harsh: Poe, he claims, "exhibits scarcely any virtue in either his life or his writings" (A. H. Quinn 672–73).

Generations of readers have wondered how someone so hostile to Poe got the job of compiling an authorized edition of his works. Griswold and Maria Clemm both claimed that Poe left written instructions that Griswold act as Poe's "literary executor," but no letter in Poe's handwriting to this effect has ever been located. It is possible that, despite their grudges against each other, Poe knew that Griswold, who had succeeded him as editor of *Graham's Magazine* and who had since edited two important poetry anthologies, was a competent editor and the kind of insider who could find a publisher for, and perhaps even promote, his collected works. If this is the case, it is still worth noting that, according to Mrs. Clemm, Poe authorized not Griswold but Willis to write his biography. Recently, Burton Pollin has questioned the truth of Clemm's and Griswold's claims, citing the lack of documentary evidence for Poe's request and contending that Clemm conspired with the man she must have known to be the author of the "Ludwig" obituary ("Maria Clemm" 211–24).

Poe may or may not have requested Griswold as his literary executor, but one thing is certain: both Poe and Griswold would have wanted his collected works to sell. The idea of appending a defamatory description of the author to his collected works may sound perverse, but it worked. Indeed, Poe had antagonized powerful editors and authors throughout his career, and had satirized the practice in his story "The Literary Life of Thingum Bob, Esq.," in which a "magazinist" rises to the top of his profession by picking fights with his rivals; he knew the value of negative publicity. While it still seems unlikely that Poe would have actually wanted Griswold to malign him when he died, he might have appreciated his rival's cunning. E. Clarence Stedman, who coedited a collection of Poe's works, argued in an 1880 *Scribner's* article that Poe "builded better than he knew" when he chose Griswold to edit his collected works for the very reason that Griswold generated interest in the supposedly depraved poet; furthermore, Griswold "paid an unstinted tribute to Poe's genius, and this was the only concession which Poe himself would care to demand" (122). In his book *Literary Blasphemies* (1927), Ernest Boyd concurred:

> The author of "The Raven" and "Annabel Lee" would have a page or two in the anthologies, and the creator of Dupin would be mentioned as the father of the modern detective story, but Poe without Griswold would be half forgotten as an American Tieck or an E. T. A. Hoffmann. . . . In the Poe universe Voltaire's phrase must be adapted. If there were no Griswold, it would be necessary to invent one. (164)

Griswold peddled his edition of Poe to several publishers before coming to terms with J. S. Redfield, whose firm put Poe's works through nineteen reprintings over the next fifteen years. According the James C. Derby, the four-volume edition sold about fifteen hundred copies per year (587), which seems reasonable given the pace at which it was reprinted.[5] While fifteen hundred copies per year is unspectacular in comparison with best-selling novels of the period like Fanny Fern's *Ruth Hall,* which sold fifty thousand copies in eight months (Hart 94), it represents very respectable (and obviously steady) sales for a writer's collected works, and is even more impressive when we consider the fact that Poe's 1845 *Tales,* the most commercially successful book of his career, went through only one print run of fifteen hundred (Ostrom 5).

Griswold was undoubtedly malicious in his obituary and memoir, and his distortions and lies tainted thousands of readers' impressions of Poe; and yet, although Boyd overstates the case, I believe Griswold did more good than harm to Poe's long-term popularity by stimulating a character debate that kept people writing about Poe for decades, keeping prospective readers curious and thereby keeping Poe very much in print.[6] He also helped to separate — just two days after Poe's death — the posthumous, pop-culture Poe from the actual, flesh-and-blood Poe. In writing his obituary, Griswold took a devious short-cut, describing Poe by quoting at length from Edward Bulwer-Lytton's novel *The Caxtons.* In fact, some of the worst things Griswold had to say about Poe were actually said by Bulwer-Lytton's narrator about the character Francis Vivian; for instance, "Irascible, envious ["arrogant" in *The Caxtons*] — bad enough, but not the worst, for these salient angles were all varnished over with a cold repellent cynicism, his passions vented themselves into sneers" (Walker, *Critical* 300). Griswold did attribute his long quotation to Bulwer-Lytton, but he dropped the quotation marks in the Memoir (as Quinn points out); the words were often quoted by others as the opinion of Poe's literary executor himself, and the length and precision of the description of Vivian tended to blur such distinctions even further.[7] More important for my focus on Poe's afterlife is the simple fact that what the public knew as "Poe," just two days after his death, was already literally a fiction, in that the words used to describe him were written about a character in a novel. To a great extent all famous people play fictional public roles, even when they are still living but especially after their deaths, when books, biopics, and the A&E network turn their lives into stories. But with Poe this story-telling and mythologizing has been unusually intense, because not only the facts of Poe's life but the very essence of his personality have been subject to debate from the beginning (debate that has not been limited to biographers and scholars), and because Poe's writing is always intriguingly autobiographical and yet never truly autobiographical, inviting intertextual readings of the Poe canon and the Poe legend.

Throughout the 1850s pundits and acquaintances of Poe debated the character issue in often hyperbolic terms, some completely whitewashing Poe and others exceeding Griswold in their contempt. This running commentary has been surveyed elsewhere, but a few examples are worth mentioning here.[8] In 1852 Richard Henry Stoddard, who would later edit Poe's collected works, wrote (anonymously) a brief biography in the mode of temperance fiction for the *National Magazine* in which the subject's name was withheld until the final sentence.[9] Stoddard's orphan boy is taken in by a good-hearted, wealthy merchant and given every advantage, but throughout his life he repeatedly squanders his money and reputation, as well as his literary talent, drinking his way to an early grave. With the final sentence, Stoddard reveals the debauchee's identity: "READER, — What you have read is no fiction. Not a single circumstance here related, not a solitary event here recorded, but happened to EDGAR ALLAN POE, one of the most popular and imaginative of writers" (365). Poe had in fact been a frequent subject of temperance articles while he was alive, and given the circumstances surrounding his death, it is not surprising that numerous temperance journals, whose influence peaked during this period, presented Poe's life as a cautionary tale.[10]

Poe's animosity toward the New England literary establishment haunted him in his afterlife as well. In 1856 the Boston-based *North*

American Review, one of the oldest and most prestigious journals in America, gave Redfield's second printing of Poe's works an extensive (eleven thousand-word) review, praising much of Poe's fiction, taking issue with his poetic theory and to claims that he was a great poet, and pointing out both the strengths and the weaknesses of his literary criticism. While the *North American* critic focuses more on Poe's literary output than on his life, he finds Poe's "critical writings" and his "personal character" to be inseparable, and he devotes several pages to an account of Poe's life lifted almost entirely from Griswold. He then imagines the ongoing debate over Poe's character as a courtroom trial, with N. P. Willis as defense attorney and Griswold as the prosecution. The only witnesses for the defense are Frances Osgood, a poet with whom Poe had carried on an intense flirtation in the mid-1840s (and whom Griswold had quoted in his Memoir), and his mother-in-law, Maria Clemm. The prosecution's long list includes Poe himself, for he admitted to "deliberate falsehood, for the sake of sustaining appearances; of insulting a respectful [Boston] audience, and a respectable literary association, solely in order to avenge himself on a small clique, who he fancied had slighted him; of making public, unjust, and untrue allegations against an individual, without any evidence," and so on (453). The verdict predictably goes against Poe, for the testimony of Osgood and Clemm, according to the *North American,* attests more to their virtue than to his. Ultimately, this judge concludes not only that Griswold's description of Poe is accurate, but that "[i]f the human brain is indeed a palimpsest . . . then most assuredly should we pray for some more potent chemistry to blot out from our brain-roll for ever . . . the greater part of what has been inscribed on it by the ghastly and charnel-hued pen of Edgar Allan Poe. Rather than remember all, we would choose to forget all that he has ever written" (455). What Dudley Hutcherson observed in his 1942 survey of nineteenth-century criticism on Poe is especially true of the 1850s: "[T]he striking characteristic of nearly all of this discussion was the inability of the authors to consider artistic matters without passing judgment also upon the personal failings which, largely through the initial instruction of Griswold, Poe was believed to have possessed" (216). Furthermore, by depicting Poe's life as a cautionary tale appropriate for Sunday School books or representing his character as the material for courtroom drama, these early commentators helped make Poe a better-known character than any of his fictional creations, establishing for him a place in American popular culture that transcends his work to a degree that has been matched only by Mark Twain and Ernest Hemingway.

Like their American counterparts, British magazines such as *Tait's* and *Chambers's Edinburgh Journal,* reviewing the Redfield edition, would summarize Griswold's Memoir, taking his "facts" at face value, and add their own appraisals of the relationship between the life and the writing. One *Chambers's* reviewer remarked, "It is more than doubtful whether the daring recklessness, the wild licence with which men like Poe sported with the responsibilities of life, have not done far more for Satan, than in their highest and purest works they have done for man. And yet the poetry of this poor inebriate is free from aught of that viciousness which marked his life; for the most part, it is the mournful wail of one whose natural endowments were never called into play without uttering unconsciously deep and touching sorrow over the wreck of the spirit of which they formed a part" ("Life" 138). Similarly, George Gilfillan, in a *London Critic* essay that was reprinted at least three times in the United States, called Poe "probably *the* most worthless and wicked of all his fraternity" of poets and, in closing the biographical portion of his essay, concluded, "He died, as he had lived, a raving, cursing, self-condemned, conscious cross between the fiend and the genius, believing nothing, hoping nothing, loving nothing, fearing nothing" (157).

The *North American*'s claims notwithstanding, Poe did have defenders other than his mother-in-law and Frances Osgood. Graham, for instance, published another sympathetic article in his magazine in 1854, "The Genius and Characteristics of the Late Edgar Allan Poe," in which he admits Poe's personal failings — with emphasis on the alcoholism — but excuses them on the grounds of Poe's poverty and the fact that his genius "was not such as to command a ready or lucrative market" (220). Furthermore, Graham made the unusual claim that Poe's vices "were in no wise reflected in or connected with his writings" (219). Other Poe partisans were more lavish in their praise and character defense. *Russell's Magazine,* published in Charleston, South Carolina, published a laughably overwrought tribute to Poe by J. Wood Davidson in 1856: "His expansive brow declared the princely power of intellect that throbbed and struggled within"; "The delicacy and accuracy of his aesthetical nature made him keenly alive to beauty in its omniscient distinctness"

(163). Davidson responds directly to the *North American Review,* and concludes by accepting as evidence of Poe's good heart the testimony of Osgood and Clemm. Another Poe partisan, Sarah Helen Whitman, published a short book, *Edgar Poe and His Critics,* in 1860, in which she politely argued against the Griswoldian depiction of Poe, citing anecdotes from Poe's life that portray him sympathetically. As for Poe's writing, Whitman suggests that he was ahead of his time: "It would seem that the true point of view from which his genius should be regarded has yet to be sought" (71). In the context of her discussion of Poe's cosmology *Eureka,* she goes further: "We confess to a half faith in the old superstition of the significance of anagrams when we find, in the transposed letters of Edgar Poe's name, the words *a God-peer,* words which, taken in connexion with his daring speculations, seem to have in them a mocking and malign import 'which is not man's nor angel's'" (78). Maintaining a Victorian sense of decorum, Whitman conspicuously avoids discussing her own broken engagement with Poe, the episode that Griswold had embellished to Poe's discredit. In fact, while Whitman writes as someone who knew Poe personally, most of her defense is based on second-hand stories and her interpretations of his poems.

But the most potent defense of Poe from this era came from the French symbolist poet Charles Baudelaire, who discovered Poe's works in the late 1840s and immediately became obsessed with the writer who was both his idol and, as he saw it, his American double: "The first time that I opened one of his books I was shocked and delighted to see not only subjects which I had dreamed of, but SENTENCES which I had thought and which he had written twenty years before" (30). Though obviously enamored of Poe, Baudelaire had no interest in testifying to his goodheartedness, and no basis for such testimony. Instead, in three essays written in the 1850s Baudelaire romanticized Poe's drinking and his irascibility as signs of his rebellious spirit. Far from trying to separate Poe's character from his works, Baudelaire claims that "what killed him is a part of that which gives us enjoyment today" (114). Poe was angry because "[p]oets see injustice — never where it does not exist — but very often where the unpoetical see no injustice whatever" (136). His drinking was not a weakness but a tool of the artist, "a mnemonic means, a method of work, drastic and fatal, but adapted to his passionate nature" (114). Baudelaire made more significant claims about Poe's artistic vision, arguing repeatedly that it defied American bourgeois values and moralism. Like Melville responding to Hawthorne's "blackness," Baudelaire cherished Poe's dark vision of human nature: "this author, product of a century infatuated with itself, child of a nation more infatuated with itself than any other, has clearly seen, has imperturbably affirmed the natural wickedness of man" (125). According to Baudelaire, Poe spent his life suffocating in a materialistic, hypocritical America that valued only moralistic works; Poe's privileging of beauty over truth made him anathema to his country-men and a hero to Baudelaire, who, like Poe, regarded didacticism as heresy. Meanwhile, Baudelaire meticulously translated five volumes of Poe's works into French, a project he began in 1848 and continued through 1865, two years before his own death. His efforts paid off in gaining Poe the admiration of French readers and the next generation of symbolist poets, especially Stéphane Mallarmé, Paul Valéry, and English poet C. A. Swinburne. Largely because of Baudelaire's efforts, by the 1870s it would become a truism among American critics and textbook writers that Poe was more appreciated in Europe than "at home."

After the Civil War, it seemed as if American literary scholars couldn't decide whether Poe was a popular writer, a great writer, both, or neither. However, the evidence virtually proves that he *was* popular: Griswold's edition went through about thirty reprintings (the publishing rights changed hands several times) before the end of the century, and after the original copyright expired in 1876, countless other editions of Poe appeared. Meanwhile, Poe continued to attract a steady stream of commentary — hundreds of magazine articles and three significant biog-raphies appeared between the end of the war and 1909, the centennial of his birth. Julian Hawthorne (Nathaniel's son) in a whimsical 1891 story about meeting the now-eighty-two-year-old Poe in a Philadelphia restaurant, assures Poe that he was now popular enough to get a dollar a word for anything he would choose to write (244).

And yet magazine writers after the war engaged in a kind of ritual hand-wringing over Poe's "place" in American literature, ultimately making Poe's alleged rejection part of his mystique. In 1893, *The Critic*, a New York literary weekly, polled its readers to compile a list of the ten best books by American authors. Not only was Poe not on it, but he was not among the thirty authors who received more than twenty votes. (Emerson's *Essays* came in first with 512 votes, followed closely by *The*

Scarlet Letter with 493.) English critic Edmund Gosse called the omission of Poe "extraordinary and sinister" (qtd. in Smith, *Repetition* 45). Poe was also overlooked by New York University's Hall of Fame committee in 1900 and 1905, prompting a more widespread outcry. Although Holmes, Cooper, and Bryant were also left off the first two inductees' lists (which totaled forty names), *Current Literature,* in an article entitled "Edgar Allan Poe and the Hall of Fame," reported that Poe's was the controversial omission. In 1910 Walter Hines Page observed that "Edgar Allan Poe might be described as the man who made the Hall of Fame famous. He made it famous for ten years by being kept out of it, and he has now given it a renewed lease of fame by being tardily admitted to it" (qtd. in Hubbell 547).

A few years earlier, Charles Leonard Moore had prompted a debate in the pages of *The Dial,* a Chicago literary magazine, with an essay entitled "The American Rejection of Poe," arguing that while Poe was "the greatest intellect America has produced," he didn't relate well to other people: "Poe, a logic machine, was absolutely incapable of those pleasing flaws and deficiencies which allow other people to have a good opinion of themselves" (41). The most potent of several responses came from John L. Hervey, who pointed out the "innumerable editions of his poems and tales, in every conceivable shape, from those in paper covers at five cents a copy to *éditions de luxe* at fancy or fabulous prices" (73). Hervey also reminds Moore that "The Raven" is as much a staple of readers and orators as "A Psalm of Life" and "The Charge of the Light Brigade," and refers to another magazine's readers' poll of the ten best American short stories, which included two by Poe (73). But after arguing that Poe is more popular than Moore suggested, Hervey concurs that he "has never been taken into the heart of his native public as, for instance, Longfellow has," a distaste Hervey attributes to the "charnel-house" atmosphere (a common phrase, apparently) of his work: "Poe's *metier* was his of deliberate choice; his atmosphere is of his own creation; there is not a breath of plain air in it" (73). These arguments over Poe's popularity convey the impression that Poe's questionable reputation — personal and literary — continued to draw readers and critics to him; paradoxically, the sense that he was unappreciated or "rejected" increased his popularity.

The late 1870s and early 1880s witnessed several biographical reassessments, in addition to a series of magazine articles contributing anecdotes to the annals of Poe biography. Eugene Didier's biographical introduction to his edition of the poems and William Gill's biography, both published in 1877, whitewash Poe, but do so with a richer collection of evidence than any previous Poe apologist had put together. Gill, who rightly claims on his dedicatory page that his is "the first complete life" of Poe, corresponded with some of Poe's friends and relatives, adding to the body of evidence regarding Poe's life but falling far short of an objective account of Poe's character. Like Poe's earlier defenders, Gill refers constantly to Griswold, whom he calls variously the "vindictive vilifier" (95), "the falsifier" (129), and "a designing and unscrupulous man" (245). Richard Henry Stoddard, author of "A Great Man Self-Wrecked," wrote a far less judgmental biographical sketch for *Harper's* in 1872, which he expanded for his 1875 edition of Poe's poems and then further expanded into a sixty thousand-word biography to introduce his *Select Works of Edgar Allan Poe* in 1880 and *Works of Edgar Allan Poe* in 1895. Stoddard's "Life" neither demonizes Poe nor whitewashes him: he alludes several times to Poe's dishonesty and drinking problem, but also quotes Poe's defenders extensively.

Anticipating to some extent twentieth-century psychoanalytic and medical diagnoses of Poe's "condition," Francis Fairfield published an article in *Scribner's* in 1875 arguing that Poe's antisocial behavior, as well as his literary output, resulted from cerebral epilepsy. Meanwhile, "reminiscences" by people Poe had swindled, threatened, or charmed appeared regularly in popular magazines. Stoddard repeatedly printed a story of Poe promising to publish his poem and then accusing him of plagiarizing it, Thomas Dunn English recalled Poe's taking money from Griswold to write a puff piece on Griswold's poetry anthology and delivering instead a "scalping" review, and C. F. Briggs, Poe's onetime partner at the *Broadway Journal,* dished more dirt on Poe's professional behavior. On the other hand, Susan Archer Talley Weiss fondly remembered Poe's gentlemanly bearing on visits he made to her home weeks before his death, and Dr. John J. Moran, the physician who attended Poe through his final days at Washington Hospital in Baltimore, turned the scene of Poe's death into another temperance tale, but one sympathetic to Poe.

But the two really significant, full-length biographies of Poe from this period were published by John Henry Ingram in 1880 and George Woodberry in 1885. Despite being based in England, Ingram collected considerably more biographical evidence — mostly through correspondence with people who knew Poe, particularly Sarah Helen Whitman — than Gill or anyone else had, but his purpose was essentially the same as Gill's, to vindicate Poe against the slanders of Griswold. Even with all the new biographical information he had gathered, Ingram relied heavily on Poe's fiction for his insights into his subject's character. For instance, "Berenice" may be "better described as an essay on its author's idiosyncrasies than as a tale" (115), and "Eleonora" is "that beautiful allegory of his life" (137). He began a tradition among Poe biographers of quoting from the description of Bransby's school in "William Wilson" as if it were part of a memoir (13–19), giving similar biographical weight to the place description in "A Tale of the Ragged Mountains" (49). Like Gill, Ingram defends Poe or shies away from unflattering evidence at nearly every turn; although Poe certainly had a drinking problem by 1835, Ingram does not mention Poe's drinking until he describes his life in Philadelphia in the early 1840s, and even then he laments that "unveiling it almost resembles sacrilege" (174).

Written for Houghton Mifflin's "American Men of Letters" series, George Woodberry's biography was not only the most objective and balanced of the nineteenth century, but it was the most readable and reliable until Arthur Hobson Quinn's in 1942. Making use of Ingram, Gill, and the various memoirs of Poe that had appeared since Griswold's, as well as his own original research, Woodberry judiciously wove together the available documentary evidence. He made some important discoveries as well, such as the fact that Poe enlisted in the army under the name of Edgar A. Perry and was stationed at Ft. Moultrie, South Carolina, for most of 1828, and the fact that Poe colluded with Thomas Wyatt to have Wyatt's *Conchologist's First Book* published under Poe's name. Unlike his predecessors, he treated Griswold as one of many sources for the facts of Poe's life, not as an adversary. As a result, Woodberry followed some of Griswold's false leads, but to his credit he avoided the partisan rhetoric and outright bias that undermined Ingram's and Gill's credibility. In his closing pages, Woodberry does seem to condemn Poe — "Solitary as he was, proud and selfish, how could he kindle his works with the vital interest of humanity?" (350) — but for most of the book he refrains from editorializing on Poe's character and delivers temperate and fair-minded evaluations of various works. For the expanded and generally improved edition published in 1909, Woodberry would even change his conclusion to reflect more favorably on Poe.

These biographies, essays, and memoirs of the late nineteenth century further fictionalized Poe even as they brought out more and more "evidence" on which to base conclusions about his character. As Scott Casper has recently shown, by the mid-nineteenth century, Americans experienced a "biographical mania." "Biography," Casper writes, "was not simply a genre of writing. In an age before radio and television, it was the medium that allowed people to learn about public figures and peer into the lives of strangers" (2). Among biography's many functions was to turn famous lives into instructive texts, somewhat in the manner of the 1990s' "virtue industry" overseen by William Bennett, and to promote nationalism by paying tribute to great Americans. Biographies of American literary figures were not as popular as biographies of, say, statesmen and soldiers; the ambitious series for which Woodberry's book was written sold poorly overall. And yet the mere fact that three book-length biographies were published within such a short span of time attests to some degree of interest in literary biography and, of course, in Poe. As his story continued to be retold, it served two of the main purposes of late-nineteenth-century literary biography: instruction (through negative example) and validation that America had produced an internationally recognized literary figure.

Another trend that characterized American biography at this time was the pre-Freudian search for the "inner man," a search that Woodberry, unlike Ingram and most writers of article-length Poe biographies, shied away from. In his preface, Woodberry remarks that "[t]he statements of fact in [existing] sources are extraordinarily conflicting, doubtful, and contested" (vi). Clarence Stedman, who with Woodberry edited a ten-volume edition of Poe in 1895, also recognized the difficulty, if not the sheer impossibility, of finding the "real" Poe. In his *Scribner's* essay (cited earlier), Stedman contrasts Frederick Halpin's engraving of Poe with "some daguerreotype taken shortly before his death." The engraving presents the noble, passionate, intelligent Poe, "his head finely molded, with a forehead and temples large and not unlike those of Bonaparte; his hands fair as a woman's, — in all, a graceful, well-dressed gentleman." In the daguerreotype, "we find those hardened lines of the chin and neck that are often visible in men who have gambled heavily, which Poe did not in his mature years, or who have lived loosely and slept ill. The face tells of battling, of conquering external enemies, of many a defeat when the man was at war with his meaner self" (108). Stedman appreciates the fact that neither of these is the one "true" Poe; he seems to have set up the contrasting portraits to suggest that "Poe" is impossible to know except through paradox. Even in his opening paragraph Stedman calls to mind the slipperiness of the word "Poe": "But as I in turn pronounce his name, and in my turn would estimate the man and his writings, I am at once confronted by the question, — Is this poet, as now remembered, as now portrayed to us, the real Poe who lived and sung and suffered, but who died little more than a quarter century ago?" (107).

Amid this ongoing discussion of Poe's character, late-nineteenth-century critics were also finding room for more sophisticated discussions of the nature of Poe's writing, although they rarely analyzed individual works at any length or offered more than cursory textual support for their claims. Occasionally a critic would try to comment on the writing without delving into biography, but for the most part what commentators found interesting about Poe's work reflected back on his personality. For many, the crucial issue was the extent to which Poe was a "mechanical," or purely intellectual, writer.

During Poe's lifetime, the image of the pedant or the detached intellectual competed with the image of the passionate, out-of-control romantic artist. Those competing images actually complement each other, in that part of Poe's supposed "madness" was his inability to sympathize — a claim made frequently by early eulogists. In December 1849, before the publication of Griswold's edition, Briggs had described Poe as "an intellectual machine without a balance wheel; and all his poetry, which seems perfect in itself, and full of feeling, was mere machine work. It was not that spontaneous outgushing of sentiment, which the verse of great poets seems to be, but a carefully constructed mosaic, painfully elaborated, and designedly put together, with every little word in its right place, and every shade of thought toned down to its exact position" (Walker, *Critical* 332). In January 1850 Evert Duyckinck claimed that Poe "thought, wrote, and dealt solely in abstractions," that "[h]is genius was mathematical, rather than pictorial or poetical" (337). The corollary to such claims was that Poe lacked human sympathy on a personal level; as John Daniel put it in his review of the Griswold edition,

Poe "could not paint men well because he did not understand them; and he did not understand them because he was not at all like them" (374).

A half century later, this same assessment prevailed, at least in American literature textbooks. Mildred Watkins, in her 1894 primer *American Literature,* suggested that "[t]he explanation of both his unpopularity as a man and of his popularity as a writer is perhaps to be found in the fact that his imagination was out of proportion to all his other faculties. It is the kindest reason we can give for his fickleness, his ugly humor, and his untruths" (57–58). Probably taking his cue from "The Philosophy of Composition," John Macy, in *The Spirit of American Literature,* was more specific about the kind of disproportionate imagination Poe possessed, describing his method as "[d]eliberate, mathematical, alert"; Poe was "a finical craftsman" who "did not sweep upward to the heights of eloquence with blind, undirected power. He calculated effects" (134). In his *History of American Literature,* Reuben Post Halleck, trying to account for the disparity between Poe's exalted reputation abroad and his rejection from New York's Hall of Fame, explained that Poe was too much a technician and not enough a moralist or sentimentalist for American tastes (305–6). Duyckinck had asserted that Poe's machine-like intellectualism would make him "a greater favorite with scholars than with the people," but as it turned out, "the people" would gravitate toward the more romantic image of Poe writing while high on opium or allegorizing his own tortured psyche in passionate poems and macabre tales, while late-nineteenth and twentieth-century scholars were increasingly drawn to Poe the engineer.

However it was explained, Poe's supposed lack of popularity "at home" seems to have been more a rhetorical claim, a way of setting up a response to a minority of dismissive critics, than anything else. Not only did Poe's works sell briskly, but in this period when monument and memorial building enjoyed its greatest boom, civic and professional organizations campaigned successfully to memorialize Poe.[11] In 1875, after ten years of planning and fund-raising, the Public School Teachers' Association of Baltimore erected an eight-foot burial marker in the cemetery of Westminster Presbyterian Church; Poe's remains were moved from an unmarked grave to a more prominent part of the grounds where the new monument was placed. In 1885, the New York Actors' Monument to Poe, a life-size, white-marble bust, was dedicated at the Metropolitan Museum of Art. The University of Virginia commemorated the fiftieth anniversary of Poe's death in

1899 by commissioning a bust of Poe by George Julian Zolnay. This memorialization of Poe continued into the early twentieth century, coming to a climax in 1909, the centennial of his birth, when several groups held ceremonies, most conspicuously the University of Virginia and the Poe Memorial Association of Baltimore. At that point the Memorial Association, which had grown out of a women's literary club, was raising money for the Poe statue by Sir Moses Ezekiel, a project that finally came to fruition in 1921 (it now stands in the Law Center at the University of Baltimore). West Point honored Poe with a marble doorway, inscribed with verse honoring Poe, in the Cadet Library.[12] Meanwhile, in the Bronx, which also hosted a Poe Centennial celebration, Poe Park was established in 1913 near the location of the "Fordham cottage," Poe's last residence and the house where Virginia died; the house itself was preserved, thanks to a campaign organized by the Shakespeare Society of New York, and moved some seventeen feet to accommodate a widened road and the new park.[13]

In some cases, considerable ceremony accompanied the unveiling or dedication, commemorated with handsome books that included the speeches, songs, and poems. The contents of these volumes repeat much of what had been offered in Poe's defense since his death, but they also reflect an effort to "Americanize" Poe as they carve his likeness into the landscape. These post-Reconstruction efforts to pay tribute to Poe as a great American writer come as no surprise. Despite the nearly continuous calls for a uniquely American literature throughout the entire century, in the decade between Poe's death and the Civil War, a decade marked by increasing national disunity, the question of whether or not Poe represented American ideals or artistic aims seems to have gone unasked; but after the war, given the national anxiety over reconciliation and nation-rebuilding, the question became more prominent in the larger discussion of Poe's status. G. P. Lathrop, in an 1876 *Scribner's* essay, maintained that Hawthorne should be ranked above Poe and Irving largely because he is the most American of the three writers. Poe, for all his genius, "has no traits that we can call American. . . . His genius was a detonating agent, which could have been convulsed into its meet activity anywhere, and had nothing to do with a soil. . . . Does this absence of roots make it more universal? Merely, I think, as the wind is more transferable than a tree" (803). Although Poe did in fact set a number of tales in the United States (particularly from about 1843 on), most of his gothic tales, as well as the Dupin trilogy, are set elsewhere, a fact that has led count-less readers and teachers to the same conclusion as Lathrop.[14]

And yet speakers commemorating Poe in 1899 and 1909 argued forcefully that Poe's art *was* essentially American. Hamilton Wright Mabie, speaking at the dedication of the Zolnay statue in 1899, turned the com-mon-sense argument about American settings inside out. Because Poe generally does not employ American settings in his best-known work, he transcends regionalism and thereby becomes a truly national author: "he went far to eradicate the provincialism of taste which was the bane of his time and section, — the bane, indeed, of the whole country" (744). Mabie casts Poe as the great emancipator of American letters who answered the "sovereign claims of art" instead of local pride, a shining example of American individualism. According to Mabie, "Equality of opportunity for the sake of preparing the way for the highest and finest individualities will bring us, perhaps, as near a perfect social order as we can hope to attain. Poe was such a personality" (743). Mabie clearly was no more a populist than Poe. As a natural aristocrat, Poe assumed the responsibility of en-lightening the average man and elevating the American "race": "One of the greatest privileges of the average man is to recognize and honor the superior man, because the superior man makes it worth while to belong to the race by giving life a dignity and splendor which constitute a com-mon capital for all who live" (743).

Several speakers at the 1909 events made similar, if less Nietzschean, claims. At the Virginia centenary, Barrett Wendell, a critic who had previ-ously dismissed Poe, argued that although "[i]t may sometimes have seemed that among our eminent men of letters he is the least obviously American . . . Poe tacitly, but clearly and triumphantly, asserts his nation-ality. No other romanticism of the nineteenth century was ever so serenely free from limitation of material condition and tradition; none, therefore, was so indisputably what the native romanticism of America must inevita-bly have been" (Kent and Patton 145, 146–47). Wendell sounds as though he is discussing American abstract expressionists as he too asserts the American-ness of Poe's insistence on freedom and purity, without regard to subject: "In this supreme artistic purity lies not only the chief secret of its wide appeal, but at the same time the subtle trait which marks it as the product of its own time, and of its own time nowhere else than here in America, our common country" (Kent and Patton 147).[15]

The remarks of Georg Edward and C. Alphonso Smith on the same occasion offered more tangible links between Poe and American culture. Edward, the German representative at the Virginia ceremonies, proclaimed that Germans consider Poe both "a thoroughly modern author, and . . . the most characteristic American poet" (Kent and Patton 83). For Edward, Poe was modern because he anticipated the symbolist and decadent movements; he was American because he was beaten down by American materialism, because he was less derivative of the English literary tradition than were the schoolroom poets, because he explored the "pathological side of the American temperament" (96–97), and because he was curious: "Curiosity is certainly a most prominent trait in American life, or interest, if the other term seem offensive. Poe's interest was directed toward the most strange and odd mysteries. . . . All that was incomplete, unsolved, unexplained, challenged him to pursuit; he was bound to complete it with his imagination; and so he has told of mysterious secret documents, of inexplicable crimes and discoveries, so he has tracked out the possibilities of mesmerism, the prospects of ariel navigation — such themes as these appealed to his interest. But when such things became realized, they became totally indifferent to him" (97). Overgeneralized though it may be, this sort of "cultural reading" — or even the acknowledgment that Poe wrote as often about technology and science (or pseudoscience) as he did about decaying mansions and premature burial — was rare in the late nineteenth and early twentieth centuries. Meanwhile, Smith took the old idea of Poe the literary engineer and cast it in a patriotic mold, ascribing to Poe "a patience and persistence worthy of Washington . . . a husbandry of details that suggest the thriftiness of Franklin . . . a native insight and inventiveness that proclaim him of the line of Edison" (Kent and Patton 163–64). According to Smith, Poe's "constructiveness" is uniquely American, and his great contribution to world poetry has been "structural" — as an exemplary American, he knew how to put things together.

Smith began his address with an anecdote sure to appeal to the audience assembled at the University of Virginia: a Romanian he met in Paris, upon discovering that Smith was American, wanted to talk only about two subjects, Poe and Thomas Jefferson. Here again, in Jefferson's company, Poe becomes the great freedom fighter: "And let the names of Jefferson and Poe, whose far-flung battle-lines intersected on this campus, forever remind us that this University is dedicated not to the mere routine of recitation rooms and laboratories but to the emancipation of those mighty constructive forces that touch the spirits of men to finer aspirations and mould their aspirations to finer issues" (Kent and Patton 160). Smith's linking of Poe and Jefferson, who were, after all, both in Charlottesville in early 1826, would remind his audience of Poe's Southern-ness as well as his American-ness. Indeed, Poe never seemed more Southern than he did during the decades following Reconstruction.

Recently, critics such as Richard Gray and Louis Rubin have examined Poe as a Southern author, but his place in the canon of Southern writers remains marginal, since he spent most of his career outside the South and rarely employed specifically Southern settings.[16] However, the idea of Poe the Southerner was commonplace, virtually a given, at the time of these commemorations. At the 1899 dedication in Charlottesville, Sidney Ernest Bashaw declared that while Poe was "[b]y accident of birth a Bostonian, he was by his training and sympathy a Southerner, and much of his work was done in the South, where he has always been recognized and very popular" (Kent 34). Several of the letters responding to the University's invitation reveal a similar regional pride in Poe: "He was Southern in ancestry and characteristics; his birth at Boston was accidental" (Robert Lee Traylor, qtd. in Kent, 65–66); witnessing the unveiling "is a privilege which no one of Southern birth can fail to prize" (Catherine Pearson Woods, 70); "I think you are doing a great and beneficient work in directing the attention of the youth of the South to our literature" by honoring Poe (Molly Elliot Seawell, 79); elsewhere he is referred to as "our Southern poet" and "the greatest literary artist of the South" (76). Smith, at the 1909 exercises, refers to Poe's conservative Southern intellectualism and his supposed affinity with John C. Calhoun: "When Baudelaire defined genius as 'l'affirmation de l'independance individuelle,' he might have had both Poe and Calhoun in mind; but when he adds 'c'est le *self-government* appliqué aux oeuvres d'art,' only Poe could be included" (Kent and Patton 177). Other Southerners commemorating the Poe centenary in Charlottesville clearly saw Poe as a regional kinsman. At the Jefferson Society celebration, DeRoy R. Fonville of North Carolina spoke on "The Pathos in the Lives of Our Southern Poets." In a letter included in the commemorative book, Professor St. James Cummings of the South Carolina Military Academy, apparently anticipating the South's rising again, called Poe "an avatar for those who have the faith to wait. . . . The

Poe world will some time be no figure of speech, but will enjoy a day and a night of its own, where the greater and the lesser light may beat in splendor against the darkness; and the God of harmony will call it good." Moreover, according to Cummings, "More than anyone else, Poe represents the South" (Kent and Patton 194).

The Southern Poe had great appeal for several reasons. As Smith's likening Poe to Calhoun suggests, many Southerners saw the Confederacy as consistent with the American ideal of fighting for independence; it was convenient to see Poe, the resolutely independent author, as part of the same tradition that produced Jefferson and Calhoun. In another letter from the Virginia centenary volume, Cummings's fellow-South Carolinian, Dr. George Armstrong Wauchope, called Poe the author of *"our aesthetic declaration of independence"* before concluding with the affirmation that "his fame is safely enshrined in the Pantheon of Southern hearts" (Kent and Patton 205, 206). Particularly if one chose Poe the apostle of beauty, the rebel against American materialism and practicality, as opposed to Poe the engineer, he could be cast from the same mold that would produce an Ashley Wilkes or a *Fugitive* poet.[17] Oliver Huckel, speaking at the Baltimore centenary celebration, concurred:

> Poe was, as all the South is, a worshipper of the beautiful. . . . He was proud but genial, handsome but grave, courtly and courteous, eloquent and kindly. . . . on his finer side, he was an embodiment of much of the genius of the South. He had the steadfast Southern devotion to ideals. He had no sordid love of money. He was never unfaithful to honor. He was always in pursuit of some noble quest. His whole ambition was literary achievement, and he never wavered, in spite of suffering, loss and defeat. (49, 52)

Moreover, Huckel claimed that Poe's poems are infused with Southern "atmosphere," that his melodic verses are "largely inspired by the soft croonings of some African mammy in childhood's days, by the gentle caressing voices of Southern women, by the whole dreamy delicious mystic atmosphere of the Southland" (52–53). Strangely, the qualities on which Huckel bases his encomium to Poe would form the basis of late-twentieth century analyses of Poe's racism and sexism: the "ideals" and way of life to which Huckel believed Poe was steadfastly devoted implicitly included white male supremacy.

However, Poe's Southernness was asserted not only by Southerners or at ceremonies held in the South. C. L. Moore, in the 1899 *Dial* article mentioned earlier, attributed the infamous American rejection of Poe to his being "of the South — the very incarnation of the South; and the South has always ordered its authors to move on, for fear they might die on the parish" (40). Moore blames the South, then, for not supporting Poe during his lifetime, but he still sees Poe as essentially Southern, the South's "greatest son," in fact (40). When American literature textbooks from this period arranged their discussion of authors by region, Poe was the main attraction in the sections on Southern literature. In *America in Literature* (1900), Walter Bronson devotes about two thirds of the chapter on Southern writing to Poe. Reuben Post Halleck, in *The Spirit of American Literature,* opens his chapter on the South with a thirteen-page discussion of Poe, far more than fellow-Southerners Simms, Lanier, Timrod, Cable, and others receive. And Woodberry, who had not emphasized Poe's Southernness in his 1885 biography, includes Poe in his chapter on the South in his brief 1903 guide *America in Literature.* After acknowledging Poe's Bostonian birth and status as a "world-artist," he makes an extended argument for Poe-as-Southerner:

> It appears to me that Poe is as much a product of the South as Whittier is of New England. His breeding and education were Southern; his manners, habits of thought, and moods of feeling were Southern; his sentimentalism, his conception of womanhood and its qualities, of manhood and its behavior, his weaknesses of character, bore the stamp of his origin; his temperament even, his sensibility, his gloom and dream, his response to color and music, were of his race and place. (144–45)

Woodberry does note that Poe's independent and cosmopolitan literary criticism could not be rooted in the "uncritical" South, but for the most part he sees Poe's personality and literary imagination as typically Southern, and he describes the intimate relationship between Poe and the South in terms that are complimentary to both.[18]

As a Boston-born Southerner who spent most of his career in Philadelphia and New York, Poe was geographically well-positioned in the decades after Reconstruction to be regarded as a great American author. At the end of the century the most celebrated American authors who were either dead or old enough to be enshrined were nearly all New Englanders —

Hawthorne, Emerson, Longfellow, Lowell, Whittier, Holmes, and Stowe would have led the list — so writers and orators hoping to do their part for national reconciliation might well have seen Poe as an ideal figure. Southern literary scholar William P. Trent, speaking at the Baltimore Centenary, argued that because of the Civil War and Reconstruction, "thoroughly normal conditions for the spread of a writer's fame have existed in this country only for a space of about thirty years" (24). He describes a New England prejudice against Poe as a thing of the past, not permanently damaging to Poe's reputation: "Their attitude toward him has doubtless somewhat retarded the spread of his fame and his influence in America; but it has also stimulated the zeal of his admirers, and it has tested as with fire the gold of his genius" (25). Because, as Michael Kammen explains, the period from 1870 to 1915 was marked both by countless public gestures toward national unity and an abiding "fierce impulse toward partisanship" (120), Poe could be seen both as a national writer free from provincialism by the mostly Northern literary establishment and as the moonlight-and-magnolias artist described by Cummings and Huckel.

But even for those who saw Poe in nationalist terms, his Southern background helped because it proved that there *was* a "Southern" author of whom the North could also be proud. Poe's usefulness as a unifying literary figure is apparent in an 1889 assessment of Southern literature written by Thomas Nelson Page, famous for his romanticized portrayals of the Southern plantation life, in the Philadelphia-based *Lippincott's Magazine*: "If we are compelled to admit that [Poe] is the one really great writer of purely literary work that the South produced under its old conditions, it is no reflection on the South or its civilization, for the North during the same period, with an educated population many times larger, can claim only three or four, whilst England herself, 'with all appliances and means to boot,' can number hardly more than a score" (115). Page claims that "Poe's poems are as distinctly Southern in their coloring, tone and temper as Wordsworth's are English," yet Poe "was limited by no boundary, geographical or other" (113). Not only was Poe a far better writer than, say, Henry Timrod or William Gilmore Simms, but he did not carry overt Confederate baggage as those writers did; this must have been part of what commentators — even Page — implied when they praised Poe's freedom from provincialism. Somewhat like Mark Twain, who came from a (marginally) Southern state, made his name in the West, and then took up residence in the Northeast, Poe emerged as an American writer who could be claimed by everyone, although in 1909 he seems to have been more Southern than anything else. Woodberry summed up the relationship between region and reputation at the Centenary event held in the Bronx: "No American name in literature is, I think, so warmly cherished. It is a pleasure, too, to recognize American genius, and today it is an added grace that Poe was a child of the South. He was, nevertheless, both in his genius and his life, remarkably free from locality. . . . Poe was a Southerner by his breeding; he was an American by his career; he was a citizen of the world by his renown" (*Torch* 323–24).

However Southern or American Poe became amidst monument-building and anniversary celebrations, he seems to have been more popular than ever by the early twentieth century. The question of Poe's depravity still lingered and probably helped maintain interest in his work, but by the time of the Centenary celebrations Griswold's memoir was long out of print, and his *Works of the Late Edgar Allan Poe* had been supplanted by several editions, including Ingram's in 1874–75, Stedman and Woodberry's in 1894–95, and the excellent "Virginia edition" of 1902, edited by James Harrison, who added a thorough, if rather dull, documentary biography as well. Poe remained controversial: renowned writers and critics still occasionally declared him overrated, and guardians of public virtue still worried about promoting the works of such a dishonest, ill-tempered, and intemperate man.[19] But this aura of mystery was good for business, and it created an open field for speculation about the "real" Poe even as it made the possibility of finding him more remote. In a 1908 textbook, John Macy saw Poe's hand in this mystification:

> If one without forewarning begins to read any life of Poe, one feels that a mystery is about to open. There seem to be clues to suppressed matters, suspicious lacunae. The lives are written, like most novels, with hintful rows of stars. A shadowy path promises to lead to the misty mid-region of Weir. But Weir proves to be a place that Poe invented [in the poem "Ulalume"]. He himself was the first foolish biographer of Poe. The "real" Poe (to take an invidious adjective from the titles of a modern kind of biography) is a simple, intelligible, and if one may dare to say it, a rather insignificant man. To make a hero or villain of him is to write fiction. (129)

While I find Poe's life considerably more interesting than Macy does, I admire his insight into the nature of Poe biography. Certainly Poe was alert to the way reputations are manufactured; he wrote several comic stories on that general theme, the best of which, "The Man That Was Used Up," literalizes the "making" of a hero. In Poe's story, the narrator, after briefly meeting the famous Indian-fighter Brevet Brigadier General John A. B. C. Smith, becomes obsessed with learning more about him, and finally visits the great man at his home. He discovers not a man but "a large and exceedingly odd-looking bundle of something" that must be rebuilt, piece by piece, every morning. Smith explains that he was chopped to pieces by Indians, and the narrator thus identifies him as the man that was "used up" — a phrase that in Poe's profession usually meant being severely attacked, one might say murdered, in print. Smith's prosthetic body parts can be read as emblematic of the cultural icon's exalted reputation: the story advances the notion that public figures are largely artificial creations, that attempts to discover the "real" Smith — or Poe — are fool's errands. The man that was used up expresses no regrets at having been dismantled by "savages," for his new parts seem to work better than those of mere mortals. Although Poe could not manage his own posthumous career in the same way Smith shops for appendages, he resembles his own Smith (whose name playfully means "maker") in that he too was used up — and then rebuilt into an ever-more-fascinating public figure.

Notes

[1] Several other papers in Baltimore, Philadelphia, Richmond, and New York gave brief notices of Poe's death on October 9, some merely copying the obituary from the *Sun*. For an extensive listing of obituaries and other printed commentary on Poe between his death and the publication of Rufus Griswold's Memoir in Volume 3 of his edition of Poe (September 1850), see Burton Pollin, "A Posthumous Assessment: The 1849–1850 Periodical Press Response to Edgar Allan Poe," *American Periodicals* 2 (1992): 6–50. See Ian Walker, ed., *Edgar Allan Poe: The Critical Heritage* (London: Routledge, 1997) for the more notable obituaries, including those by Griswold, Willis, and Hirst, and reviews of *The Works of the Late Edgar Allan Poe,* including those by C. F. Briggs, George Ripley, George Rex Graham, and John Neal. See also Arthur Hobson Quinn, *Edgar Allan Poe: A Critical Biography* (1941. Reprint, New York: Cooper

Square, 1969), 642–95; and Ian Walker, "The Poe Legend," in *A Companion to Poe Studies,* ed. Eric W. Carlson (Westport, CT: Greenwood, 1996), 24–27.

[2] See Patrick F. Quinn, *The French Face of Edgar Allan Poe* (Carbondale: So. IL UP, 1957), esp. 3–65.

[3] Arthur Hobson Quinn (*Critical Biography,* 660) points out that Griswold, not Lowell, might have revised Lowell's 1845 article on Poe, but finds the evidence inconclusive.

[4] See Dwight Thomas and David K. Jackson, *The Poe Log: A Documentary Life of Edgar Allan Poe* (Boston: G. K. Hall, 1987), 778–80, and Quinn, *Edgar Allan Poe,* 581–87, for the documentary evidence relevant to the breaking of Poe's engagement to Whitman.

[5] While Derby's claim seems reasonable, I should note that he is not an entirely reliable source, given some of his other statements concerning Griswold, received second-hand from Redfield.

[6] On Griswold as editor of Poe, see Killis Campbell, *The Mind of Poe and Other Studies* (1933. Reprint, New York: Russell and Russell, 1962), 93–98.

[7] Walker, *Critical Heritage,* n. 302; Quinn, *Edgar Allan Poe,* 647. See, for example, an anonymous article, "Edgar A. Poe," originally published in *Tait's Magazine,* reprinted in *The Eclectic* in 1852, in which the quotation from *The Caxtons* is attributed to Griswold (118).

[8] See Alice L. Cooke, "The Popular Conception of Poe, 1850–1890," *University of Texas Studies in English* 22 (1942): 145–70; Dudley R. Hutcherson, "Poe's Reputation in England and America, 1850–1909," *American Literature* 14 (1942): 211–33; and Walker, "The Poe Legend."

[9] Esther F. Hyneman, in *Edgar Allan Poe: An Annotated Bibliography of Books and Articles in English, 1827–1973* (Boston: G. K. Hall, 1974), 52, identifies the anonymous author as Stoddard. For more on Stoddard's career as a Poe commentator, see Burton Pollin, "Stoddard's Elegaic Sonnet on Poe," *Poe Studies* 19 (1986): 32–34.

[10] See Pollin, "A Posthumous Assessment," 7–8; and Burton Pollin, "The Temperance Movement and Its Friends Look at Poe," *Costerus: Essays in English and American Language and Literature* 1972: 119–44.

[11] On monument-building and sectional politics during this period, see James W. Loewen, *Lies Across America: What Our Historical Sites Get Wrong* (New York: New Press, 1999), esp. 38–39; and Michael Kammen, *Mystic Chords of Memory: The Transformation of Tradition in American Culture* (New York: Vintage, 1993), esp. chs. 4 and 7.

[12] See Clifford Krainik, "The Sir Moses Ezekiel Statue of Edgar Allan Poe in Baltimore," in *Myths and Reality: The Mysterious Mr. Poe,* ed. Bejamin F. Fisher, 48–58 (Baltimore: Edgar Allan Poe Society, 1987). I would like to thank William F. Hecker III for his description of the doorway at West Point, which, as of 2003, "frames a blank piece of plywood and, ironically, leads nowhere."

[13] See Burton Pollin, "Woodrow Wilson and Julian Hawthorne on Poe: Letters from an Overlooked Scholaraly Resource," *Poe Studies* 12 (1979): 35; and Frederick M. Hopkins, "Shall We Preserve the Poe Cottage at Fordham?" *Review of Reviews* 13 (1896): 458–62.

[14] See J. Gerald Kennedy, *The American Turn of Edgar Allan Poe* (Baltimore: Edgar Allan Poe Society and the Library of the University of Baltimore, 2001).

[15] Jay B. Hubbell, in *Who Are the Major American Writers?* (Durham, NC: Duke UP, 1972), 548, points out that Wendell became gradually more friendly to Poe. See also Wendell's chapter on Poe in his *Literary History of America,* esp. 217–18, for similar comments on Poe's American traits.

[16] Richard Gray (*Southern Aberrations: Writers of the American South and the Problems of Regionalism* [Baton Rouge and London: Louisiana State UP, 2000]) and Louis Rubin (*The Edge of the Swamp: A Study in the Literature and Society of the Old South* [Baton Rouge and London: Louisiana State UP, 1989]) expand and revise the work of [Jay B.] Hubbell, who focused on Poe's Southern background and on New England critics' bias against him in his 1954 survey of Southern literature, *The South in American Literature, 1607–1900* (Durham, NC: Duke UP), 1954.

[17] See Gray, *Southern Aberrations,* 21.

[18] One notable exception to the presentation of Poe as a Southern author is Barrett Wendell, who in *A Literary History of America* (New York: Scribner's, 1900), categorizes Poe under "Literature in the Middle States From 1798 to 1857," along with Brown, Irving, Cooper, Bryant, and the Knickerbocker School. In his deprecatory remarks on Southern literature, he claims that Poe is Southern "only by courtesy" (487).

[19] For example, William P. Trent, in his Poe Centenary address ("The Centenary of Poe," *Edgar Allan Poe: A Centenary Tribute* [1909], ed. Heinrich Ewald Buchholz, 45–54 [London: Folcraft Library, 1972]), told of having a school principal reject his American literature guidebook from his library "for the reason — not that I had treated Poe too harshly or too favorably — but that I had treated him at all. School children, according to my correspondent, ought not to know that such a life was ever lived" (21).

2: A Dream Within a Dream: Poe and Psychoanalysis

There has never been much doubt that something
was very much the matter with Edgar Allan Poe.
— Philip Young (1951)

IN 1909, the year Poe was celebrated as a great American and a true Southerner at centennial celebrations in Charlottesville and Baltimore, Sigmund Freud visited the United States; as he arrived in New York, Freud is reported to have remarked to Carl Jung, "They don't realize we're bringing them the plague" (Gallop 58). Indeed, in 1909 few Americans were aware of the revolutionary theories that would "plague" their faith in human rationality and self-control, although over the course of the decade following Freud's visit his theories would make their way not only into scholarly journals but also, in somewhat distorted and popularized forms, into *Good Housekeeping* and *The Ladies' Home Journal* (Morrison 27). One could argue, though, that Americans never did see "Freudianism" as a plague, despite the controversy it generated; while psychoanalysis took root as a profession, for the laity Freud's theories could be translated as a rationale for liberation from sexual repression and guilt (Dumenil 146). Almost immediately literary writers and critics began to incorporate Freud's ideas into their work. As we have seen, most commentary on Poe in the nineteenth century was concerned with biography and character assessment, sometimes with a psychological emphasis on Poe's alleged insanity or a more specific diagnosis such as "cerebral epilepsy" (Fairchild 691).[1] Psychoanalysis at first must have seemed like nothing more than a new set of tools that could be used to perform the same old tasks of author study, enabling critics to make bolder claims about, in this case, Poe's "mind" and "character." Yet by 1933, when Marie Bonaparte published her seven-hundred-page *Edgar Poe: Étude psychoanalytique,* it was clear that psychoanalysis could inspire new and inventive ways of reading literature. In this chapter I will focus on questions about the value of psycho-analysis and "inner biography" for literary study, arguing for the enduring significance of Bonaparte's magnum opus (translated in 1949 as *The Life and Works of Edgar Allan Poe*), particularly in light of later readings by Daniel Hoffman and Jacques Lacan.

In 1910, Ernest Jones virtually founded the "school" of psychoanalytic literary criticism with "A Psychoanalytical Study of *Hamlet*" for *The American Journal of Psychology* (he would revise and expand the essay, ultimately publishing the landmark book *Hamlet and Oedipus* in 1949).[2] Not only did psychoanalytic criticism catch on almost immediately afterward, but, according to Claudia Morrison, debates about the validity of applying psycho-analysis to literature proliferated in the decades following Jones's *Hamlet* essay, as scholars raised many of the same questions we raise today:

> Was the artist a neurotic individual who found release for his emotional problems in artistic expression, or was he a superior individual endowed with a greater than normal ability to harness unconscious emotional forces and transform them into universally communicable images and themes? To what extent did art represent a "wish-fulfillment" of the artist's unconscious needs and desires? What part did consciousness play in the creative process? If the source of creativity was the unconscious, how were the artist's personal symbols rendered meaningful to his audience? To what degree was the effect of the art work on its audience a result of the unconscious appeal of its content and to what extent was it a result of purely formal qualities? (Morrison 43–44)

Theorists and critics quickly recognized the opportunities Poe presented for psychoanalytic study, given his fiction's emphasis on hidden motives and detection, altered states of consciousness, sadism, and obsession, as well as the self-destructive tendencies he exhibited in his own life. In 1920, in the same journal that had published Jones's article on *Hamlet,* Lorine Pruette contributed "A Psychoanalytical Study of Edgar Allan Poe," a multifaceted analysis of Poe's character based on biographical information gleaned from Ingram, Woodberry, and Harrison, and theories of behavior associated with Alfred Alder, Carl Jung, and Freud, all of whom she cites. No single concept unifies Pruette's expansive study; if the question was "What was the matter with Poe?" Pruette's answer was "A lot." Poe's "will-to-power" made him perpetually jealous and demanding; his stories reflect his own suppressed necrophilia, sadism, and death wish; and his marriage to Virginia, motivated by his need for the mother-figure Maria Clemm, was "perhaps an unconscious manifestation of the incest desire" (378). Pruette moves back and forth between biography and fiction for evidence of Poe's neuroses, and her attempt to locate causes for these impulses is rather feeble: early in the essay she suggests that Poe's only-child upbringing in the Allan household was detrimental to his character, and later she points out that Poe's behavior later in his life was symptomatic of syphilis, but that's about all.

Like Bonaparte and, one might argue, virtually all psychoanalytic critics, Pruette shows no interest in her subject's conscious act of creation, the formal qualities of the poetry and fiction; this neglect is one of the standard complaints against Freudian approaches to art. And yet, also in keeping with better, later examples of psychoanalytic criticism, Pruette makes at least some of her bold claims plausible by connecting biography and literary writing. For example, the relationship between Poe's idealization of women (his mother, stepmother, Helen Stanard, Virginia, Francis Osgood, Sarah Helen Whitman, "Annie" Richmond) and his representation of women in his poetry and fiction, which continues to intrigue biographers and critics today, is depicted in presumptuous but logical terms by Pruette:

> His nature demanded the adoration and approval of "woman," rather than sexual conquests, and he worshiped in his poems a feminine idealization to which he ascribed various names. These women are never human; they are not warm flesh and blood, loving, hating, or coming late to appointments — they are simply beautiful lay figures around which to hang wreaths of poetical sentiments. His emotional interest lay in himself, rather than in outer objects; he wished to be loved, rather than to love. (380)

Pruette builds on this point, which seems more obvious today than it must have in 1920, first affirming Lowell's famous quip that Poe's "heart somehow seems all squeezed out by the mind," then exploring the connection between sex and death in Poe's stories. She catalogues color imagery (gold, red, and black) and the frequent mention of draperies and curtains in Poe's tales, as well as references to tombs and worms, before concluding that a necrophilic impulse informed the writing of Poe's tales. Thus Pruette, who cares about Poe's tales only as vehicles to explain his neuroses, nonetheless observes patterns in those tales that no one had written about before, and which are interesting and valid to readers who see the interpretation of the *texts* (apart from author-analysis) as an end in itself. Having cited references in six different works to black or sable draperies, she continues:

> From contemplation of the coffin, the funeral pall or the draperies came to have a peculiar significance, and when he wrote of rooms in which terrible deeds transpired he hung those rooms with the draperies of the dead. Not only that, but the curtains stir, to sad music, to strange winds, heightening the effect of horror, as the breezes which lift the pall over the face of the dead, increasing the agony of the spectator by giving the semblance of life where life has fled. (389)

Several years before the New Criticism took hold, psychoanalysis was replacing the nineteenth-century model of writing about literature — concerned primarily with value judgments and author biography — with a model of close reading.

The assertion that modern literary criticism begins with psychoanalysis should not be surprising, given the often-noted parallel between the work of analysis and the work of literary interpretation. Freud himself referred to poets as the "real pioneers in the exploration of the unconscious," likening artistic creation with the dreams that the analyst interprets (Meisel 4–5); he also likened his case histories to short stories (Bloom 13–17). John Crowe Ransom similarly argued in 1924 that while even "naive" realist literature "is full of psychoanalysis," modernist literature "has sprung up to welcome the new learning" (40, 41). If literary works explored the workings of the unconscious — characters' and authors' — without formally adopting the language of analysis, then the critic's job was indeed similar to the analyst's. According to Clive Bloom, "[T]o Freud each 'patient' was a text, whose fictional life was available for interpretation, whose words, syntax, and style were subject to a 'reading' which would reveal hidden and more profound depths" (13). However much English teachers chuckle over students' insistence on the phrase "hidden meanings," with its implication that texts should be approached like word puzzles or "Where's Waldo" books, we continue to reinforce this conception of literary interpretation by opposing the "shallow" reading of works (reading for plot or literal comprehension, empathizing with characters) to the "deeper" reading that comes out of formal classroom study. Similarly, what fascinated enthusiasts of Freudian analysis in the twenties (and afterward) was the idea that the psychoanalyst could find the hidden (unconscious) meaning of one's dreams, fantasies, aberrant behavior, and slips of the tongue. If biblical exegesis provided one model for pre-deconstructionist close reading, the secular realm of psychoanalysis provided the other.

Pruette, then, had begun to apply psychoanalytical principles to Poe's tales and poems, the project Bonaparte would take up a decade later. In the interim, two other books on Poe would make clinical claims without really adopting the model of psychoanalysis or venturing very far into Poe's works. John W. Robertson's *Edgar A. Poe: A Psychopathic Study* (1923) goes to unnecessary lengths to argue that Poe was dypsomaniac, and that because this disease was inherited, critics and biographers are wrong to hold Poe morally responsible for most of his "abnormal" behavior. To his credit, Robertson avoids the defensive tone of earlier Poe apologists, and, more importantly, he's right to regard Poe's alcoholism as a disease in the clinical and not merely metaphorical sense. But most of his study is a tedious biographical narrative focusing on Poe's alcohol use, and, as his title suggests, Robertson is concerned with psychopathology rather than psychoanalysis. He takes pains to situate himself within what was by then a seventy-three-year-old debate over Poe's moral character by including a ninety-two-page assessment of previous biographers, from Griswold to Harrison; despite his use of modern theories, Robertson's concerns are those of nineteenth-century author study.

In *Edgar Allan Poe: A Study in Genius* (1926), Joseph Wood Krutch criticized Robertson for his simplistic explanation, insisting that "the only really significant question" is "What was the cause of that disease? . . . If we could get, not at the facts, but at the cause of the intemperance we might at least have some inkling of the secret of his genius" (50). Krutch unfairly discounts or simply misses Robertson's point that Poe's "intemperance" was biologically based alcoholism, but correctly perceives that "biological inheritance" is an unsatisfying answer when the question is what made Poe tick, that in biography as in fiction a more titillating, "deeper" explanation is needed not just to explain Poe but to explain his writing. He refers to the "silly farce" of believing that "the most fantastic and abnormal writings in all literature are assumed to be ingenious toys without meaning, and in which the whole process which created them is dismissed as irrelevant" (17). But Krutch's solutions to the mysteries of Poe's life and work are poorly supported and ultimately reducible to a moralistic judgment of Poe's "abnormality." In Poe's tales "there is never from the first to the last any recognition of the existence of *normal* amorousness" or any of "the other interests of *normal* life" (83); his marriage to Virginia goes to show that "the *abnormality* of Poe's literary expression had its roots in the very center of his being" (52); despite the apparent similarity in the works of Poe and Ambrose Bierce, "unlike Poe [Bierce] would often base . . . horror on the exaggeration of a *normal* emotion" (205; italics added in each case). Krutch does make some specific conjectures regarding Poe's "abnormality" — that he was impotent, that the household he (more or less) maintained with Muddy and Virginia fed the twin fictions by which he lived, "the sexless phantom and the illusion of unquestionable supremecy" (128), that he "invented the detective story in order that he might not go mad" (118) — but he goes to little trouble to support or explain these theories. And despite his contention that Poe's psyche provides the key to understanding his works, he has almost nothing to say about those works. Krutch's most important claim is that Poe's poems and tales should be appreciated on their own aesthetic terms, without reference to the "normal" outside world; for all his seeming disparagement of his subject, he maintains that Poe is a great artist, and he clearly aspires to a balanced view of Poe that neither whitewashes his flaws nor devalues his art because of its decadent subject matter. And yet, apparently heedless of his stated goal, he settles for the explanation that Poe was neurotic and "abnormal," which is no more of an explanation than that Poe was dypsomaniac.

Like Robertson's, Krutch's study of Poe hardly qualifies as psychoanalytic. Although Claudia Morrison claims that for Krutch Freud and psychoanalysis "were taken for granted" (194), Krutch not only doesn't mention Freud but writes about the mind in a way that shows little familiarity with psychoanalysis, his frank conjectures about Poe's impotence and its causes notwithstanding. In his chapter on Poe in *Studies in Classic American Literature* (1923), D. H. Lawrence doesn't mention Freud either, yet his reading of Poe's personality, conflated with those of a handful of Poe's narrators, has a distinctively psychoanalytic feel to it; although at times preposterous, it is a groundbreaking interpretation, perhaps the earliest reading of Poe's fiction that is of more than historical interest to students of Poe in the twenty-first century. Lawrence seems to have shared Freud's belief in the existence and importance of the unconscious but disagreed with Freud regarding its nature; Lawrence repeatedly referred to the Holy Ghost, a guiding force that should be not only acknowledged but obeyed, unlike Freud's unconscious, which Lawrence regarded as "a huge slimy serpent of sex, and heaps of excrement, and a myriad repulsive little horrors spawned between sex and excrement" (qtd. in Morrison 204). As if opposing the destructive urges of the id against his Holy Ghost, Lawrence argues that the trouble with Poe and the male lovers who narrate several of his stories is that they refuse to "listen in isolation to the isolate Holy Ghost": "The Ushers, brother and sister, betrayed the Holy Ghost in themselves. They would love, love, without resistance. They would love, they would merge, they would be as one thing. So they dragged each other down into death. For the Holy Ghost says you must not be as one thing with another being" (85). Out of context, this quotation sounds perversely moralistic rather than psychoanalytic, and to some extent it is, but Lawrence's larger argument is that Poe and his narrators are controlled by an insatiable need for love, and that this craving as represented in Poe's tales is symbolic not merely of the author's urges but of "man's": "the first law of life [analogous to the reality principle?] is that each organism is isolate in itself . . . . Yet man has tried the glow of unison, called love, and he *likes* it. It gives him the highest gratification. He wants it. He wants it all the time. He wants it and he will have it" (72).

In this respect Lawrence's reading is similar to Krutch's (which it predates), but Lawrence does not make Poe's "abnormality" his focus but rather universalizes the motives that underlie the action of Poe's tales; he recognizes, for instance, that "[a]ll this underground vault business in Poe only symbolizes that which takes place *beneath* the consciousness" (85) — not Poe's consciousness but *the* consciousness. Moreover, Lawrence, more creatively and more thoroughly than Pruette, actually interprets a group of stories, with particular emphasis on "Ligeia" and "The Fall of the House of Usher." Lawrence's provocative, nonacademic style and imposition of his personal psychological system onto Poe's (and other "classic" American authors') texts are off-putting today as they must have been in 1923, and yet they also achieve, at least partially, what Jacques Lacan would call for decades later: like a Lacanian analyst, Lawrence "exposes the illusions" of his authority "without renouncing [his authority], so as to permeate the position itself with the connotations of its illusoriness" (Gallop 21). Lawrence's audaciousness is both an assertion of authority and an invitation to disagree.

The same cannot be said of Marie Bonaparte's *Life and Works of Edgar Allan Poe,* which is not surprising since in the early 1950s Bonaparte would square off against Lacan for leadership of the Paris Psychoanalytic Society. Although she shows occasional awareness that she may be straining her readers' credulity, she writes with the authority of, well, a princess, which she was, and a close friend and follower of Freud, which she also was. A great-grand-niece of Napoleon I and wife of Prince George of Greece, Bonaparte persuaded a reluctant Freud to meet with her in 1925 and quickly won his respect and lifelong friendship (Appignanesi and Forrester 338–39). In turn, Bonaparte proved a valuable friend: she used her enormous wealth to establish psychoanalysis in France through publishing and other ventures, and in 1938 she paid the "exit tax" required by the Nazis to get Freud safely out of Austria (and helped close to two hundred others escape Nazi persecution during the war [Bertin 200, 202]).

Bonaparte's "conversion" to Freudian analysis suggests why people were so fascinated with the "new science." At the same time, it provides a kind of model for Bonaparte's reading of Poe's fiction. Bonaparte related to Freud a dream in which she sat on a small bed watching a couple making love on a large bed. When Freud suggested that she had, as a child, seen her parents make love, Bonaparte explained that her mother died when she was a month old; Freud then encouraged her to focus on early childhood memories of nannies. Marie related this memory, recorded in her copy-book:

> I am sitting very low down, on a little chair or box, in Cours la Reine, in my wet-nurse's room. She is standing before the mirror on the chimney piece, where the fire is burning; I am looking at her attentively. She is putting cream on her parted black hair. The pomade, in a little white jar, is on the marble mantel-piece: It is black. I feel disgusted. My nurse has a long yellowish face and looks like a horse. (Bertin 28)

According to Appignanesi and Forrester, "Freud picked apart the elements in the dream — the nanny's uncharacteristic horselike face, indicating a displacement from a man who dealt with horses; the fire, sexual relations; the sooty fireplace, the cloacal inside of the woman's body, and so on — to imply that Marie must indeed have seen her nanny in coitus with the family groom and that this scene provided her with her first perception of sexual difference" (340–41). Bonaparte tracked down the former groom, eighty-two years old, and questioned him; eventually he revealed that he and the nanny had repeatedly engaged in sexual intercourse in front of Marie, from her infancy to about age three (341). Bonaparte's reading of Poe's stories, while more elaborate than Freud's breakthrough interpretation of her own dream, are nearly always in this vein: she invokes displacement and other associations of images, particularly phallic and vaginal symbols, with child-hood memories and trauma to interpret Poe's tales as dreams.

Today *The Life and Works of Edgar Allan Poe* is commonly discussed or excerpted in literary criticism text books as an example of old-school, pre-Lacanian psychoanalytic textual analysis. Bonaparte's discussion of "The Purloined Letter" is included as the first example of psychoanalytic criticism in Shirley Staton's *Literary Theories in Praxis*; her work on Poe merits a five hundred-word summary in Oxford's *Handbook of Critical Approaches to Literature,* where it is referred to as "one of the most widely known psychoanalytic studies of literature" (148); Morton Kaplan and Robert Kloss devote five pages to Bonaparte in their book *The Unspoken Motive: A Guide to Psychoanalytic Criticism*; and Shoshona Felman's critical survey of psychoanalytic approaches to Poe, which includes a substantial discussion of Bonaparte, can be found in Charles Kaplan and William Anderson's *Criticism: Major Statements,* a popular classroom anthology. Since its publication, Bonaparte's book has been hailed as tour de force and ridiculed for its relentless pursuit of Oedipal motives and genital imagery. Only a few commentators have condemned Bonaparte's reading of Poe without paying homage to her inventiveness and tenacity, or to praise the book without acknowledging Bonaparte's tendency to push every reading too far or to ignore the role of Poe's conscious artistic decision-making.[3] A gently condescending comment by Felman probably represents the current consensus: "Like Krutch, [Bonaparte] comes up with a clinical 'portrait of the artist' that, in claiming to account for the poetry, once again verges on caricature and cannot help but make us smile" (141).

And yet Bonaparte's book is, I think, one of the great achievements of Poe scholarship, for a number of reasons. Bonaparte was the first critic to write extensively (by which I mean hundreds of pages) on the Poe canon, covering most of the fiction and poetry as well as *Eureka* with an eye for detail — she was a close reader of the first order. Not surprisingly, then, she simply found things in Poe's works that have since become part of standard readings. Readers tend to remember her more far-fetched Oedipal interpretations, but we should also acknowledge, for instance, that her analysis of the dying woman tales was groundbreaking: "In order that Poe might become the kind of artist he was, a woman had first to die," she writes, equating Usher and Egaeus and the narrators of "Ligeia" and "The Oval Portrait" with Poe but still establishing the framework for many subsequent discussions of these stories. She also took the comic stories seriously long before most other critics. Her exhaustive analysis of "Loss of Breath" is, to my knowledge, the first to regard Mr. Lackobreath's loss as a loss of sexual potency — again, she attributes the impotence back to Poe himself, but that basic insight unlocked the story for future readers and commentators. And throughout her book, Bonaparte painstakingly works through the details of a general statement that today is a given: that although Poe was hardly the first to do so, he dramatized to a startling degree a number of the concepts Freud would name and establish as the fundamentals of modern psychoanalysis. Bonaparte's study makes clear that when it comes to psychoanalytic interpretation, Poe is not just another writer.

Another impressive feature of Bonaparte's work is her ability to connect Poe's works — via Freudian concepts, of course — to a range of myths and anthropological studies. In her provocative discussion of "The Gold-Bug," she supports her contention that buried gold represents both feces and fetus by referring to children's stories such as the goose that laid the golden egg. The fact that Mr. Lackobreath loses his breath while shouting in his wife's ear Bonaparte relates to a mythological tradition of conception through the ear, citing not only the Immaculate Conception but also Rabelais's Gargantua, Hera's being made pregnant by the wind, and "Shigemuni, the Mongol savior [who] . . . having chosen the most perfect of earthly virgins, Mahaenna or Maya, for mother, impregnated her while she slept by entering her right ear while, in the Mahabharata, Kunti, the very pure virgin and later mother of the hero Karna (whose name signifies breath), is similarly impregnated by the sun god" (381). I find these digressions valuable not so much for what they add to our understanding of the stories but for the way they situate Poe in a larger intertextual web, much the way John Irwin's *Mystery to a Solution* (1995) would do half a century later. To put it simply, this approach reinforces the notion that all roads somehow lead back to Poe.

Finally, Bonaparte comes much closer than any of her predecessors and most of her successors to writing a convincing inner biography of Poe, an anatomy of his unconscious. Granted, the book is not "scientific," as she seems to have believed, but if we read it as a work of biography — that is, an attempt to try to understand Poe by using the evidence she had available to her — it's a remarkable effort. Consider for instance the fact that Bonaparte's basic contention — that the death of Elizabeth Arnold had such a profound effect on Poe that virtually everything he wrote, and everything he did, can be traced back to it — recurs as the primary theme of the most respected recent biography of Poe, Kenneth Silverman's *Edgar A. Poe: Mournful and Never-ending Remembrance*. Particularly in her opening section, "Life and Poems," Bonaparte reads biographical evidence as if it were a literary text: while she notes that the name "Muddy" is derived from the German "mutter," she also suggests that the name evokes the humble tasks to which Poe's aunt devoted herself. In her discussion of Poe's drinking, Bonaparte seizes upon the fact the Poe always drank away from home: "In effect, whenever Poe was tempted by living women, drink cleared the way for 'flight' and kept him faithful to his dead mother" (86). Noting (as did Krutch) that Poe allegedly drank himself out of relationships with Mary Devereaux and Helen Whitman, Bonaparte links this "flight" through alcohol to latent homosexuality. Assertions of this sort, along with claims of Poe's impotence and repressed necrophilia, seem overly aggressive — her leaps from evidence to conclusion are indeed likely to "make us smile" (141). But that aggressiveness is perhaps the book's greatest virtue — Bonaparte may not be right, but she's passionate without being moralistic, she is sincerely trying to comprehend Poe and make him comprehensible, and she constructs a surprisingly consistent argument to that effect.

The most trenchant criticisms of Bonaparte raise the same questions I quoted from Claudia Morrison's book earlier, and they reveal the limitations, but also the attraction and wider possibilities, of Freudian literary criticism. Allen Tate, Floyd Stovall, Roger Forclaz, and Kaplan and Kloss all raise essentially the same objection to *The Life and Works,* that Bonaparte reduces genius to neurosis or ignores the role of consciousness in the creation of art. For Stovall, psychoanalytic studies of Poe "are not literary critiques at all, but clinical studies of a supposed psychopathic personality" (183). Forclaz, in a thorough critique written in 1970, takes offense at Bonaparte's treating her investigation as a scientific study: "A system that pretends to explain literature only by means of the unconscious and of early childhood, without taking into account literary movements or the intellectual climate of an era or country, can hardly be called scientific" (188). These critics rightly point to this limitation of Freudian theory and criticism, but in doing so they imply that one mode of criticism denies the relevance of all others, that readers who find Bonaparte's book persuasive would necessarily believe that her insights completely explain Poe's poetry and fiction and render all other criticism obsolete. Even Bonaparte, true believer that she is, does not go that far. She admits that *how* some men with mysterious gifts turn their dreams into works of art "is an aesthetic problem still unsolved" (664). She does not deny that Poe wrote about what he consciously knew — for instance, "The actual impetus to write *The Gold Bug* was doubtless communicated to Poe by his poverty, and the wish to change it for something better" (666). Moreover, her mentor Freud, in his foreword, writes, "investigations such as this do not claim to explain creative genius, but they do reveal the factors which awaken it and the sort of subject matter it is destined to choose" (xi). For the purposes of her book, Bonaparte is not interested in Poe's conscious artistic or life decisions, but she doesn't deny their existence, nor would any sensible reader. Moreover, as Felman points out, "this conception of the mutual exclusiveness, of the clear-cut opposition between 'conscious art' and the unconscious, is itself naive and oversimplified," much like the rigid lines both early psychoanalytic theorists and their critics draw between normality and abnormality, sanity and insanity (143).

But while focusing on the writer's unconscious motives seems perfectly valid, that doesn't mean Bonaparte's readings are "correct." Given the fact that unconscious drives work with or through or against conscious artistic decisions, how can we know *the extent* to which tale X, character Y, or image Z truly reflects Poe's personal inner life, as opposed to reflecting, say, something he had just read or even a dream related to him by Virginia? Is it possible, for instance, that the loss of breath suffered by the narrator of "Loss of Breath" does reflect Poe's fear or awareness of his own impotence, but that the decapitation of Toby Dammitt in "Never Bet the Devil Your Head," while suggestive of castration, does not necessarily point specifically to *Poe's* fear of castration? It seems clear now that Poe's tales can have psychological depth without necessarily being all about Poe himself. Forclaz suggests that, rather than follow Bonaparte's strictly biographical method, one could more profitably explore Poe's work through Jungian depth psychology, an approach a few more recent critics have successfully taken (194).[4] A more radical alternative is to read psychoanalytically while abandoning the notion of a stable "self" that biography takes for granted — that is, to move in the direction of Jacques Lacan.

But before moving in that direction, I would like to consider why biographical readings, whether grounded in psychoanalysis or not, remain so attractive. Kaplan and Kloss argue that for all the virtues of Bonaparte's book, ultimately it is "not a literary explication, but rather a clinically detailed case study of a highly neurotic man who *happened to be a writer*" (193). Kaplan and Kloss are right — Bonaparte's true subject is Poe himself. But the fact that Poe happened to be a writer makes all the difference to Bonaparte, and to the students and fans who are fascinated with the kinds of connections between life and art that Bonaparte explores. As any teacher can tell you, interest in Poe's life often overwhelms the study of his poems and tales; readers of all types are drawn to his biography, his personality and image. It can be frustrating, as a teacher, to see Poe's most complex stories reduced to a Krutch-like thesis statement ("Poe reveals his own insanity through the narrator of 'The Tell-Tale Heart'"). It's also a little unsettling how often students substitute Poe's name for "the narrator" or "the speaker" or even a character's name when writing about a story or poem. And yet I sympathize with my students' desire to make Poe a character in his fiction, and to take as much interest in his life-story as in his stories — they have admirable precedents in Lawrence and Bonaparte. Not only does Poe's life — or, rather, the textual evidence related to it — provide the raw material for a number of good narratives, ranging from anecdotes to the three dozen or so full-length biographies; biographical evidence and speculation provide an important set of intertexts that complicate and expand the effects Poe's works have on us.

For example, prior to the 1920s, the question of Poe's relationship with Virginia was part of the sometimes heated debate over his moral character. Poe's defenders — from Sarah Helen Whitman to John Henry Ingram to Susan Archer Talley Weiss — represented the relationship as chaste, a sign of Poe's "purity." "Patiently and uncomplainingly he bore his unhappy lot," Weiss conjectured in her 1907 *Home Life of Poe*, "and it is to be noted to his credit that howsoever he might at times go astray, no word or act of unkindness toward the wife and mother who loved him was ever known to escape from him" (225). Although his notes indicate some skepticism, Weiss's contemporary George Woodberry accepted this view: "From the beginning his marriage was, in a sense, no marriage; it was a family arrangement. His love for his wife was never that of man for woman" (185). If, as these and other writers assumed, Poe never had sexual relations with other women, his own purity was preserved by this "family arrangement," a belief that supports a key claim on behalf of Poe's poetry at the end of the nineteenth and early twentieth century, that it is "pure," because Poe was essentially an apostle of beauty.

When, in the 1920s and 30s, the psychoanalytic critics I've been discussing reinterpreted his motives for marrying Virginia, they turned Poe's "purity" inside out. Krutch, as we have seen, argued that Poe married in order to avoid sex:

> Doubtless he was aware in his own mind of nothing except the charm which feminine beauty divorced from any suggestion of conscious sex had for him and he would call his admiration for Virginia a worship of purity: but when we consider the distaste which his writings reveal for the whole idea of sexual passion and the unhappy history of his constantly frustrated flirtations with other women we may guess that this abnormal absorption in purity was but one of the outward signs of a deep-lying inhibition and we may guess also the function which Virginia was to perform in his life. (53–54)

Hervey Allen, in his biography from that same year, implied that Poe's attraction to Virginia was rooted in neurosis: "The truth seems to be that he was a type which is so hypersensitive as to be somewhat revolted by the fully developed womanly form, and for some of its more hearty implications" (291). Lawrence, acknowledging no distinction between Poe and his narrators, read Poe's marriage as the blueprint for the marriages in "Ligeia," "Berenice," and "Eleonora," as well as the incestuous relationship of the Ushers. Bonaparte, though unaware of Lawrence's work on Poe, accepts and develops the conjectures of Allen and Krutch:

> Virginia, of all the women in Poe's life, was most fitted to evoke Elizabeth Arnold and unconsciously make him feel that, while loving another, he continued true to his first love.
>
> Firstly, her name was Virginia and in the State of that name he had seen his never-to-be-forgotten mother languish and die; there too, Frances Allan, his second mother, gave him a home and there he knew his "Helen." Again, Virginia was of the same blood, almost a sister, one whom he called his "Sis"; there was a touch of incest about their union. As with his mother, the incest barrier seemed to keep them apart, not as then, because he was too little, but because Virginia was too young. . . . The "mother" relived in Virginia as in the second Morella and as, in Rowena, she re-embodied Ligeia. (82)

Granted, Bonaparte makes too much of the coincidence of Virginia's name (as she does with Muddy's — see above), but that sort of linguistic wordplay and evocation of the uncanny would certainly appeal to Poe, much as it probably did to Freud.

Later commentators have been more responsible than the early Freudians, and far less provocative on the subject of Poe's marriage. Several biographers have insisted that there is no dirty little secret, that despite the age difference and Virginia's illness, the marriage was healthy and, at some point, consummated. William Bittner, in his 1962 biography, imagined Edgar and Virginia in 1841, before Virginia's tuberculosis set in, alone in Philadelphia while Muddy was visiting friends in New Jersey: "He and Virginia were alone, having passed without awareness from the infatuation and impulse that had led to their marriage to the deep contentment of affectionate companions and companionable lovers. Virginia was no longer a child, but a young woman and wife of four years' maturity [she would have been eighteen, Poe thirty-two]. Theirs was a family in more than church vows . . ." and so on (158). Arthur Hobson Quinn, not a biographer given to wild speculation, says little about the relationship but depicts the marriage in surprisingly sentimental terms: "As she matured, the adoration of the child he had married grew into the devotion of the woman, and the physical attraction for the handsome young cousin she worshiped blossomed into a spiritual passion which his love had nurtured and which, in its turn sent its roots deeper and deeper into his life" (346) — a view he later supports by printing an acrostic valentine poem Virginia wrote for Edgar in 1846. One of Poe's most recent biographers, Jeffrey Meyers, adamantly claims that "Autobiographical elements in Poe's works suggest that their sexual life was *normal*" (86). Kenneth Silverman, in what is probably the most psychologically driven biography to appear since Bonaparte's, never really addresses the question at all. Thus, there are three basic responses — pre-Freudian, Freudian, and post-Freudian — to the question of Poe's relationship with Virginia, sexual and otherwise: that Poe made an unfortunate (and probably sexless) marriage but, noble man that he was, remained chaste and true to Virginia; that Poe married Virginia specifically to avoid sex, because he was afraid of mature women; and that the marriage began as an expediency but grew into a healthy relationship — presumably, when Virginia's health and Muddy's whereabouts permitted it, a sexual one. The last interpretation is clearly the most responsible, but the Freudian reading remains the most compelling.

But why does any of it matter? What is the proper relationship between biography and literary analysis, and, more specifically, what does Poe's sex life, the "purity" or impurity of his relationship with his wife, have to do with Poe's literary productions? It's a truism of biography that it borrows heavily from the novel for its structure and style; literary biography has the even greater challenge of not just making sense out of countless fragments of information but including the author's writing within that coherent whole — the life and mind of, in this case, Poe. The attempt to integrate the poetry or fiction into that larger picture is the great challenge — it's where literary critics often find fault with literary biography, and yet it's what critics and for the most part the public want from literary biography. What we think about Poe's relationship with his wife has some bearing on the way we interpret the stories — whether "we" are students or teachers, fans or scholars.

Take, for instance, "Morella," a tale with many relatives in the Poe canon, the most immediate of which are "Berenice," "Ligeia," and "Eleonora," the stories named for the women who die in them, narrated by the men who love them, objectify them, torture them, possibly kill them, and grieve for them. A number of critics, notably Cynthia Jordan, Leland S. Person, Joan Dayan, and J. Gerald Kennedy, have analyzed the gendered power relations in these stories, and all to some degree take up the question of whether Poe endorses or exposes the misogynist fantasies that create the central conflicts. Most critics who consider this group rightly focus on "Ligeia," the most complex and problematic of the four. "Morella," if regarded as more than a warm-up exercise for "Ligeia," is analyzed as a commentary on competing philosophical conceptions of identity and an example of Poe's interest in metempsychosis. But "Morella" is also a perverse love story. Written in 1835, at a time when Poe might well have been engaged to his young cousin (published four months before the alleged secret marriage in Sept. of 1835), the story reflects a fear of a loveless marriage. I think we should take with a grain of salt assertions such as Hervey Allen's that Virginia was the "prototype of Poe's heroines," particularly since one thing nearly every commentator agrees on is that Virginia was not intellectually gifted, whereas "Morella" is virtually defined by her intellect. However, in contrast with the narrator of "Ligeia," the narrator of "Morella" repeatedly tells us his was a passionless relationship: "the fires were not of Eros," he says in the first paragraph; "I never spoke of passion, nor thought of love" (234). Her physicality — the touch of her cold hand and the sound of her singing voice — makes him shudder; when she becomes ill, he admits that he wishes she were dead. Freudian biographers and critics, as we have seen, pin a great deal on Poe's fear of sexual intercourse and attribute his marriage to that fear. In that regard, "Morella" stands out as the only dying-woman story in which the narrator insists he does not love the title character, at least not in her first incarnation, and it is the only one in which Poe explicitly indicates that the two have had sex: Morella refers to her daughter as "thy child and mine" (236).

Marriage in this story is a perverse impulse. The consequences of its consummation are the wife's death — she dies in childbirth — which the narrator wishes for but which thrusts him into a world of guilt and sorrow; the daughter haunts him and forces him to love his wife now that she is gone, because in what seems to be an instant after her birth, and right after he names her (or acknowledges her as) Morella, she too dies. We can read this along with Bonaparte: "Since love, from its infancy, for Poe, had worn death's aspect, it was an erotic necessity for him that, in her turn, the second Morella should die, as did the little Virginia some few years later, in the same manner as Elizabeth Arnold" (222). Speaking of his daughter, the narrator tells us, "I loved her with a love more fervent than I had believed it possible to feel for any denizen of earth. But, ere long, the heaven of this pure affection became darkened, and gloom, and horror, and grief, swept over it in clouds" (237). Why does the narrator love the daughter even as she develops into an exact replica of the detested mother? Perhaps because eros is not part of the equation, his love for the daughter is "pure." To that extent I think the Poe's Freudian commentators were right: however much it might have been endemic to his Southern male upbringing, Poe seems to have internalized a need to deny all sexual passion for women as unseemly; "Morella," like the other tales of dying women, takes this male neurosis to an extreme, exposing what Leland Person refers to as "the objectifying, even murderous powers of the male gaze" (141). Ultimately, we might just as easily regard Morella as the kind of woman Poe was afraid of as a woman for whom Virginia was a model — that is, she's an adult, and an intellectual, and someone with whom a husband must have sex — and therefore a bad choice. We might also complicate the Freudian reading of Poe's relationship with Virginia (and perhaps affirm the claims of later critics that eventually the marriage was consummated) by contrasting "Morella" with the later story "Eleonora" (1841), in which an implied sexual encounter evokes a Whitmanesque change in the landscape: "Strange brilliant flowers, star-shaped, burst out upon the trees where no flowers had been known before" (640). But what's important, I think, is that we recognize that even as Poe exposes the dangers of objectifying women in this group of stories, he describes, consciously or unconsciously, his own strange relationship with the inseparable concepts of purity and perversity, and a psychoanalytic reading of Poe's experience with women (which in a fuller discussion would not be restricted to his wife) helps to unfold that paradox, which is of course both fictional and real.

In this rather sketchy outline of a biographical reading of "Morella," I make no claim to having discovered the secret embedded in the story or the "correct" reading, but rather have suggested that some interplay between biographical and fictional texts can enrich our understanding of both: that suggestion is somewhat different from Bonaparte's project of analyzing Poe's inner life using his fictions as dreams. Her attempt to explain it all with clinical precision is admirable and courageous, but as we have seen, it leaves her vulnerable to a number of criticisms. One final objection I would like to address came in an early review by Mario Praz, who ridiculed *The Life and Works* as an example of how psychoanalysis "cheats": "Now a card game in which any card can be a trump to suit one of the players, would obviously not make sense. But psychoanalysis is just such a preposterous game" because any image can be interpreted, through "chains of association," to mean whatever the analyst wants it to mean. You go looking for an Oedipal fantasy, you're going to find one. But to a great extent, the same could be said of virtually any critical approach; indeed, a standard assignment in lit-crit classes is to choose a literary text and describe how each of the following "schools" would interpret it: psychoanalytic, Marxist, feminist, etc. Such assignments are useful in testing "course mastery" but they also underwrite a cynical attitude toward literary criticism — it's all a big game — and give the impression that the only real choices critics make are what school to adhere to and what texts to plug into the party line, when in fact much of the best literary criticism is eclectic and nonformulaic. The question Praz raised in the 1930s, of "validity in interpretation," was debated with particular vehemence in the 1970s and 1980s, when the term "reader-response" was applied to a range of approaches that challenged the stability of literal meaning and valid interpretations. The idea that the text is "in the reader" or even in the reader's interpretive community would seem to make all interpretation as tautological as psychoanalytic reading seemed to Praz. If the goal of interpretation is to get to the one true meaning of the text, then Praz is right, because Bonaparte *is* stacking the deck. But if the goal is to widen the range of plausible meanings or just to make the object of study more interesting, then "cheating" in the sense that Praz uses the word is a moot issue, and what we're left with is not so much a failed reading of Poe but a fascinating rewriting of his tales.

But then, I am in effect rewriting Bonaparte by representing her analysis in this way. The fact remains, as Peter Brooks observes, that "[t]he reference to psychoanalysis has traditionally been to close rather than open the argument, and the text" (3). I contend that Bonaparte wants to close the argument but opens it despite herself. Brooks, in "The Idea of a Psychoanalytic Literary Criticism," formulates a model that would regard reading itself as the object of analysis, rather than the usual suspects — author, reader, and fictional characters. Employing the concept of Freudian transference, which "actualizes the past in symbolic form so that it can be repeated, replayed, worked through to another outcome" (13),

Brooks argues that "meaning . . . is not simply 'in the text,' nor wholly the fabrication of a reader (or a community of readers), but in the dialogic struggle and collaboration of the two, in the textual possibilities in the process of reading. . . . As in reading, hypotheses of construal prove to be strong and valuable when they produce more text, when they create in the text previously unperceived networks of relation and significance, finding confirmation in the extension of the narrative and semantic web" (14–15). Thus Bonaparte, who like Poe grew up in the shadow of her biological mother's death, and whose relationships with both her father and husband were strained and lacking in affection, and who found in Freud both a father-figure and mentor, is in a sense writing the narrative of her conversion to Freudian analysis in *The Life and Works,* affirming again and again that childhood trauma and fantasy underwrite the adult's worldview, that eros and thanatos are the driving forces of our lives.[5] Although Bonaparte intended her analysis of Poe to be what Brooks is urging us to move away from, I think her book, despite her intentions, models in many ways the dialogic struggle he refers to.

For Brooks, "Psychoanalysis is not an arbitrarily chosen intertext for literary analysis but rather a particularly insistent and demanding intertext, in that mapping across the boundaries from one territory to the other both confirms and complicates our understanding of how mind reformulates the real, how it constructs the necessary fictions by which we dream, desire, interpret, indeed by which we constitute ourselves as human subjects" (17). The best psychoanalytic readings are a dialogue between the analyst and the text-as-analysand (or perhaps the text–as–analyst and the critic-as-analysand) in which insight into the human experience that transcends both analyst and analysand emerges in the process. Several post-Bonapartian psychoanalytic readings of Poe achieve this insight, most notably Daniel Hoffman's *Poe Poe Poe Poe Poe Poe Poe.* As unorthodox in his approach as Bonaparte was orthodox, Hoffman enters and re-enters Poe's writing by way of his own memories of earlier encounters with Poe, associating his old high school with the house of Usher, recalling a recurring nightmare inspired by Poe's spoof "A Predicament," and, as a student, having scrawled "I hate Poe" across the flyleaf of his copy of Poe's works. Hoffman does not exactly present himself as a psychoanalytic critic; in the early chapters of the book especially, he approaches the poems, the poetic theory, and the detective tales more in the formalist manner of fellow poets Richard Wilbur and Allen Tate. But as he goes on, Bonaparte's influence becomes increasingly palpable, as Hoffman refers to her repeatedly in terms that show both respect and skepticism. Referring to Bonaparte's reading of "The Cask of Amontillado," in which the wine cellar symbolizes the mother's sex organs and womb and the murder of Fortunato represents the killing of the father-figure, Hoffman writes, "Come to think of it, how can we deny the thesis? But, thinking further, how can we accept it as a full exposition of the narrator's horrible purpose, his malignancy, his compulsion fifty years ago so to act, his obsession now to confess his action?" (219) That response epitomizes Hoffman's relationship with Bonaparte: he agrees with her, but he insists on more nuanced and less strictly Freudian readings. At one point — perhaps the only point where he directly criticizes her — he writes, "Were we to take Mme Bonaparte as literally as she takes Poe, would we have any right or reason to take either of them seriously?" (254) Rather than responding, as many readers do, that Bonaparte goes too far, he regards her readings as "literal" starting points from which to expand.

Hoffman expands the old-school Freudian reading of Poe by focusing less on Poe's unconscious and more on the collective unconscious he tapped into. The story of his own fascination with Poe becomes a treatise on why millions of readers are similarly fascinated and moved:

> But the hapless accidents of one miserable scrivener's biography are in "Ligeia" successfully mythologized, universalized, raised to the level of archetype. Strange though the combination seems, in Poe, of ideality with necrophilia, here he has imagined a condition of blessedness, its loss, the loser's search for its recurrence in another love-object, the intensification of that love into hatred for its substitute and longing for that lost love, and a final apotheosis in which the lost love seems to reappear. (256)

Several paragraphs later, he puts a sharper point on this claim: "Thus as fiction, as myth, as psychological archetype, the pattern of imagined action in 'Ligeia' is not only fantastic but self-consistent — and true, in its kinky way, to human experience as well as to the accidents of one particularly blighted life" (257). Hoffman returns repeatedly to that point in his reading of the Poe canon. While operating within the triad of author, character(s), and reader that Brooks wants criticism to escape from, Hoffman, by keeping all three of those balls in the air, avoids the trap of simply putting

Poe or his characters on the couch. And by writing about his own experience as a reader, he avoids making empty or pretentious claims about "the
reader." And yet, when he suggests that the obsessions and perverse impulses Poe knew and wrote about in some ways affect us all, I don't think
he is reaching for a larger significance that isn't there.

Hoffman is particularly insightful regarding Poe's explorations of the
relationship between love and death, also a preoccupation of Bonaparte's
and a leading contender for Poe's most obsessive theme. "I could not love
except where Death / Was mingling his with Beauty's breath," wrote Poe
in the "Introduction" to the 1831 *Poems,* and the protagonists of some of
his most famous works ("Ligeia," "The Raven," and "The Fall of the
House of Usher" among them) share this fate — or psychic need. Bonaparte argued convincingly that the loss of Poe's mother when he was two
years old established this pattern in his inner life and his fiction. Building
on Bonaparte's claims, Hoffman describes *Eureka* as

> a brilliant projection outward upon the universe of the conflict between
> Eros and Thanatos, between the life-wish and the will to self-
> destruction. . . . The rhythm imposed upon experience by the conflict
> between these irreconcilable instincts we recognize in its other mani-
> festations too: in the impulsion and expulsion of breathing (so frequent
> a motif in Poe's tales!); it is characteristic also of the sexual act, as,
> metaphorically, of the entire life history of a species or individual. It is
> imprinted in nature in the double helix, it is reproduced in art in the
> shapes of forms. It is the deepest, the simplest, the most unitary truth
> of our natures. A double truth. (289)

Hoffman is equally adept at explicating the paradoxes of love and death
represented in Poe's tales and poems. More recently, to cite a few examples, J. Gerald Kennedy has explored these same tensions in *Poe, Death,
and the Life of Writing* (1987), to be discussed in the next chapter;
Kenneth Silverman has made the motif of mourning — Poe's experience
of love primarily through loss — the unifying theme of his 1991 biography; and Elisabeth Bronfen, in an ambitious essay linking Freud, Poe
("Ligeia"), and Hitchcock (*Vertigo*), expounds on the paradox that "[t]o
recover a lost love object in the embodiment of another entails acknowledging precisely the loss that one is reinvesting libidinal energy to deny"

(103). Freudian psychoanalysis, then, has proved essential to opening up this discussion of Poe's treatment of love and death.

Those works just mentioned, like Hoffman's, succeed because they recognize the ways that Poe's tales, for all their abstraction and stylized gothicism, convey profound insights into human experience without focusing narrowly on Poe, his characters, or "the reader." And a good case could be made that psychoanalysis is the best way to discover how, in Hoffman's words, from "conditions so willed, contrived, and unactual, he succeeds in evoking real terror, real love, real hatred, real guilt, the real Imp of the Perverse" (325). In an essay published in 1993, Christopher Benfey divides commentators on Poe into two camps: "those who claim to have keys to the puzzles, and . . . those who find the puzzles to be impossible or unworthy of solution" (27), equating the first group with psychoanalytic and "psychologically astute" critics. Benfey's dichotomy is rather limiting, but his own reading, which refers to Wittgenstein and J. L. Austin rather than Freud or Jung, nonetheless places him in the camp of the psychologically astute puzzle solvers. Benfey investigates why the narrators of "The Tell-Tale Heart" and "The Black Cat" kill the ones they either love or are loved by. He provides original, subtle readings of both stories in light of twin fears: of being misunderstood (both narrators are driven by an intense need to explain themselves) and of being isolated from other people. Relating Poe to Rainer Maria Rilke and Robert Frost, he suggests that a fear of intimacy inheres in the fear of isolation, perhaps as its perverse opposite (his logic is not altogether clear on this point), and he concludes with what sounds like psychiatric counseling of a very sobering kind:

> Poe seems, like Frost, to be saying, These fears are always with us — the fear of love and the fear of isolation. Taken to extremes, they both lead to disaster: one cat avoids us and is blinded, another cat follows us and is killed. To live life is to steer a dangerous course between these extremes and there is no point at which the current widens. To declare oneself safe — as the imp of the perverse tempts us to do — is to be lost. (43)

Poorly handled, this kind of reading can easily become preachy and reductive, but Benfey's application of Poe's tales to "real life" is hardly moralistic, and, perhaps more importantly, it is sensitive to the texts themselves. Like Hoffman, though, he realizes that most people read literature for insights into what Faulkner famously called "the problems of the human heart in conflict with itself" (273), and sees his job (I presume) as articulating those conflicts as they are represented in literature.

The psychoanalytic readings I find most compelling all share a strong authorial presence: Lawrence imposes his personal psychotheology on his reading of Poe; Hoffman introduces his interpretations with accounts of his own nightmares and childhood memories; Bonaparte is less forthcoming, but when read in light of her own biography, her analyses are no less personal than those others. This readerly approach to psychoanalytic criticism is epitomized by Norman Holland, whose 1980 essay on "The Purloined Letter" greatly exceeds Hoffman's in personal revelation in order to make a larger point about the subjectivity inherent in reading and interpretation:

> I read this story when I was thirteen and I also had something to hide, something that is perfectly known to anyone who knows anything at all about thirteen-year-old boys. Most obvious, yet most carefully concealed. In the Prefect's phrase, "This is an affair demanding the greatest secrecy, and . . . I should most probably lose the position I now hold were it known that I confided it to any one." . . . [T]he villainous D— "is, perhaps, the most really energetic human being now alive — but that is only when nobody sees him." Can a thirteen-year-old boy find something of himself in D—? (310)

Holland then compares himself to Bonaparte, who does not reveal her own secrets in the course of her explication of the same tale: "Like most readings from first-phase or symbolic Freudianism, it costs nothing. It costs me something to admit to you that I masturbated, even thirty-nine years ago and at an age when all boys do. It costs nothing to say a little brass knob stands for the clitoris" (311).

Holland wants to expose the way most literary criticism pretends to be objective, pretends that there is a normal or standard way of interpreting texts when in fact every reader's response is unique; he implies what I have already argued here, that Bonaparte read Poe the way she did largely because of her traumatic childhood experiences and, of course, her involvement with Freud. Holland foregrounds his own biography to show why he reads "The Purloined Letter" as he does; Bonaparte does not. For Holland, these self-references are more than a rhetorical gesture; they exemplify what he calls transactive criticism, "in which the literant builds the response, and the text simply changes the consequences of what the literant brings to it" (319). As opposed to a psychoanalytic reading of the text or the author, transactive criticism recognizes that the psychology of the literant (formerly known as the reader) determines what the text will mean. This is a great theory, but a hard one to put into practice: literary criticism based on the critic's emotional baggage is likely to be solipsistic and boring (I had a black cat once, but its name wasn't Pluto), or maybe interesting but embarrassing (For me, "Ligeia" evokes fantasies of Mortitia Addams). And yet, how can we deny the validity of Holland's basic claim? If reading were really text-active (that is, if meanings inhered in texts), then it "would be an anomalous procedure, quite different from our other acts of interpreting the world around us" (318). Responding to literature is a highly personal activity, but how can it lead anyone other than the individual free-associating reader to a fuller understanding of "The Purloined Letter" or any other text?

Holland asks and answers this same question in his essay. It is a risky venture, he admits, but the critic's job is to try to make his or her own "feelings and associations" operative for other readers. For instance, though the rest of us did not read the story in Holland's thirty-nine-year-old perma-gloss-bound paperback copy of Poe's tales,

> [we] can take the association through "The Purloined Letter" by reading the story as a contrast between such tight, spatially defined texts as my paperback or the letter that Dupin physically removes and the indefinite texts of all the different narrations, the Prefect's story, Dupin's story, the narrator's story (which extends outward to include two other Dupin stories) and, I would say, extends even to the Perma-Gloss binding of my thirty-nine-year-old copy. Can you get a richer experience of this story by thinking of it as a prototype of all stories — both physically defined but conceptually and emotionally infinite — open to a million different transactions of it? (320)

No? Then try this one: "I can also feel in [the story] the exuberance of human development. Like magic tricks [Holland discussed his teenage interest in magic earlier in the essay], we give up something, the lost card, the cut rope, in order to get something even more precious, the knowledge that is power. Is that a feeling you can take through the story?" (321). Yes, I would answer.

Obviously transactive criticism is a hit-or-miss enterprise, but I am impressed by how closely it resembles my own and many of my colleagues' teaching methods. In class I often bring up personal and pop-culture references that I hope will connect and help students find an entry into a difficult text or another way of looking at a text they are too comfortable with. Students, in turn, are likely to offer their own associations, tempered, no doubt, by what they think their classmates will accept. These are not exactly "free associations" because they are limited by audience and a collective sense of classroom decorum. But our goal as a class is to find — or even to make — a range of reasonable meanings out of literary texts, and the class-discussion format often achieves that goal. I think it is harder to achieve with written and published literary criticism because a writer's audience is more of an abstraction than a class participant's audience; responses will be slower in coming, if they come at all, to this book than to my offhand classroom examples. (Listserve discussions fall somewhere in between.) However difficult and awkward it may be to practice Holland's transactive criticism in print, it offers a valuable reminder that no criticism is truly objective and that all interpretation contains an element of psychoanalysis: as we interpret texts, we interpret ourselves.

Holland chose "The Purloined Letter" as the focus for his essay largely because that story had already been used as a model for analysis by two of the most influential intellectual figures of the late twentieth century, Jacques Lacan and Jacques Derrida. Holland wrote his essay, which includes several paragraphs of response to Lacan and Derrida, for a collection entitled *The Purloined Poe: Lacan, Derrida, and Psychoanalytic Reading*. As the book's title suggests, "The Purloined Letter" has been appropriated as a testing ground for theories of language, analysis, and reading. (As if to underscore this point, the book's cover depicts a hand lifting Poe's head off his collar, with a fountain pen aimed at the neck like an instrument of decapitation — and yet, the editors clearly approve of the "purloining" of Poe). Lacan's discussion of "The Purloined Letter" in a 1956 seminar on *Beyond the Pleasure Principle* is largely responsible for the influence he has had on literary studies since the 1970s (Muller and Richardson vii); its importance was magnified when Derrida, the theorist most closely identified with deconstruction as a philosophical and literary practice, wrote an extended response in 1975. By the time Muller and Richardson compiled their book in 1988, they were able to include previously published commentary by Barbara Johnson, Shoshana Felman, and Jane Gallop on the seminar and Derrida's response, to which they added new analyses by Irene Harvey and Muller.

The most striking feature of Lacan's "Seminar," and his writing in general, is its difficulty. According to Karl E. Jirgens, "Lacan claimed that he structured his papers [written for oral reading at seminars] in a particular manner in order to suggest the shifting structures of dreams and the unconscious. His predilection for language play, puns, and associative leaps in logic illustrates and enacts the relationship of mind to language" (397). Jane Gallop argues that Lacan's use of language "mirrors" his theory in a particularly Lacanian sense: In opposition to the traditional conception of mirrors as reflectors, "Lacan posits that the mirror constructs the self, that the self as organized entity is actually an imitation of the cohesiveness of the mirror image. . . . Lacan's trick with mirrors suggests that the preposterous difficulty, only apparently secondary, actually constructs the theory, constructs the image of the theory, the notion of its coherent identity" (38). What a Poe-esque reversal! It should come as no surprise, then, that Lacan should choose a Poe story as an allegory of his psychoanalytic theory. The "Seminar on 'The Purloined Letter'" is one of Lacan's best-known lecture/essays, certainly the best-known among literary scholars, and yet because of its complexity, commentators on Lacan and the Lacan-Derrida exchange typically qualify anything they say about them with the observation that they are not attempting to write a summary or thorough analysis: "I will not enter here into the complexity of the psychoanalytic issues involved in Lacan's 'Seminar on "The Purloined Letter"'" (Shoshana Felman 144); "The theories [of Lacan] are so complex and couched in such convoluted and, at times, inspissated prose that here there is space to make but two points" (*The Penguin Dictionary of Literary Terms and Literary Theory* 334); "Any attempt to do 'justice' to three such texts [Poe's, Lacan's, and Derrida's] is obviously out of the question" (Barbara Johnson 214); "Because Lacan's and Derrida's essays defy concise summary, and because this continuing discussion has more to do with theories of language and writing in general than with 'The Purloined Letter' specifically, I will not attempt to summarize their arguments" (Scott Peeples 129). Since here my subject is not "The Purloined Letter" but psychoanalytic approaches to it, I cannot use that excuse again; nonetheless, I would like to invoke the ritual disclaimer that my comments here are not an attempt to "cover" Lacan's seminar or Derrida's response.

While it is important to keep in mind that Lacan was not concerned with contributing to Poe scholarship with a literary explication of "The Purloined Letter" — he was writing, or rather speaking, primarily for psychoanalysts — he did in fact alter the course of commentary on Poe's story by pointing out the mathematical structure of the two scenes of theft. He represents the two scenes as triangles, with a character at each angle. In the first scene, in the royal boudoir, the royal personage who Lacan presumes is the King occupies the position of *blindness*: he takes no note of the letter. The female "royal personage," presumably the Queen, is the holder (but not the possessor) of the letter and one who can see the king's blindness to it. The Minister D— occupies the third angle, from which he sees the letter for what it is and sees the king's blindness to it; he is therefore in a position to take the letter and put a facsimile in its place. In the second scene, the Queen's agent, the Prefect of Police, is in the position of blindness (can't find the letter); D— as the holder of the letter, is in the position formerly held by the Queen; like the Queen in scene one, he can see the Prefect's blindness but is vulnerable to the greater perception of the third party, which in this scene is Dupin, who, like D— who previously occupied the third corner, sees the letter in the cardrack for what it is and sees the Prefect's blindness to it. Shoshana Felman provides this diagram:

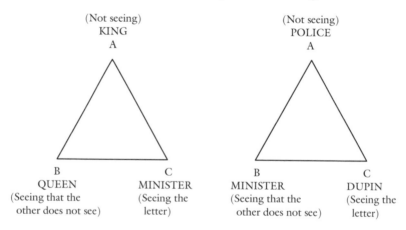

(Not seeing)   (Not seeing)
KING   POLICE
A   A

B   C   B   C
QUEEN   MINISTER   MINISTER   DUPIN
(Seeing that the   (Seeing the   (Seeing that the   (Seeing the
other does not see)   letter)   other does not see)   letter)

Such an observation could lead to an astute traditional reading of "The Purloined Letter," as it did in the case of Liahna Klenman Babener, who, without any help from Lacan, published a fine essay on the tale's doubling motif in 1972 (the same year Lacan's "Seminar" was published in English). But for Lacan, this repetition, like the repetitions Freud discusses in *Beyond the Pleasure Principle,* points to the primacy of the "signifying chain," in which the "pure signifier" has no signified but is closely associated with the phallus, not the sexual organ itself but, in Lacan's formulation, a locus of never-to-be-fulfilled desire. The pure signifier's analogue in the story is the letter, whose content (the non-existent signified) is never revealed and whose "itinerary" determines where the players position themselves in the triangle. Lacan describes the signifier/letter's strange power: "For the signifier is a unit in its very uniqueness, being by nature symbol only of an absence. Which is why we cannot say of the purloined letter that, like other objects, it must be *or* not be in a particular place but that unlike them it will be *and* not be where it is, wherever it goes" (39). As for the characters who occupy the triangle, Lacan likens them to ostriches, "the second believing itself invisible because the first has stuck its head in the ground, all the while letting the third calmly pluck its rear" (32). A few pages later he connects this set of relationships, dependent on the signifier/letter, to "what happens in the repetition automatism. . . . [i]t is not only the subject, but the subjects, grasped in their intersubjectivity, who line up, in other words our ostriches, to whom we here return, and who, more docile than sheep, model their very being on the moment of the signifying chain which traverses them" (43). Near the end of the seminar, Lacan reasserts the primacy of the signifier as the driving force of the unconscious:

> So runs the signifier's answer, above and beyond all significations: "You think you act when I stir you at the mercy of the bonds through which I know your desires. Thus do they grow in force and multiply in objects, bringing you back to the fragmentation of your shattered childhood. So be it: such will be your feast until the return of the stone guest I shall be for you since you call me forth." (52)

Although drawing that connection between Poe's story and Lacan's theory is, I think, the main purpose of the seminar, other lines of thought spin out from Lacan's non-linear argument. For instance, Gallop and Felman explain the implications Lacan's reading of "The Purloined Letter" hold for the practice of psychoanalysis itself. "Lacan condemns ego psychology as hopelessly mired in the imaginary because it promotes an identification between the analysand's ego and the analyst's," explains Gallop. For Lacan, the imaginary is the stage, or register, where the analysand strongly identifies with the analyst, a stage associated with "transference," which in laymen's terms is often reduced to "falling in love with your analyst." Gallop goes on: "The ego, for Lacan, is an imago," which she defines as "an unconscious image or cliché 'which preferentially orients the way in which the subject apprehends other people'" (60–61).[6] In ego psychology, "[t]he analysand has no way of grasping the working of his imagoes. He has simply substituted the analyst's imaginary for his own" (Gallop 61). For Lacan, the goal of psychoanalysis is to reach the register of the "symbolic," in which the analyst acts as a mirror for the analysand but in such a way that the analysand sees the analyst as a *neutral* mirror, works through the imaginary but can see it *as* the imaginary — that is, sees the mirror itself and not just the reflection — and is not under the spell of the analyst. This advanced degree of insight seems to parallel the position of D— in the first scene and Dupin in the second. Recognizing this, Felman diagrams Lacan's stages of perception as they correspond with (but are not identical to) Freud's categories of superego, ego, and id:

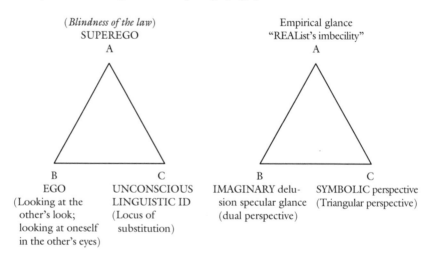

(*Blindness of the law*)		
SUPEREGO		
A		
B	C	
EGO	UNCONSCIOUS	
(Looking at the	LINGUISTIC ID	
other's look;	(Locus of	
looking at oneself	substitution)	
in the other's eyes)		

Empirical glance	
"REAList's imbecility"	
A	
B	C
IMAGINARY delu-	SYMBOLIC perspective
sion specular glance	(Triangular perspective)
(dual perspective)	

The difficulty with this application of the twin triangles in "The Purloined Letter," though, is that in the logic of the story — and the logic of Lacan's reading of it — to be in position "C" is to be one inevitable move away from position "B," as Muller and Richardson point out: "The paradox is that . . . the 'acting accordingly' of the third position tends to catch the subject up in the dynamics of repetition that drag him into the second position, and so forth, without any conscious intention on his part" (63). And yet to recognize this problem is to appreciate another link between Poe and Lacan, their sense that to feel oneself safe is itself a great danger, to believe that one has arrived at the truth is to be deluded, to declare one's mastery over a situation or body of knowledge is to declare one's blindness to the forces that overwhelm or control us all.

Derrida accused Lacan of just that sort of hubris/blindness in his essay "Le facteur de la verité," translated into English as "The Purveyor of Truth." As the sarcastic title suggests, Derrida, deconstructor of the notion of stable truth, sees Lacan as one who sets himself up as a truth-merchant, the man with all the answers: "Lacan leads us back to the truth, to a truth which itself cannot be lost. He brings back the letter, shows that the letter brings itself back toward its *proper* place via a *proper* itinerary, and, as he overtly notes, it is this destination which interests him, destiny as destination" (181). Throughout the essay, Derrida demonstrates what Lacan leaves out of his reading of "The Purloined Letter" in order to make the story fit his purposes; in particular, he argues that Lacan's triangles should be rectangles that include the narrator's role. As Barbara Johnson demonstrates, Derrida's critique of Lacan depends on the same slights-of-hand that he exposes in Lacan's essay: "Derrida's repetition of the very gestures he is criticizing does not in itself invalidate his criticism of their effects, but it does problematize his statement condemning their existence" (218). Holland puts the case succinctly: "Derrida, I think, writes out of a need not to believe, a need to *dis*trust. Yet, as with Lacan, I feel the absence is itself a presence. Disbelief is itself a belief in disbelief" (316). Derrida demonstrates that even a writer like Lacan, who seeks to undermine the authority of the (psycho)analyst as all-knowing, ultimately only reasserts that authority and becomes himself a "purveyor of truth," — and yet, by doing so, Derrida places himself, like the Minister D—, in a spot where his own reading can be deconstructed by Barbara Johnson.[7]

For the purposes of this chapter, Derrida's most important dig at Lacan may be his claim — cast in the sneering rhetorical questions Poe liked to use in similar circumstances — that Lacan more or less plagiarized part of his reading from that other rival, Marie Bonaparte: "Why then does the seminar refind, along with the truth, the same meaning and the same topos as did Marie Bonaparte when, skipping over the text, she proposed a psychobiographical reading of 'The Purloined Letter' in 1933? Is this a coincidence?" (187). More specifically, he claims that "[f]or Bonaparte too, the castration of the woman (of the mother) is the final sense, what 'The Purloined Letter' means. And truth means a readequation or reappropriation as the desire to stop up the whole" (188). Derrida must simplify Lacan's conception of the signifier (as castration) to make this claim, but he rightly points out Bonaparte's influence on Lacan and the complexity of *her* argument: "But Bonaparte does what Lacan does not: she relates 'The Purloined Letter' to other texts by Poe. And she analyzes the gesture of doing so" (188). It is difficult not to suspect that only his rivalry with Lacan would lead Derrida to speak up for Bonaparte, a "purveyor of truth" if ever there was one. Felman, on the other hand, itemizes the essential differences between Bonaparte and Lacan to emphasize how Lacan's approach represents a breakthrough in psychoanalytic reading. She points out that Bonaparte, because she assumes the stable identity of the individual, works through the repetitions in Poe's texts in order to confirm her diagnosis of Poe's malady, whereas Lacan assumes that identity is under reconstruction in analysis and focuses on how repetitions "make a difference" that can "bring about a solution to the problem"; that Bonaparte's approach is biographical while Lacan's is textual; and that Lacan breaks down oppositions and hierarchies that earlier psychoanalysts and literary critics assumed.

This last point, I think, is most significant. As Felman explains, "There seemed to be no doubt in the minds of psychoanalytic readers that if the reading situation could be assimilated to the psychoanalytic situation, the poet was to be equated with the (sick) patient, with the analysand on the couch. Lacan's analysis, however, radically subverts not just this clinical status of the poet, but along with it the 'bedside' security of the interpreter" (150). Although no one would mistake Lacan's approach for Hoffman's or Holland's, they too sought to subvert the authority of the critic by laying bare their own subjective associations with Poe's tales and poems. But for Lacan, not only the analyst/author and doctor/patient relationships are creatively disrupted; so is the traditional relationship between literature and psychoanalysis, for psychoanalysis is not being *applied* to literature but rather *integrated* with the literary text: "Poe's text serves to reinterpret Freud just as Freud's text serves to interpret Poe . . . psychoanalytic theory and the literary text mutually inform" (Felman 152). Jane Gallop similarly emphasizes this realignment: "Rather than teach psychoanalysis as a basis for understanding literature, Lacan might see psychoanalysis as a regional branch of literary studies" (24).

Felman and Gallop are such good readers of Lacan that they make him sound far more accessible than he is; even so, the "Seminar on 'The Purloined Letter'" and its apparatuses make earlier (and most later) psychoanalytic readings of Poe seem naive and outdated (despite the fact that Lacan gave his seminar almost fifty years ago), which is unfortunate because it reduces the meticulous and insightful readings of Bonaparte and others to the implicitly unsophisticated "pre-Lacanian" category. While those more traditional Freudian approaches remain valid (as I have argued here), Lacan's subversions of the analyst/critic's authority and the application model of psychoanalytic reading have liberated more recent scholars like Brooks, Bronfen, and Shawn Rosenheim to read fiction and psychoanalysis intertextually. Brooks argues, "Psychoanalysis matters to us as literary critics because it stands as a constant reminder that the attention to form, properly conceived, is not a sterile formalism but rather one more attempt to draw the symbolic and fictional map of our place in existence" (17), an observation that applies to Bonaparte and Hoffman as well as Lacan. While not written in regard to Poe, Brooks's statement might help us to connect Poe's formalism with his psychopathological concerns. But more importantly, it confirms the need for critics to continue to facilitate the dialogue between Poe's texts and psychoanalytic theory.

Notes

[1] See also Philip Young, "The Earlier Psychologists and Poe," *American Literature* 22 (1951): 442–54. For more on the popularity of psychoanalysis in the 1910s and 1920s, see Claudia C. Morrison, *Freud and the Critic: The Early Use of Depth Psychology in Literary Criticism* (Chapel Hill: U of North Carolina P, 1968), ch. 1.

[2] See Morrison, *Freud and the Critic,* 161–75.

[3] See, for instance, Mario Praz, "Poe and Psychoanalysis," *Sewanee Review* 68 (1960): 375–89; Patrick F. Quinn, *The French Face of Edgar Allan Poe* (Carbondale: So. IL UP, 1957); and Shawn Rosenheim, "Detective Fiction, Psychoanalysis, and the Analytic Sublime," in *The American Face of Edgar Allan Poe,* ed. Shawn Rosenheim and Stephen Rachman, 153–76 (Baltimore and London: Johns Hopkins UP, 1995), 167.

[4] See, for instance, Valentine C. Hubbs, "The Struggle of Wills in Poe's 'William Wilson,'" *Studies in American Fiction* 11 (1983): 73–79; and Stephen K. Hoffman, "Sailing into the Self: Jung, Poe, and 'MS. Found in a Bottle,'" *Tennessee Studies in Literature* 26 (1981): 66–74.

[5] Freud reportedly told Bonaparte that her dreams reflected her belief that she had killed her mother in childbirth and that her mother would one day "come back, an Oedipal ogress, to take revenge" (Bertin 163). See Silas L. Warner, M. D., "Princess Marie Bonaparte, Edgar Allan Poe, and Psychobiography," *Journal of the American Academy of Psychoanalysis* 19 (1991): 446–61, for more on the relationship between Bonaparte's psychological biography and her reading of Poe.

[6] Gallop's definition of "imago" is quoted from Jean Laplanche and Jean-Baptiste Pontalis, *Vocabulaire de la psychoanalyse* (Paris: PUF, 1967), 196.

[7] See John T. Irwin's discussion of the Lacan-Derrida-Johnson exchange in *The Mystery to a Solution: Poe, Borges, and the Analytic Detective Story* (Baltimore and London: Johns Hopkins UP, 1994), 3–12.

3: Out of Space, Out of Time: From Early Formalism to Deconstruction

Textual analysis, by punctuation, word, phrase, line, paragraph, and by total effect, with the eye undeviatingly upon the object, but with reference to collateral and comparative data, has become the standard method with many important American critics. A rigorous exclusion of generalization and a minimizing of tangential observations, characterize the return to a view of critical method which Poe would have applauded.
— George Snell, 1945

BY THE 1920s, literary scholars were trying to move away from the "character issue" that had been central to commentary on Poe up to that time. As we have seen, psychoanalytic critics of this period would announce that they had come not to judge Poe's character but to explain it, and yet they fueled readers' lurid interest in Poe's substance abuse and sex life (or lack thereof). Other academic critics, particularly those associated with the New Criticism, sought to shelve biographical and historical concerns and focus on The Text. But as William Elton pointed out in 1948, "The Revolution of the Text was accomplished by men of no single creed; strictly speaking, there was no 'New Criticism,' as its enemies supposed, but several new criticisms mingled with several old ones" (4), a point that is particularly important to keep in mind when surveying their responses to Poe. Not only did the rubric of New Criticism cover a range of beliefs about literature's function, but its interpretive methods spilled over into what textbooks typically label mythological and archetypal approaches, as well as readings focused more on ethical and philosophical traditions.

Poe has been regarded as a forefather of critics who emphasized textual unity and whose readings demonstrated how various elements in a poem or short story work together to produce a subtle but ultimately coherent meaning.[1] Partly because of this emphasis on unity, New Critics generally valued lyric poetry and short fiction over drama and the novel, just as Poe had done in his review of *Twice-Told Tales* and elsewhere. Poe regarded didacticism a heresy a century before Cleanth Brooks declared that "the poet is a maker, not a communicator" (*Well-Wrought Urn* 74–75); in avoiding didacticism, Poe kept readers off balance through his use of irony, the deployment of which Brooks and Warren, in their introduction to *Understanding Fiction*, identify as the common denominator of great literature. On the other hand, for critics who sought to elevate literary study to the same level of respectability as the sciences, Poe's work must have seemed embarrassingly popular. His poems lent themselves to memorization and recitation, and his fiction could be filed under "gothic," "detective," and "science-," the realm of the "sub-literary." Moreover, Poe was often self-consciously mechanical in his approach, and to the extent that his his works had "meanings," they were perhaps more equivocal or amoral than the conservative neo-humanist wing of American formalists could accept.

Not surprisingly, then, responses to Poe highlight some of the differences among the major mid-twentieth-century formalist critics. In some respects their disagreements resemble the nineteenth-century arguments over Poe's value as a writer (see chapter 1), only without the hand-wringing over his moral character. Emerson had famously called Poe "the Jingle Man" in 1859,[2] and in the heyday of modernism Poe's poems sounded more jingly — that is to say, gimmicky, meretricious, hackneyed — than ever. Although not usually identified as a New Critic, Aldous Huxley made the case against Poe's poetry in "Vulgarity in Literature" (1930) in terms that later New Critics would adopt:

> The substance of Poe is refined; it is his form that is vulgar. He is, as it were, one of Nature's Gentlemen, unhappily cursed with incorrigible bad taste. To the most sensitive and high-souled man in the world we should find it hard to forgive, shall we say, the wearing of a diamond ring on every finger. Poe does the equivalent of this in his poetry; we notice the solicism and shudder. . . . It is when Poe tries to make it too poetical that his poetry takes on its peculiar tinge of badness. (161)

Huxley went on to parody Poe's style, imagining what Poe would have done with the following passage from *Paradise Lost*:

Like that fair field
Of Enna, where Proserpine gathering flowers,
Herself a fairer flower, by gloomy Dis
Was gathered, which cost Ceres all that pain
To seek her through the world.

Poe's version, according to Huxley:

It was noon in the fair field of Enna,
   When Proserpina gathering flowers —
   Herself the most fragrant of flowers —
Was gathered away to Gehenna
   By the Prince of Plutonian powers;
Was born down the windings of Brenner
   To the gloom of his amorous bowers —
Down the tortuous highway of Brenner
   To the God's agapemonous bowers. (163)

It's all there, in the anapestic trimeter of "Ulalume": Poe's relentless, mechanical rhythms, strained rhymes, repetitions, inexplicable use of words like "agapemonous." For Huxley, the poetic conventions of Poe's time are no excuse, because artistic standards are eternal: "Many nineteenth-century poets used these metrical short-cuts to music, with artistically fatal results" (162).

Yvor Winters's attack, published in *American Literature* in 1937 and incorporated into his classic study *Maule's Curse*, went further than Huxley's, describing the flaws in Poe's poetic theory and prosody in detail. Winters combines a new critical reverence for the text with a neo-humanist insistence on moral edification through literature. His tone is that of a crusader, intrepid and unwavering from the first sentence, which reads, "I am about to promulgate a heresy: namely, that E. A. Poe, although he achieved, as some of his admirers have claimed, a remarkable agreement between his theory and his practice, is exceptionally bad in both" (176–77). For Winters, of course, the real heresy is propagated by those who would allow Poe into the temple of high literary art. He is so disdainful of Poe that he enumerates all the passages in Poe's poetry and fiction that are "fairly well-executed, if one grants him temporarily his fundamental assumptions about art" (199). He can find only six. After quoting five other passages he regards as representative of Poe's style, Winters declares, "This is an art to delight the soul of a servant girl; it is a matter for astonishment that mature men can be found to take this kind of thing seriously" (200).

The blatant sexism and classism of that remark helps to expose Winters's assumptions about who and what literature is for. But at the same time, Winters, like Huxley, makes a valid point about the clunkiness of Poe's prosody: Poe does wear his rings on every finger, which may be why Homer and Bart Simpson are among the most successful interpreters of his most famous poem. But what bothers Winters even more than Poe's style is the amorality of Poe's theory: "It is obvious, then, that poetry is not, for Poe, a refined and enriched technique of moral comprehension. It can be of no aid to us in understanding ourselves or in ordering our lives, for most of our experience is irrelevant to it" (185). Poe's avoidance of didacticism, his talk of merely *suggesting* larger meanings, amounts to "an aesthetic of obscurantism" (188). In that respect, too, Winters is right about Poe, but the question remains, should we condemn Poe's — or William Carlos Williams's, or Wallace Stevens's — obscurantism? Winters believes that Poe has simply failed to see that poetry can convey human truth without being didactic, but surely Poe knew that, or why would he have written about, for instance, the almost ecstatic pain of mourning ("The Raven," "Ulalume," "Annabel Lee") or the frustrations of the creative mind ("Romance," "Israfel")? Winters is most convincing when he holds up Poe's poetry to the aesthetic standards of modernism and shows them lacking, as Huxley had done with his parody. He is less convincing in attacking Poe's theory, not only because the attack reveals his own narrow-minded insistence on poetry as a vehicle of truths beyond the reach of "servant girls" but because he takes Poe's own theories too seriously and too literally — especially "The Philosophy of Composition," which is as much hoax and mystification as it is a sincere attempt to articulate a theory of writing.

And what of Poe's fiction, the body of work on which his reputation would later come to rest? Winters has much less to say about it, but here too he reads Poe's theory (specifically, the *Twice-Told Tales* review) too narrowly, too literally:

Now the word *effect,* here as elsewhere in Poe, means impression, or mood; it is a word that connotes emotion purely and simply. So that we see the story-teller, like the poet, interested primarily in the creation of an emotion for its own sake, not in the understanding of an experience. It is significant in this connection that most of his heroes are mad or on the verge of madness; a datum which settles his action firmly in the realm of inexplicable feeling from the outset. (195)

In fact, I would venture that the emotion people typically feel in reading Poe (or William Faulkner or Toni Morrison, for that matter) is not devoid of understanding — quite the contrary. Faulkner writes the first section of *The Sound and the Fury* to immerse us in Benjy's consciousness: for emotional effect or understanding? For both, clearly; the same answer would apply to, say, "The Black Cat." If anything, that story (as well as "The Tell-Tale Heart," the dying woman tales, "The Cask of Amontillado," and others) is directed more at our understanding than at our emotions, but understanding the experience in the tales requires that we dissociate Poe from the narrators, a point James Gargano would illustrate in a landmark 1963 essay. One *can* read Poe's fiction as rigidly moral, in fact: if the detective doesn't solve the crime, the murderer will turn himself in, kill himself, or be eaten away by remorse. No one gets away with *anything* (with the exception of the vengeful Hop-Frog, whom Poe depicts as a kind of monster). But Winters, taken in by the doctrine of effect, is offended by Poe's lack of a clearly stated moral purpose.

Among modernist poet/critics of this era, T. S. Eliot and Allen Tate offered more temperate, nuanced assessments than Huxley and Winters. Writing in 1948, Eliot credited Poe with two major contributions to the literary tradition, one of which would become an article of faith for New Critics. Eliot quotes Poe's disciple Baudelaire — "A poem does not say something — it is something" — then adds, "that doctrine has been held in more recent times" (215). Poe's other contribution is laying the theoretical groundwork for a poetry that is only about its own making — *la poésie pure* — which Eliot sees as having inspired some great work (not Poe's, particularly) but which he objects to as a theory: "I believe [*la poésie pure*] to be a goal that can never be reached, because I think that poetry is only poetry so long as it preserves some 'impurity' in this sense: that is to say, so long as the subject matter is valued for its own sake" (216). While not outraged as Winters was, Eliot too maintains that poetry, even if it can't be paraphrased, ought to avoid the extreme self-consciousness of, for instance, Valéry, whom he regards as Poe's literary descendent. And yet, Eliot appreciates Poe's contribution to the development of modern poetry, however flawed Poe's own verse may be. Throughout his opening paragraph especially, he explains why Poe should be dismissed, only to double back and declare that he can't be dismissed, as if Poe were a skeleton in the closet of The Tradition: "Can we point to any [English or American] poet whose style appears to have been formed by a study of Poe? The only one whose name immediately suggests itself is — Edward Lear. And yet one cannot be sure that one's own writing has *not* been influenced by Poe" (205).

In "Our Cousin, Mr. Poe," an address to the Poe Society in 1949 (the centenary of Poe's death), Allen Tate similarly concedes that "It is easy enough to agree with Aldous Huxley and Yvor Winters" in regard to the defects of Poe's style (468), but like Eliot he sees Poe as somehow inescapable: "I confess that his voice is so near that I recoil a little, lest he, Montresor, lead me into the cellar, address me as Fortunato, and wall me up alive" (470–71). Writing in the late 1940s, at a point when others had shown the specific deficiencies and limitations of Poe's work, Eliot and Tate could reassert Poe's importance, his effectiveness, despite his already acknowledged clumsy rhymes and contradictory theories. Both are impressed with Poe's literary afterlife, in which he appears not as a second-string romanticist but a modernist before his time — for his experimental style and theory, according to Eliot, and for his subject matter, which in the atomic age strikes Tate as uncannily contemporary:

> I do not hesitate to say that had Poe not written *Eureka*, I should have been able, a man of this age, myself to formulate a proposition of "inevitable annihilation." I can only invite others to a similar confession. Back of the preceding remarks lies an ambitious assumption, about the period in which we live, which I shall not make explicit. It is enough to say that, if the trappings of Poe's nightmare strike us as tawdry, we had better look to our own. (470)

Tate, who would pursue his interest in Poe's apocalyptic writings in a later essay ("The Angelic Imagination"), is a transitional figure in the history of Poe criticism, associated as he is with a formalist approach that tended mainly to expose Poe's stylistic defects but pointing the way for other critics who would take a long view of Poe's work and argue that something like a philosophical system undergirds his entire corpus.

Meanwhile, the New Critical approach had become entrenched in college literature classes, and in their influential primers of the late 1930s and early 1940s, Cleanth Brooks and Robert Penn Warren spread the word that Poe was overrated. In *Understanding Poetry* (1938), they suggest that Poe has gotten a free ride from previous generations of readers who were insufficiently attentive to form: in "Ulalume" Poe creates "a kind of atmosphere that we can accept only if we do not inspect its occasion too closely — for dank tarns and ghoul-haunted woodlands are stage-sets, we might say, that are merely good for frightening children" (359–60). To accept them is to willingly "forego our maturity" (360). Poe's hokey place names — Weir, Auber, Mount Yaanek — are meaningless, the references to ghouls confusing, and the poem's rhythm is "monotonous," a point they reinforce in the second edition by reprinting Huxley's parody.[3] Their interpretation of "The Fall of the House of Usher" in *Understanding Fiction* (1943) acknowledges the story's skillful construction, noting the parallels between the description of the house and the description of Roderick Usher. But, like Winters, they regard Poe's "effect" as superficial: "The horror is relatively meaningless — it is generated for its own sake" (204–5). In their readings of Poe, then, Brooks and Warren focus not so much on how his poems and tales work as on why these texts fail to measure up to the standards of great literature. The discussion questions that follow "The Fall of the House of Usher" are designed to lead students to disparage Poe, in case they missed the point in Brooks and Warren's interpretation: "Can it be said that 'The Fall of the House of Usher' suffers from overwriting? . . . Can one justify the conclusion of the story against the charge that it is melodramatic? . . . Does the story 'say' anything which the poem ["The Haunted Palace"] does not 'say' in more concentrated form? If so, what?" (205).

In reading Brooks and Warren on Poe, one senses their hostility toward his popularity: it is as if they are saying to students, "Look, we know you like this Poe, and you're proud of your liking him because he's supposed to be a great writer. But when you learn to read more carefully, like a grown-up, you'll see that he's only a little better than the pulp fiction you read for pleasure." And yet, despite the wide distribution of the *Understanding*s, Poe's reputation among academics, as well as his popularity among general readers, remained high through mid-century. New Critics were not alone in questioning his status — in *Expression in America* (1931), Ludwig Lewisohn argued that Poe was greatly over-rated, and Hemingway, predictably, dismissed him in *The Green Hills of Africa* (1935) — but Poe maintained a secure place in the canon in an era when critics were quite conscious of recent and ongoing shifts in literary reputations. In 1926, before New Criticism had taken hold, a poll sponsored by *Golden Book Magazine* asked four hundred high school and college literature teachers, "If some condescending international critic were to intimate that the United States had not yet produced anything really worthy of a place beside the acknowledged masterpieces of fiction, — which ten works by American writers could be selected that would best represent our bid for a permanent place in this section of the world's literature?" (Hubbell, *Who* 289). The most popular response was Poe. The reference to the "condescending international critic" probably worked to his advantage, since by this point most teachers would have known that Poe was highly regarded in France and that European literary men had scorned the Hall of Fame's rejection of him prior to 1910. In 1949, a more elite panel of twenty-six professors of American literature and cultural history still placed Poe a close second to Hawthorne in a poll sponsored by UNESCO. (Hawthorne, incidentally, had placed second to Poe in the *Golden Book Magazine* poll.) It is worth noting that the major New Critics were not on the panel, perhaps because they tended not to specialize in American literature (Hubbell 300–302); still, the poll indicates a continuing consensus among academics of Poe's importance. Throughout that period, critics commenting on the state of the American literature canon consistently recognized Poe as a major writer. Carl Van Doren, describing what he saw as dramatic changes to the canon in a 1932 essay, referred to Poe as a mainstay in the pantheon; Dumas Malone in 1937 ranked Poe fifth (behind Emerson, Hawthorne, Twain, and Whitman) among American men of letters;[4] and responding to Malone, whose list he regarded as outdated, Bernard DeVoto claimed that Poe was now of interest only to scholars, but in making that curious point ventured that Poe was "more widely and more exhaustively studied than any other American writer" (8). By 1956, when the MLA published the canon-shrinking *Eight American Authors,* Poe still made the cut.

As these polls and rankings of American authors suggest, the period associated with New Criticism was also marked by a resurgent self-consciousness over the American-ness of American literature, the importance of identifying a national literary tradition. Here, too, critics were divided. F. O. Matthiessen, whose approach combined New Critical attention to form and language with broader cultural concerns, neglected Poe in his enormously influential book *American Renaissance* in 1941, but a few years later he wrote the chapter on Poe for what would become a standard reference for decades, Spiller and Thorp's *Literary History of the United States* (1948). His chapter consists mostly of an account of Poe's career, but in his conclusion Matthiessen hints at why he did not discuss Poe in his earlier study: Poe's influence was felt more strongly in France, and he made his mark on American poetry indirectly through the *symbolistes*. Matthiessen implies that Poe was the most important writer *before* the "American Renaissance," hailing him as "one of the few great innovators in American literature" and comparing him favorably to Cooper and Irving. Significantly, the editors placed Matthiessen's chapter just before the section that includes chapters on the five authors he examined in *American Renaissance*: Emerson, Thoreau, Hawthorne, Melville, and Whitman. That chapter's title, "Literary Fulfillment," also suggests that Poe was merely a precursor to the real (American) thing.[5]

While for Matthiessen the American literary tradition begins in earnest the year after Poe's death, William Carlos Williams, in *In the American Grain* (1925), *ends* his chronological study of American literature with a chapter on Poe (followed only by a one-page essay on Lincoln). Like R. W. B. Lewis in his later work *The American Adam*, Williams sees the destruction of old-world aesthetics and values, making way for "the new," as a defining gesture, and for that, Poe is quintessentially American. Poe's criticism "is a movement, first and last to clear the GROUND" (216); Poe declared, "Either the New World must be mine as I will have it, or it is a worthless bog" (219); "Poe could look at France, Spain, Greece, and NOT be impelled to copy. He could do this BECAUSE he had the sense within him of a locality of his own, capable of cultivation" (225). Williams's idea is not entirely new — Barrett Wendell and C. Alphonso Smith made similar claims for Poe's American-ness at the 1909 centenary commemoration at the University of Virginia (see chapter 1) — nor does it lead him to any New Critical close reading of Poe; but it is significant because it bases the claim to Poe's American-ness strictly on form. "On him is FOUNDED A LITERATURE," writes Williams (223), a literature in which subject matter is subordinated to composition or "method." The following year, Lewis Mumford similarly placed Poe in the American grain on the basis of form, but he was less inclined than Williams to celebrate it: "With no conscious connection with the life about him, Poe became nevertheless the literary equivalent of the industrialist and the pioneer. . . . Poe's meticulous and rationalistic mind fitted his environment and mirrored its inner characteristics far more readily than a superficial look at it would lead one to believe" (76). Notice how easily Poe's position in regard to American culture can be reversed: Baudelaire and others had seen him as a rebel against American pragmatism and materialism, while for Smith, Mumford and Williams, the hyper-rationalistic Poe was a pure product of America — not because of his subject matter but because of the formal qualities of his writing.[6]

In 1941, the same year Matthiessen published *American Renaissance,* Arthur Hobson Quinn's massive biography of Poe appeared. Quinn's meticulous documentation of the verifiable facts of Poe's life and his careful, New-Critical interpretations of the more important works made a strong case for Poe's importance while suggesting new possibilities for readings of the entire Poe canon. By the end of the decade, N. Bryllion Fagin attempted to unite Poe's poetry, short fiction, and a portion of his criticism by examining them all in terms of Poe's theatrical background in *The Histrionic Mr. Poe* (1949). The fact that Fagin seems overly defensive regarding Poe's worth underscores the lingering controversy over Poe's place in the pantheon, but the publication by Johns Hopkins University Press of a book-length study whose main focus was not biography was itself an affirmation of the claim made by Quinn. In his early chapters, Fagin goes to a great deal of trouble to establish points that aren't hard to grasp: Poe was histrionic in his personal life, he wrote a drama and some dialogues that tend to give way to monologues, and he was an astute drama critic, a job he took seriously. The chapters on the poetry and short fiction are more perceptive, however. After establishing that Poe's poetry is dramatic and elocutionary, Fagin attempts to reconcile the creative/mathematical schism highlighted in "The Philosophy of Composition" through an analogy with acting: "It is safe to say that there were always two Poes, one playing his part as poet, as storyteller, or as critic, the other watching him play it" (141). He later discusses Poe's theatrical settings, the "lighting designs" (188), and the use of color in his stories, suggesting that as a fiction writer Poe thought like a set designer. In short, Fagin was reading Poe's work closely not to depreciate it, as Brooks and Warren had done, but to treat it like other aesthetically rich fiction.

By the 1950s, the stage was set for major thematic readings of American literature that would include Poe. Charles Feidelson discussed Poe briefly in *Symbolism and American Literature* (1953), echoing Eliot in maintaining that Poe's theories were more sophisticated and successful than his practice (38). At the same time, Feidelson anticipated Richard Wilbur's argument that Poe's fiction and poetry depicted a struggle between rationalism and irrationalism — death, for instance, is associated "with the inverted world, the opposite of reason" (41). Similarly, Harry Levin, in *The Power of Blackness* (1958), observed that Poe "is a rationalist, seeking to cast enlightenment on dark places. But the forces of the irrational have their revenge in jeopardizing the status of reason itself" (137). Levin devotes two chapters to Poe's fiction: one to Poe's motif of the journey as a quest for self-knowledge (with the emphasis on *Pym*) and one to his treatment of death. While Levin's chapters often read like a series of plot summaries rather than analysis, they nonetheless represent a new set of assumptions that would inform mainstream Poe criticism from the late 1950s to the 1970s. Focused on fiction rather than poetry and for the most part unconcerned with judging literary merit, Levin, like other late-1950s critics, looks for patterns and coherent themes that run through the Poe canon. He concludes the chapter entitled "Notes from Underground" with a shrewd insight into Poe's obsession with death:

> Poe's cult of blackness is not horripilation for horripilation's sake; it is a bold attempt to face the true darkness in its most tangible manifestations. If life is a dream, then death is an awakening. The dreamer coexists with another self, who may be his accuser or his victim, or his all too evanescent bride. His house may be a Gothic ruin or a home-like cottage; but any sojourn must be temporary; and the journey thence . . . leads downward toward the very closest circumspection of space, the grave. (163)

However much Levin and other critics of this period were still devoted to the idea of the Author as a unified subject, they clearly shifted the focus away from evaluating Poe's writing and relating it to his life, toward finding an idea or cluster of ideas that unify Poe's work.

Allen Tate, in his lecture "The Angelic Imagination," suggested that a key to "Poe" (which by the 1950s was more likely to signify the Poe canon than the man) might be found in such obscurities as "The Conversation of Eiros and Charmion," "The Colloquy of Monos and Una," "The Power of Words," and *Eureka*. From these unclassifiable life-after-death conjectures we learn what the angels already know, that words are literally creative, and that "Man is not only an angel, he is God in the aspect of his creativity" (251). Tate hedges slightly near the lecture's end: "I have not discussed Poe from what is commonly known as the literary point of view. I have tried to expound one idea, the angelism of the intellect, as one aspect of one writer" (254). What did Tate mean by the "literary point of view"? He may have been suggesting that by examining Poe's ideas rather than his style, content rather than form, he was moving away from the New Critical view of literature, or he might simply have meant that his purpose was not evaluative. At the same time, while he asserts that this is only "one idea" one might find in Poe, his search for a single figure in the carpet, the larger meaning in Poe, was, by the late 1950s, typical of what mainstream literary critics were doing.

Indeed, by the end of the decade something like an academic "Poe industry" had developed, running parallel (literally, with no intersection) to the pop-culture Poe industry spearheaded by Roger Corman's early films and Classic Comics adaptations of Poe's tales (to be discussed in chapter 5). In addition to numerous groundbreaking articles by scholars such as Darrel Abel ("A Key to the House of Usher") and Clark Griffith ("Poe's 'Ligeia' and the English Romantics"), three landmark academic books, Patrick F. Quinn's *The French Face of Edgar Poe* (1957), Edward Davidson's *Poe: A Critical Study* (1957), and Richard Wilbur's edition of Poe's poems for the Laurel Poetry Series (1959), cleared the way for future generations of Poe scholars. Quinn's study is largely metacritical, focusing on Baudelaire's career as a Poe devotee and translator for about a third of the book, but also describing, and generally endorsing, Bonaparte's then-recently translated interpretation, and glossing a wide range of other French commentators and poets influenced by Poe. Bonaparte looms large over Quinn's chapter on *Pym* in particular, which he sees as "remarkably coherent in its management of structure and theme" (176): Pym's adventures trace a pattern of revolt against authority, but the real journey is interior and highly autobiographical. Quinn concludes the chapter by arguing for *Pym*'s influence on *Moby-Dick*, laying out for the first time a number of themes and devices common to both novels. In his chapter on Poe's short fiction, he places less emphasis on French responses to Poe and develops, better than anyone up to that time had, an argument for the centrality and meaning of the *doppelgänger* motif in Poe's fiction. He sees, for instance, that the narrator of "The Man of the Crowd" is unaware that his attraction to the old man stems from his identification with him, and that the same unacknowledged projection of self-on-other motivates the murder in "The Tell-Tale Heart." Quinn's conclusions, while very general, summed up why the French appreciated Poe and why Americans should follow suit: through the themes of "the Double, Premature Burial, and Metempsychosis . . . Poe found it possible to embark on an imaginative exploration beyond the frontiers of conscious knowledge. . . . [W]hen we read his stories, with an awareness of what his ambitious intention was, we too may in some degree take part in this imaginative exploration" (274).

For better or worse, Quinn comes across as old-fashioned, even by 1950s standards, and even as he is urging his American audience to "catch up" with the French. In fact, the very premise of his book — that the French rightly recognize Poe's greatness — places the emphasis on judging the author. Early on, he explains, "However true it is that the final and defining task of literary criticism is the task of evaluation, it is certainly true also that the initial work that must be done is to determine as exactly as possible *what is there*" (26), suggesting that, like a scientist, a literary critic will establish correct explications of stories that will lead to the proper placement of the author in the pantheon. Perhaps because he was so immersed in the work of Baudelaire and Bonaparte, Quinn maintained that Poe's work revealed his personality, and saw that explication of "Poe the man" as an important task as well: "There can be little doubt that we find the author in Usher rather than in Dupin, an indication that, despite his pretensions to a universal sort of mind, Poe's true bent was towards the darker regions of the psyche" (224); "Poe could not be the detective, the hunter, for he was too radically the criminal, the prey" (225).

By contrast, Edward Davidson generally avoids stumping for Poe's great-author status and makes a point of *not* reading his work biographically. For example, having glossed the biographical context for Poe's first major poem, he turns away from it: "[W]e might, however, look for the subject of 'Tamerlane' elsewhere than in Poe's disappointed love affair, his eviction from the Allan household, or conjectures on his own emergent manhood and artistic sensibility" (5–6). Instead, he tells us, we might look to Wordsworth's theory of childhood and memory (7). Similarly, the first "To Helen" is "not about *a* woman, Mrs. Stanard, Mrs. Allan, nor even Helen of Troy. Its subject is the way the mind can move toward the past and, in some such symbol as the indefinable beauty of woman, is able to comprehend a world and culture long vanished from this earth" (33). The mental "fracture" in much of Poe's work, the split between "inner self and outer world" (51), is not a symptom of his own split personality but rather "part of the major stream of intellectual and artistic life from the seventeenth until well into the nineteenth, and even into the twentieth, century" (52). These are not empty rhetorical gestures: Davidson takes Poe's work, Poe's ideas, more seriously than any critic up to that time, and as a result wrote what in my opinion is the best book-length study of the Poe canon prior to the 1970s.

Davidson might be described as an "old historicist" in that he tries to illuminate not economic and political concerns of Poe's time but intellectual issues, placing Poe within a history of ideas. He offers insights into some facets of cultural history as well — recognizing, for instance, that in antebellum America, death not only became sentimentalized but served as a locus for eroticism (120) — but he concerns himself more with trends in philosophy and aesthetic theory, namely Romanticism and the tension between idealism and Lockean rationalism. Davidson, then, shares with the New Critics a distrust of biography and psychoanalysis, but unlike them he is concerned more with content than form, and his philosophical grounding is less concerned with values (in the manner of a New Humanist like Yvor Winters) than with basic questions of the mind's relationship to the material world and the meaning of death. He does relatively little close reading, in fact, yet his interpretations are clearly informed by a careful study of Poe's poetry, fiction, and literary theory.

Like Tate, Davidson sees Poe's imagination as angelic but defiant; in Poe's poetry, he "plays heaven and hell, God and Satan, and tends more and more to enter a private world from which reality and even meaning, normally considered, are excluded" (13). In Poe's manifestation of the Romantic Agony, the artist destroys the material world but does not re-create it; instead, he creates art (47). Poe's art-world is a closed system, one which plays by its own rules and remains independent of the material world. Appropriately, given that focus, Davidson ends the book with a chapter on *Eureka,* again expanding on the ideas advanced by Tate a decade earlier: "[I]n order to remain 'pure,' art had to disavow any connection with science, with the world as it is, with the forlorn hope that it can in any way direct the lives of men. *Eureka* . . . affirmed that the work of art is like the creative act of God: a special, a private auton-omy, a unique disclosure of idea and fact, word and idea" (252–53). If this sounds vaguely post-structuralist, it is fair to say that Williams, Tate, and Davidson perceived a Poe much like the one critics of the 1980s would (re)discover. Almost, but not quite, as Davidson ascribes to poetic language what a deconstructionist would likely claim for all language:

> Poetic language exists not in substance nor in the poetic mind which may have made the poem but in a neutral world, a kind of farther dimension wherein the mind or imagination functions as mediating between external reality and itself. Language, to rephrase our problem, is real and not real at the same time; in expressing an idea a poet is not expressing his view of that idea, for words are not inward nor even, as it were, mental. . . . [A] poet might even be permitted to invent his own vocabulary — a vocabulary, it must be insisted, that could not be altogether his. (72)

Among earlier critics, only Bonaparte had made as compelling an ar-gument for some organic unity to the Poe canon. But whereas Bonaparte had rested most of her case on the tales and *Pym,* Davidson devotes three chapters to poetry and poetic theory, one to Poe's handling of Eros and Thanatos, two to the tales, and one each to *Pym* and *Eureka.* Thus Da-vidson pays relatively little attention to the tales, seeing them as psychic dramas closely related to the poems. He examines only a handful of stories closely, but his observations are shrewd. For example:

> The central problem of "William Wilson" is the nature of self-identity: is the self born isolated and alone, as was the early theme of "Usher," or is it permissively designed to order its own way in the world? . . . Usher saw around him the infinite interrelations of the self and the

> world outside; he lived in such terror that his private mind-being might
> be destroyed that he created the outer protective shell or the house.
> Wilson, on the other hand, is the Romantic individualist for whom the
> world is nothing but the externalization of the self. (199, 201)

Poe's work exists "out of space, out of time" not because Davidson
regards literary texts as well-wrought urns divorced from social context
but because he saw Poe's project as one in which art, like the artist
Roderick Usher, deliberately removed itself from the material world and
from real human contact.

In his introduction to the Laurel Poetry Series paperback collection of
Poe's poems, Richard Wilbur makes a similar argument for the larger
coherence of Poe's work around the idea of art aspiring to leave the dull
earth behind for a higher realm of beauty. He makes a strong case for the
inextricability of the tales from the poems; in fact, he devotes most of his
introduction to a discussion of the tales, reserving most of his commentary
on the poems for detailed end-notes. The poems are deliberately obscure,
he argues, but the stories provide their "narrative basis" and help to make
sense of them. More specifically, all of Poe's work revolves around two
related myths: the Cosmic Myth, developed at length in *Eureka,* and the
Myth of the Poet's Life. The first of these myths closely resembles Tate
and Davidson's central motif of the artist as destructive angel:

> Since the poet's business is to help *undo* phenomena toward unity,
> dreaming the oak of creation back to its original acorn, his negation of
> human and earthly subject-matter becomes in Poe's cosmic theory
> positive; his destructiveness becomes creative; his exclusiveness a condi-
> tion of his inclusiveness; his vagueness a consequence of his unearthly
> subject-matter; his denial of Intellect a means to ultimate Truth. In
> short, Poe's myth of the cosmos presents his every apparent limitation
> as an advantage. (12–13)

The closely related Myth of the Poet's Life is expressed most clearly in
poems such as "Alone" and "Israfel" and stories such as "Eleonora" and
"Usher." The poet lives in a fallen world and makes poetry a vehicle for
reclaiming the "primal harmony" of his pre-existence, or at least early
childhood. Both myths involve a loss of wholeness and harmony and the
return — cosmic and personal — to that perfect, Edenic state.

For Wilbur, these myths explain such questions as why Poe's poems are not clearer (because poetry should "move us not to contemplation but to a state of strange abstraction in which we seem, for a moment, to apprehend an unearthly beauty" [34]), why Ermengarde and Rowena are contrasted with Eleonora and Ligeia (because "[t]he poet may *use* Earthly Beauty as a means of reconceiving or remembering Psyche" [17]), and why dreams and dreamlike states are invoked so frequently in Poe. Wilbur developed his answer to this last question in more detail in his Library of Congress lecture "The House of Poe," delivered the same year as his edition of Poe's poems. The "hypnagogic state" of transition from wakefulness to deep sleep, like the moment of death or near-death, is analogous to the poet's dimly lit view of paradise. According to Wilbur, "Poe regarded the hypnagogic state as the visionary condition par excellence, and he considered its rapidly shifting abstract images to be — as he put it — 'glimpses of the spirit's outer world'" (265). Wilbur's analysis is less expansive than Davidson's, and his "book" on Poe is inconveniently spread out over the Laurel introduction, the Library of Congress lecture, an essay on Poe in *Major Writers of America* (1962) and an introduction to a 1973 edition of *Pym* (the last three of which are reprinted in his collection *Responses*); and yet he writes more clearly than Davidson — the twin myths, for instance, are a nice hook — and ultimately is more helpful in explaining individual works. Together, these two critics make a powerful case for an over-arching "project" that unifies the wide range of modes, genres, and rhetorical postures found in the Poe canon.

As much as the concerns of literary criticism have shifted over the years, the work of Quinn, Wilbur, and Davidson has echoed through Poe scholarship since the 1950s. Ten years after Wilbur's edition of Poe's poems, John Lynen thickened the plot in a chapter on Poe in his book *Design of the Present* (1969), placing *Eureka* at the center of Poe's aesthetic of annihilation and discussing several stories and poems that focus on some sort of apocalypse or descent into nothingness. He differs from his predecessors in insisting that the destruction of the material world — the house of Usher, for instance — is not merely an allegorical figure for mental or spiritual collapse. Rather, "Usher" demonstrates "that the world of mind and the world of matter are in truth one realm, which exists in the process of developing toward an annihilating unity" (231). That is, the fall of the house does not *represent* the fall of the family; the two falls are "the same event" (234). Lynen's subtle and intricate discussion of time and language in Poe concludes with an analysis of the poetry, ultimately endorsing T. S. Eliot's assessment that Poe's verse was crude but influential on generations of less crude modernists.

David Halliburton, in *Edgar Allan Poe: A Phenomenological View* (1973), also works within the tradition of Wilbur and Davidson, arguing that Poe's writings progress steadily toward *Eureka*'s transcendence. Halliburton distinguishes his method from New-Critical claims of scientific objectivity on one hand and Freudian privileging of author over text on the other. The result, though, is a kind of melding of those two approaches: while acknowledging readerly subjectivity, Halliburton tries to minimize its role; and while reading the intentions of text rather than author, he ultimately arrives at an assessment of Poe's artistic and philosophical consciousness. Not that there's anything wrong with that, but from the perspective of 2003, this strategy seems much more conventional than it must have before deconstruction and reader-response theory had their impact. Throughout his careful study, Halliburton does offer a number of original insights and careful readings of some of Poe's major tales, and his book demonstrates well the phenomenological approach to literary study.

David Ketterer further developed the idea of the destructive imagination in *The Rationale of Deception in Poe* (1979). What Wilbur had called the "hypnagogic state" became for Ketterer the "half-closed eye" or the evocation of "arabesque reality." For Ketterer, Poe's project is "to blur the outlines and allow everything to fuse into everything else — in fact, to destroy the external universe as usually perceived and eradicate the barriers erected by time, space, and self. With the destruction of the reasoned world, the world of the imagination can take over" (28). Ketterer's significant contribution to this tradition of Poe scholarship was to connect this visionary reading of major Poe works to the concept of deception, and in so doing reach many more texts in the Poe canon. One limitation of Davidson's study, as well as Wilbur's, that became apparent by the late 1970s was the virtual omission of minor stories, reviews, and miscellaneous prose. The larger umbrella of deception covers those works that had presumably not seemed worthy of discussion in the 1950s. Ketterer's approach is a bit more plodding, as it requires a good deal of plot summary, but his completeness — with chapters on Poe's life, his reviews, the poetry, and

Eureka, of course, but with the greatest emphasis falling on the tales, both major and minor — leaves little doubt in the reader's mind that deception and "vision," whether one calls it arabesque or hypnagogic, are closely related and inform virtually everything Poe wrote.

The 1960s and 1970s saw a proliferation of intelligent readings consistent with this tradition, regarding the texts as objects of study independent from their author but in dialogue with literary and philosophical traditions. Some focused on Poe's style and aesthetics, others on specific motifs, symbols, and themes. A complete listing would be prohibitively long, but the titles of some of the most important articles from the period suggest both the range of interests and the continuation of the basic concerns laid out by Quinn, Davidson, and Wilbur: Stephen Mooney's "Poe's Gothic Wasteland" (1962), Joseph Patrick Roppolo's "Meaning and 'The Masque of the Red Death'" (1963), Richard P. Benton's "Is Poe's 'The Assignation' a Hoax?" (1963), James W. Gargano's "Poe's 'Ligeia': Dream and Destruction" (1962) and "The Question of Poe's Narrators" (1963), James M. Cox's "Edgar Poe: Style as Pose" (1968), David H. Hirsch's "The Pit and the Apocalypse" (1968), Liahna Klenman Babener's "'The Shadow's Shadow': The Motif of the Double in Edgar Allan Poe's 'The Purloined Letter'" (1972), J. Gerald Kennedy's "The Limits of Reason: Poe's Deluded Detectives" (1975), and David W. Butler's "Hypochondriasis: Mental Alienation and Romantic Idealism in Poe's Gothic Tales" (1976). Essays with such traditional focuses have become less fashionable since the 1970s, but one cannot say they've died out.[7] Monographs with traditional focuses *have* at this point nearly died out, but the 1980s did see two highly regarded books that considered Poe in light of aesthetics and philosophy: Kent Ljungquist's *The Grand and the Fair* (1984) examined Poe's treatment of landscape, providing new insight into his aesthetic principles and intellectual background, while Joan Dayan's *Fables of Mind* (1987) depicted Poe as a skeptic immersed in but reacting against Enlightenment philosophy, particularly that of Locke and Jonathan Edwards.

With so much being written about Poe's craft and ideas in the 1960s and 1970s, scholars might well have wondered if there was anything more to say about him. In 1972, Daniel Hoffman not only titled his book *Poe Poe Poe Poe Poe Poe Poe* (discussed in the previous chapter) as if to suggest a kind of exhaustion, but began it, "What, another book on

Poe! Who needs it?"(ix). And yet Hoffman did find new and useful ways to discuss Poe's work, as did G. R. Thompson in *Poe's Fiction: Romantic Irony in the Gothic Tales*, published the following year. Thompson, like Davidson and others, believes Poe must be understood in light of the Romantic movement, but he emphasizes a particular element of Romanticism — Romantic Irony — generally overlooked by his predecessors. Thompson uses that concept to reverse the prevailing consensus that Poe's "serious" investigations of human psychology were separable from his hoaxes and satires, which were less successful and less interesting. Instead, he demonstrates that in Poe's employment of Romantic Irony — "what Friedrich Schlegel called 'self-parody' and 'transcendental buffoonery,' which involves achieving a mystical sense of an 'ideal' state beyond our limited earthly one by playing, as it were, a cosmic hoax on both the world and oneself" (10) — he dissolves categories, often spoofing his own style in an ostensibly serious tale or making a "serious" claim about human understanding or the afterlife in a hoax or broadly comic tale. Anticipating Ketterer, Thompson argues that "Poe's subject is the precariously logical human mind which is capable of gross misperception, unreal construction, and instant irrationality" (103).

One of Thompson's important contributions to our understanding of Poe is his detailed discussion of terms such as "Gothic" (distinguishing between German supernatural Gothic and the "explained" and "ambiguous" forms developed by later American writers), "grotesque," "arabesque," and "irony," all in the context of European, mostly German, theorists with whom Poe would have been familiar. His other great contribution consists of his lucid, detailed readings of individual stories. His sixteen-page discussion of Poe's first published tale, "Metzengerstein," uncovers previously unnoticed patterns of repetition and layers of irony; he argues that this "carefully flawed tale is a paradigm for Poe's subsequent Gothic hoaxes" (67), for it demonstrates Poe's "power to touch the unseen, unconscious life, to render forcefully certain dark psychological states, to suggest the demoniac in mankind and in nature — and yet at the same time to bring a cool rationality, an ironic skepticism, and even mockery to bear on all that he examines" (67). Elsewhere he expands on Clark Griffith's 1954 article claiming that part of Poe's purpose in "Ligeia" was to mock the transcendentalism Ligeia represents, pointing out the living Ligeia's resemblance to a death's head, ironizing her "apparent love of life" (87). The Gothicism of "Ligeia" and "Usher," according to Thompson, are deliberately hackneyed, which is not to say that these are really comic, satiric tales but that they contain within themselves ironic readings of the very materials they are constructed from. Ultimately, Poe's irony exposes the illusions of ultimate meaning, as *Eureka* and *Pym* particularly direct readers to apprehend "nothingness." In Thompson's reading, Poe emerges from his Romantic context as a proto-Existentialist, expressing both the absurdity of the universe and the freedom that accompanies one's awareness of that absurdity.[8]

For all their differences, the writers described so far in this chapter share at least one basic assumption, articulated in 1982 by John Carlos Rowe: "a good work of literature ought to demonstrate internal coherence and narrative consistency" (92). That belief's implied corollary, according to Rowe, is "that criticism is a process of making difficult or extraordinary texts intelligible" (92). By the time he made these observations in his book *Through the Custom House,* an increasing number of critics, Rowe included, were challenging those assumptions. As the academic community embraced — or, alternately, reacted against — deconstruction in the 1970s, new studies of old authors sought to show how the internal coherence and consistency of "extraordinary texts" unraveled under close inspection, that instead of arguing for a particular meaning, one might more interestingly demonstrate how meaning is endlessly deferred, how texts only appear to be windows on the world but are in fact opaque and teasingly self-referential. If deconstruction's claims were valid, they could be applied to any author, virtually any text, and yet, as had been the case with psychoanalytic criticism, Poe's "world of words" (to borrow a phrase from his poem "Al Aaraaf") seemed especially fertile ground. Lacan's "Seminar on 'The Purloined Letter'" (discussed in chapter 2) not only revolutionized psychoanalytic interpretation but launched a series of deconstructions — Derrida's "The Purveyor of Truth," Barbara Johnson's "The Frame of Reference," as well as further metacommentary by Joseph N. Riddel, Irene Harvey, John T. Irwin, and others. However, those essays were only tangentially related to Poe; with Jean Ricardou's "Le Caractère singulaire de cette eau" (1967; translated as "The Singular Character of Water" in 1974) critics began to describe Poe's textual world in the language of deconstruction. The lightning-rod text was *Pym,* which Ricardou saw as a "journey to the bottom of the page" (5) and to which Rowe devoted his chapter on Poe.

As I've tried to suggest in my discussion of the 1950s critics, the move to deconstructive readings of Poe was not the complete break from tradition that it might seem to be. Eliot, Tate, Wilbur, and Davidson — all "traditional," formalist critics — had already zeroed in on Poe's avoidance of transcendent truths, particularly in his poetry. They recognized Poe's linguistic playfulness, his attraction to codes, his self-referentiality. Furthermore, one might argue — and many readers have — that deconstructive readings make "decentering" a kind of center, the denial of metaphysical truth the ultimate (metaphysical) truth. For instance, Rowe's argument concerning *Pym* — "Forever holding out the promise of a buried signified, *Pym* offers a sequence of forged or imitation truths: delivered messages, deciphered hieroglyphs, a penultimate vision" (93) — sounds like an effort to make an extraordinary, difficult text intelligible, the goal of criticism from which he implicitly sought to break. Just as 1940s be-bop now can be classified as "traditional" jazz although it seemed wholly defiant of tradition at the time, deconstruction has been absorbed into the critical vocabulary in ways that make it look now like part of the larger close-reading, formalist/post-formalist "tradition." The fact that the word "deconstruction" and its variants are (at the time of this writing) watered down and overused is a clear sign of this absorption.

And yet, while it seems fairly clear now that the deconstructive literary criticism of the seventies and eighties is in most cases a continuation of the formalist project rather than a complete rejection of it, there's no denying the difference (or *différance*) between the new (1980s) way of reading and the old. Ricardou, Rowe, John Irwin, Gerald Kennedy, and Dennis Pahl all concern themselves with Poe's presentation of texts and writing in *Pym* to a much greater extent than previous critics: the diary format, the editorial Preface and concluding Note, the forged note that gets Pym on board the *Grampus,* the note Augustus writes in blood (written, perhaps, on the reverse side of the forged note), and the hieroglyphic writing engraved into the landscape of Tsalal foreground the acts of reading and interpreting. The other deceptions and misapprehensions in the novel can also be read as "misreadings" of the textual world that underscore the instability of signification. For example, Rowe argues that "the Preface and Note formally define Pym's metaphysical adventure by questioning beginnings and endings. Within this frame, the text explores the nature of writing in such a way as to render ambiguous what we thought we had understood to be Poe's gnostic philosophy of composition" (97–98). He carefully examines *Pym*'s scenes of writing and interpretation, concluding that Poe's writing unravels the theory of unity and idealism that Poe promoted and that Wilbur explicated. The various deconstructive readings of *Pym* spurred other critics, such as Douglas Robinson and Richard Kopley, to argue more inventively for a unifying principle in the novel. Kopley, in a series of articles, explicated the novel's biblical allusions, arguing that the *Ariel* (another name for Jerusalem) represents the destruction of the Holy City and that the white figure — which is actually the figurehead of the *Penguin* (Welsh for "white head") — "signifies Christ in the Vision of the Seven Candlesticks, come to prophecy" ("Very" 157).[9] This renewed interest in the novel led to a *Pym* conference in 1988 as well as new classroom editions from Oxford World Classics in 1994 and Penguin in 1999; appropriately, the former was edited by Kennedy, whose approach to the novel was essentially deconstructionist, and the latter edited by Kopley.

Of course, deconstructionists were not limited to *Pym*, nor were their readings interchangeable with one another. Joseph Riddel's 1979 essay "The Crypt of Edgar Poe," republished in 1995 as a part of his book *Purloined Letters*, remains one of the best and most challenging articulations of Poe as proto-deconstructionist. Early in the essay he gives credit to William Carlos Williams for seeing Poe's writing as a rebellion against mere representation and sentimentality (123) and positions his own close-reading of Poe in relation to the tradition of New Criticism: "In Poe the images of nature are already metonymic substitutions for words — or substitutions for substitutions. It is all the more strange that Eliot and Tate, those fathers of New Critical formalism, would be enchanted by the force of his madness, and equally repelled by it" (124). Riddel and his contemporaries were not repelled but rather fascinated by the primacy of words — "The Power of Words" suddenly became another key Poe text — and, like William Carlos Williams, saw Poe not as a distant cousin but as more of a brother. According to Riddel, Poe's "realm of dream" is the "realm of language," always pointing to the "absence of the ideal" (126). He uncovers displacements and subversions of origins in "Usher," *Eureka*, and "The Purloined Letter," arguing that the tautological conclusions of these fictions are endlessly deferred by metaphor (134).

To state a rather obvious point, these poststructuralist analyses were simply harder to process, harder to *read,* than the New Critical interpretations that preceded them, and many debates over poststructuralism's legitimacy hinged on whether its specialized language was a necessary vehicle for subtle, self-conscious writing about writing, or jargon that served mainly to intimidate outsiders and display the critics' (implicitly pointless) virtuosity. This concern, too, relates closely to Poe's preoccupation with textual mystification, particularly its use in games of one-upmanship and revenge. For that reason, deconstructive analyses that strove for rhetorical clarity even while writing about obscurity and the deferral of meaning were particularly helpful. Dennis Pahl and Michael J. S. Williams, who belong to the first academic generation to absorb poststructuralism in graduate school, offered lucid deconstructive discussions of Poe in books based on their dissertations. Pahl's *Architects of the Abyss* (1989) included chapters on "Usher," "The Assignation," and *Pym,* in each case offering new insight into Poe's use of "indeterminacy." The general point that the house of Usher parallels Poe's textual "house" had been made before, but Pahl teased out some new implications of the inside/outside opposition and the trope of construction (which is always already a deconstruction) created by that basic parallel. His chapter on "The Assignation" demonstrates the way Byron "becomes that interpretive fiction into which Poe reads himself" (40); similarly, the *Pym* chapter deals with Poe's simultaneously announcing and concealing himself through a text that only pretends to refer to a non-textual world.

In *A World of Words* (1989), Williams bridges the gap between the old New Critical tradition and the post-structuralists, demonstrating how Poe's fiction again and again destabilizes logocentrism, and along with it Enlightenment notions of selfhood. He avoids sustained discussion of *Pym* and "Usher," wisely so in light of the number of poststructural treatments they had already received, offering instead inventive but responsible readings of stories ranging from the obscure "X-ing a Paragrab" (which really does seem designed for deconstruction) to "Morella" to "The Gold-Bug," as well as usual suspects such as the Dupin tales and "William Wilson." Like G. R. Thompson, Williams limits his study to the fiction and *Eureka,* and he grounds his discussion in the philosophy with which Poe would have been conversant, especially that of Locke. Williams, again like Thompson, sees Poe's fiction as deeply ironic, his outlook skeptical, but he adds a strong emphasis on the play of language that thickens earlier readings. Take, for example, Williams's conclusion of a fourteen-page discussion of "Ligeia": "In an ironic fulfilment of the narrator's desires for full presence, the name "Ligeia" is attached not to the pure, the wise, the lofty, the ethereal Ligeia but to a corpse that has undergone the 'wild change' of progressive decomposition" (104). That's fairly consistent with Thompson's reading of the story, but Williams emphasizes Ligeia as name, as linguistic symbol, so that the story's irony might be seen as a lacuna of *language*: "The symbol, then, does not offer access to the infinite, but is a blank, or rather, like the corpse, it is mute, accepting a significance imparted to it by the interpreting mind" (104).

Poststructuralism had a wider impact as the new emphasis on textuality and the subversion of all manner of stable meaning infused readings grounded in social and intellectual history. John Irwin's *American Hieroglyphics* (1980) turns Matthiessen's *American Renaissance* upside down; dealing with essentially the same list of authors, Irwin devotes more than half the book to Poe, who had been all but written out of Matthiessen's. Like *Renaissance, Hieroglyphics* reads literature against the backdrop of American culture, but the reading orientation has shifted from New Critical to poststructural. Both *American Hieroglyphics* and Irwin's later book *A Mystery to a Solution: Poe, Borges and the Analytic Detective Story* (1994) set out to answer questions that seem simple — What was the impact of the decipherment of Egyptian hieroglyphics on the "American Renaissance" writers? How did Borges appropriate Poe's Dupin tales in his own trilogy of detective stories? But such questions lead Irwin, and his readers, into labyrinths of intertextuality. While his American contemporaries were "using" deconstruction as if it were a new toy, Irwin in 1980 wrote as if he'd had the new approach to textuality in his back pocket for some time. The history of hieroglyphic decoding leads to a larger discussion of codes, cryptography, origins of language, doubling and repetition, as they appear in Poe and as they appear in numerous texts that surround Poe, both precursors and contemporaries. Poe's voyages, especially *Pym*, receive the most attention; Irwin builds on references to classical philosophy, Christianity, the Narcissus myth, Borges's story "Funes the Memorious," and Melville's *Pierre*, in addition to nineteenth-century Egyptology, to reach a surprising, original conclusion regarding the novel's ending: the hieroglyphic human form carved into the chasm on Tsalal, whose pictographic doubling of the body's shape is in turn phonetically doubled by the shape of the chasm spelling the root of the word "shadow," not only foreshadows (that is, temporally doubles) the appearance of the giant figure in the mist but also points to the fact that that figure is itself a spatial double, a white shadow that has undergone the color reversal characteristic of the opaque image's translation into the immortal soul. . . . What the ending of Pym acts out, then, is "a certain tendency of the human intellect" (inscribed within it by the very structure of its birth) to try to survive death by projecting an image of itself (the self as image) into the infinite void of the abyss. (205)

Irwin begins his next chapter supporting his contention that the white figure is Pym's own shadow with "numerous examples of the trope of the white shadow in Romantic tradition" (205), and the exploration of *Pym* within the world of ideas and texts continues. *The Mystery to a Solution* proceeds similarly: Irwin reads Poe and Borges not only against each other but against an array of texts on calculation, games, doubling, and detection.

While his argument takes a more linear path than Irwin's, J. Gerald Kennedy in *Poe, Death, and the Life of Writing* similarly brings a deconstructive approach to a reading of Poe in relation to changing cultural attitudes toward death. Kennedy's focus, like Irwin's, extends beyond the Poe canon. The cultural and philosophical history isn't really background anymore; instead, Poe emerges as both representative of a "culturally shared disquietude" about premature burial (along with all its existential implications) and prescient in his awareness of modern and postmodern death anxiety: "The contemporaneity of Poe's writing . . . comes from the perception of death as an absolute horizon of existence; though he invented dialogues between spirits and worked variations on the motif of resurrection, the essential horror of his writing resides in the blankness and silence, in the perception of emptiness at the core of being" (211). And yet, writing is paradoxically redemptive, "a way of translating his isolation into coherence, of recovering through his own creative gesture a purpose and significance no longer apparent in the universal scheme" (212). Kennedy deftly probes the relationship between death and writing as an eternal problem at the same time that he contextualizes Poe's representation of that problem. Poe's infamous obsession with "the death of a beautiful woman" resembles the author's anxiety over the "loss" of his own text through publication and distribution. Poe's revenge plots hinge on attempts to silence one's adversary "through a foreclosure of language" (116). In a chapter on Poe's letters, Kennedy foregrounds rhetorical parallels between the desperation in his appeals to John Allan and Sarah Helen Whitman and the dread of his condemned or imperiled narrators. The convergence of death — or the fear of death — and writing is particularly revelatory in *Pym*, where Kennedy sees Pym's insistence on providential design crashing against "the ubiquity and purposelessness of death" in a book that, like the man of the crowd, "does not permit itself to be read" (176, 174).

While the tradition outlined in this chapter tends to discuss "Poe" as a collection of writing rather than an author in the traditional, pre-Roland Barthes sense, many critics, with varying degrees of sympathy with poststructuralist thought, continued to investigate "authorship," although what that word means had become an open question by the 1980s. Jonathan Auerbach, Donald Pease, and Kenneth Dauber, for instance, included chapters about Poe's narrative strategies, the stylistic maneuvers that set him apart from other writers, in their late-1980s studies of canonical nineteenth-century American authors. Louis Renza, in an essay first presented in 1983, both questioned postmodern strictures against reading autobiographically and utilized deconstructionist strategies in making the case for a "secret autobiography" forged by Poe's persistent calling-attention-to-himself-as-author, and to the written-ness of his texts:

> I do not mean to claim that [Poe's tales] are "autobiographical" in the sense of symbolically outlining his extratextual, perverse spiritual autobiography through, say, the experiences of his many haunted narrators or the various incognito subterfuges afforded by the discourse of fiction. Rather, I mean something akin to Paul de Man's notion of autobiography as a figure of reading as opposed to genre of writing, but here revised as a figure of Poe's reading of his own texts as he imagines them being misread by others. . . . (60)

Like Kennedy and Williams, Renza retains, or reclaims, a fairly traditional notion of what an author is but examines that author's works with a poststructuralist's eye for textual play. The gesture that comes to represent Poe in Renza's reading is the anagram of Poe's title for a short tale later called "Silence": "Siope"/"is Poe." Poe seems to disappear, and yet he haunts his own texts, encrypting messages that only he can enjoy, privately. In his 2002 book on Poe and Wallace Stevens, Renza explores further Poe's conception of privacy, demonstrating how often Poe creates a hard shell of textuality that readers never really crack. He also re-examines obscurities such as "The Philosophy of Furniture" and "The Domain of Arnheim" alongside "The Pit and the Pendulum" and "The Murders in the Rue Morgue" as indicators of Poe's concern with the nature of and need for privacy and his fear of losing it. Renza's analysis of privacy in Poe is hardly ahistorical, and he repeatedly makes the point that privileging the private is not a rejection of the public sphere (on the contrary, he finds that it makes meaningful public discourse possible); still, like Kennedy's *Poe, Death, and the Life of Writing*, *The Poetics of American Privacy* is concerned primarily with issues of language and the nature of writing, and so I place it, somewhat hesitantly, in this chapter as part of the tradition of formalist/deconstructionist criticism.[10]

While studiously avoiding the tired questions of Poe's character and the unconscious motives behind his art, formalists and poststructuralists still affirmed something that uniquely "is Poe." Recall the assessment of C. Alphonso Smith, cited in chapter 1 as a celebrant of Poe's American genius, who argued that Poe's "constructiveness" was his most valuable and most American trait. Smith may have been right after all, for the rigorous attention to literary form that unites the various readings glossed in this chapter is crucial to the study of Poe. In the first half of the twentieth century, critics who either held that Poe's reputation rested on his poetry or who were distracted by his gaudy gothic effects failed to appreciate the pervasive ironies and the textual and philosophical patterns that a study of his entire literary output revealed. But the practice of close reading in the service of finding the larger unifying idea — or the creative destruction of such an idea — brought new meanings to Poe's work (or, perhaps, uncovered meanings that were there all along). Only a few of the critics discussed in this chapter made more than passing reference to race, gender, or class, the publishing world of antebellum America, P. T. Barnum, or Andrew Jackson (those who did will show up again in the next chapter); and the image of Poe fostered by New Criticism (and to some extent continued by deconstruction) — an isolated artist, "out of place, out of time" — misled generations of students. At the same time, no psychoanalytic or historicized reading of Poe cancels out the profound insights of critics in the grain of William Carlos Williams, Wilbur, Davidson, and their successors in the "tradition" outlined here. These were the critics who taught the rest of us how to read Poe.

Notes

[1] See, for instance, George Snell's "First of the New Critics," *Quarterly Review of Literature* 2 (1945): 333–40, as well as the more recent *Handbook of Critical Approaches to Literature,* ed. Wilfred L. Guerin, et al., 4th ed. (New York: Oxford UP, 1999), which also cites Poe as a forerunner of the New Critics (79).

[2] Emerson's famous remark was related by William Dean Howells in *Literary Friends and Acquaintance: A Personal Retrospect of American Authorship,* ed. David F. Hiatt and Edwin H. Cady (Bloomington and London: Indiana UP, 1968), 58.

[3] Despite their low regard for Poe's poetry, Brooks and Warren included three poems, "Ulalume," "The Sleeper," and "To Helen" in both the 1938 and 1950 editions of *Understanding Poetry* (New York: Henry Holt). In the 1976 edition, they excluded the latter two poems, included only the first verse of "Ulalume," and cut most of their discussion, but retained Huxley's parody.

[4] See Jay B. Hubbell, *Who Are the Major American Writers?* (Durham, NC: Duke UP, 1972), 272–73.

[5] While F. O. Matthiessen does not place Poe solidly within the American tradition, in "Edgar Allan Poe," in *Literary History of the United States,* ed. Robert E. Spiller and Willard Thorp, 321–42 (New York: Macmillan, 1948), he acknowledges the argument "that has sometimes been advanced that the materialism of so many of Poe's interests, his fondness for inventions and hoaxes, and his special flair for journalism make him more 'representative' than Emerson or Whitman of ordinary Americans" (342); he also recognizes Poe's place in the American Gothic tradition, along with Brockden Brown, Bierce, and Faulkner.

[6] See also Charles L. Sanford, "Edgar Allan Poe," *Rives* 18 (1962): 1–9; reprinted in *The Recognition of Edgar Allan Poe,* ed. Eric W. Carlson (Ann Arbor: U of Michigan P, 1966), 297–307.

[7] For examples as recent as 2000–2001, see Brett Zimmerman, "Allegoria and Clock Architecture in Poe's 'The Masque of the Red Death,'" *Essays in the Arts and Sciences* 29 (Oct. 2000): 1–16; Frederick L. Burwick, "Edgar Allan Poe: The Sublime and the Grotesque," *Prisms: Essays in Romanticism* 8 (2000): 67–123; Roberto Cagliero, "Poe's Interiors: The Theme of Usurpation in 'The Cask of Amontillado,'" *Edgar Allan Poe Review* 2 (Spring 2001): 30–36; and William Freedman, "Poe's Oval Portrait of 'The Oval Portrait,'" *Poe Studies* 34 (2001): 7–12.

[8] For more perspectives on Poe as satirist and hoaxer, see Dennis Eddings, ed., *The Naiad Voice: Essays on Poe's Satiric Hoaxing* (Port Washington, NY: Associated Faculty, 1983).

[9] Richard Kopley ("The Hidden Journey of Arthur Gordon Pym," in *Studies in the American Renaissance* 1982, ed. Joel Myerson, 29–51 [Charlottesville: UP of Virginia, 1982]), builds on Wilbur's interpretation in his introduction to the Godine edition of *Pym,* going into greater detail and emphasizing the reappearance of the *Penguin* as the

white figure. William Mentzel Forrest's *Biblical Allusions in Poe* (New York: Macmillan, 1928) is a foundational book for studies of Poe and the Judeo-Christian tradition. For another impressive treatment of Poe and biblical prophecy, see David H. Hirsch, "The Pit and the Apocalypse," *Sewanee Review* 76 (1968): 632–52. For a summary of visionary readings of *Pym*, see J. Gerald Kennedy, "*The Narrative of Arthur Gordon Pym*" and the Abyss of Interpretation (New York: Twayne, 1995), 18–23.

[10] Shawn Rosenheim's *The Cryptographic Imagination: From Edgar Poe to the Internet* (Baltimore: Johns Hopkins UP, 1997) investigates the pursuit of privacy through cryptography, relating Poe's extensive use of ciphers to secret writing and decoding throughout history. Rosenheim makes Poe the touchstone for consistently intriguing and informed discussions of detective fiction, science fiction, spiritualism, espionage, and digitization of information and images. It is perhaps a tribute to *The Cryptographic Imagination* that I could not make it fit properly into this or any other chapter (although I mention it briefly in the afterword), but it comes closest to fitting here, alongside the work of John T. Irwin (*The Mystery to a Solution: Poe, Borges, and the Analytic Detective Story* [Baltimore and London: Johns Hopkins UP, 1994]), Kennedy (*Poe, Death, and the Life of Writing*), and Louis A. Renza (*Edgar Allan Poe, Wallace Stevens, and the Poetics of American Privacy*).

4: The Man of the Crowd: The Socio-Historical Poe

> *The whole period, America 1840,*
> *could be rebuilt, psychologically*
> *(phrenologically) from Poe's "method."*
> — William Carlos Williams (1925)

IN THE LAST CHAPTER, I surveyed what might be called "traditional" readings of Poe that, with a few exceptions, pay little attention to the material contexts for his writings, focusing instead on form, irony, "timeless" themes and philosophical issues. While the great disruption *within* this tradition came from deconstruction, the real challenge to traditional Poe studies, and to traditional literary studies generally, since the 1980s has come from critics who focus attention on representations of race, gender, and class, usually by positioning the literary text in question to other texts from the same period. Chronologically, these more sociological approaches overlap with deconstruction: to the extent that they're separate movements, they shared center stage in literary criticism throughout the 1980s. The two approaches often shared practitioners as well, as deconstruction came to be regarded less as an end in itself than as a tool to dismantle texts that reinforce oppressive social structures or to show how texts that appear to endorse such structures actually undermine them. At the same time, literary critics tend not to look, for instance, only at gender to the exclusion of race and class. However, in order to give some structure to this chapter, I will proceed from race to gender to class and economics, considering discussions of Poe's role in the publishing pre-industry as part of that last, large category.

Two critics in particular, John Carlos Rowe and Joan Dayan, exemplify the late-1980s shift in emphasis toward seeing race as a key point of discussion in Poe studies; indeed, they made the early, polemical arguments that forced many scholars to consider a new cluster of issues.

Rowe had written an influential deconstructive analysis of *Pym* in his 1982 book *Through the Custom House* (discussed in chapter 3). Ten years later, in a collection of essays on *Pym* culled from a 1988 conference, his focus on *Pym* had shifted, as he argued that Poe must be re-read as a pro-slavery Southerner, and that the analyses of Poe's "world of words" that locate him outside of history, particularly antebellum Southern history, were complicit in Poe's "racist strategy of literary production" (118).[1] In 1987 Dayan published *Fables of Mind,* a complex re-examination of Poe's philosophy and aesthetics, an expansive revision of Richard Wilbur's reading of the Poe canon, with *Eureka* at the forefront. But two years later, at the annual lecture sponsored by the Poe Society of Baltimore, she made a case, similar to Rowe's, for re-reading Poe in the context of antebellum slavery and racism. Dayan referred to a review praising two pro-slavery books in the *Southern Literary Messenger* as Poe's "most disturbing, because most authentic, 'love poem'" (96) and proceeded to suggest ways that "The Black Cat," "The Murders in the Rue Morgue," "Hop-Frog" and *Pym* concern race and slavery. A decade later, both critics would be included in a landmark collection, *Romancing the Shadow: Poe and Race,* which demonstrates how far and in how many directions the discussion had gone in a relatively short time.

As we saw in chapter 1, Poe's "Southern heritage" had drawn attention before, in the early twentieth century, but with the object of promoting more favorable images of both Poe and the region. The speakers at the centenary events had no interest in connecting Poe with slavery even as they declared him a true son of the South. While the overblown, overtly pro-Southern claims of the centenary orators had faded by mid-century, a number of writers held on to the image of the Southern Poe without suggesting that his background implicated him as a racist, or that such an implication mattered. V. L. Parrington wrote passionately about the evils of slavery in *Main Currents in American Thought* (1927) and classified Poe as a Southern author, yet he declared that Poe's social and political beliefs weren't worth exploring: "Southern though he was in the deep prejudices of a suspicious nature, his aloofness from his own Virginia world was complete. Aside from his art he had no philosophy and no programs and no causes" (57). Killis Campbell compiled considerable evidence of Poe's American-ness and, more particularly, his Southern-ness for a 1923 essay, expanded into a chapter of *The Mind of Poe* (1933). But while

Campbell notes Poe's defense of slavery in his *Southern Literary Messenger* reviews, he mentions it only briefly and shows no anxiety over how that particular part of Poe's Southern background might influence one's reading of his fiction or poetry, unless we count his repeating Clarence Stedman's suggestion that Poe's musical verse owed a debt to "the Negro" (115). Campbell thought enough about Poe's relation to African-Americans to write a brief article on "Poe's Treatment of the Negro and of the Negro Dialect" in 1936, in which he itemized and summarized Poe's racist representations without describing them as racist: "The trait of the negro slave which Poe makes most of both in his tales and in his reviews is that of the negro's loyalty and faithfulness to his master. . . . Furthermore, he insists upon the slave's carelessness in dress and upon his unprepossessing appearance — his wooly hair, his large mouth and eyes, his bow legs, and his clumsiness both in speech and in appearance" (114).[2] And that's the last sentence of the essay.

In a 1934 article, "Poe as Social Critic," Ernest Marchand states directly that "Poe received his views on slavery and swallowed them whole, unseasoned by criticism" (37). And yet Marchand considers Poe's approval of slavery only a little longer than Campbell had — about two pages of a fifteen-page article — and doesn't touch the issue of race in Poe's fiction. A 1952 survey/textbook, *The Literature of the South*, includes Poe in the section on "The Confederate South" but makes no mention of slavery and concludes that "Poe cannot be treated as fundamentally a Southerner" (109). Jay B. Hubbell's chapter on Poe for *The South in American Literature, 1607–1900* (1954) makes a fairly strong case for a Southern Poe but mentions slavery only to exonerate Poe of having written the "Paulding-Drayton Review" (536). By mid-century, then, Poe was still being classified as Southern, but it didn't seem to matter: aside from Allen Tate and Ellen Glasgow, who called Poe "a distillation of the Southern" in *A Certain Measure* (1943), no one seemed able to do much with the idea of a Southern Poe anymore.[3]

And yet, in the late 1950s, amidst what might be called the first *Pym* revival as well as the emergence of American Studies, critics began to argue that Southern race relations and slavery were vital to the Tsalal episode and the ending of *Pym*. Harry Levin noted the implications of the racial antipathies in *Pym*, speculating that in Poe's unconscious, "there must have been not only the fantasy of a lost heritage, but a resentment and a racial phobia" (121). Levin treads lightly, even as he traces Poe's phobia through "The System of Dr. Tarr and Professor Fether" and "Hop-Frog." He concludes that if Poe "shared those benighted sentiments of interracial hostility which have made the black man so tragic a victim of our history, then he deserves some credit for having concealed them under the strata of his symbolism" (123). Leslie Fiedler in *Love and Death in the American Novel* (1960) and Sidney Kaplan in his introduction to a popular edition of the novel (1960) are more aggressive, as both read the Tsalal episode as an allegory of Southern racism and slavery. Fiedler's discussion of *Pym* is brief — about eight pages — but groundbreaking: "Insofar as *Gordon Pym* is finally a social document as well as a fantasy, its subject is slavery; and its scene, however disguised, is the section of America which was to destroy itself defending that institution. It is, indeed, to be expected that our first eminent Southern author discover that the proper subject for American gothic is the black man, from whose shadow we have not yet emerged. . . . [T]he book projects his personal resentment and fear, as well as the guilty terror of a whole society in the face of those whom they can never believe they have the right to enslave" (397, 399). As much a psychoanalytic reader as a historicist, Fiedler suggests that, as in *Benito Cereno,* the specter of race in *Pym* evokes what one might call a national uncanny, haunting not only Pym but the republic for which he stands: "At this point, the darkness of 'Nigger-town' merges at last into the darkness of the womb which is also a tomb, an intestinal chamber from which there is apparently no way of being born again into a realm of light" (399).

Whereas Fielder saw Pym's voyage to the South as a trip back to "Ole Virginny" (398), for Sidney Kaplan, "Tsalal is Hell" (xix) because the black people of the earth are, in Poe's mythology, damned. For Kaplan, then, the ending of *Pym* is nothing less than a quasi-biblical defense of the peculiar institution: "To be sure, the 'great men' among the Tsalalians are Wampoos or Yampoos — a blend of Swift's Yahoos and the race of Ham . . . whose posterity (as Genesis has it) occupied the southernmost regions of the world" (xix). Levin's introduction is perhaps the most condemnatory essay on Poe and race that has been written, since it claims not only Poe's complicity with slavery but a deepseated personal racism, taking Pym's impressions as an expression of Poe's manichean belief that black people were demonic.

And there the matter stood, more or less, for about thirty years, when Rowe and Dayan renewed the discussion.[4] Many of the "old guard" of Poe devotees and scholars objected to their insistence that race matters — greatly — in the study of Poe, that his personal pro-slavery views, his "Southern" disposition toward race infuses much — all? — of his writing, not just those isolated minstrel-show caricatures in "The Gold-Bug" and "A Predicament."[5] Like most canonical authors, "Poe" became a battleground in the culture wars that raged in academe and popular media throughout the 1990s, so much so that in 1995 an episode of the television show *Northern Exposure* literalized the war metaphor in a dream sequence depicting Poe as one of the beleaguered soldiers defending a besieged Western tradition ("Graduate"). While neither Rowe nor Dayan proposed expelling Poe from the canon, both explicitly challenged traditions of scholarship and appraisal that supported Poe's aesthetic, which they regarded as complicit in maintaining white male privilege a century and half after his death. Having argued that Poe's fantasy of power accruing to the most able readers underwrote a status quo dependent on human oppression, Rowe suggests that "Poe was profoundly clairvoyant, even if . . . his was a perverse vision. Today one's class identification and one's virtual earning power are tied intimately to the 'Power of Words'" ("Poe" 138). Dayan's essay "Amorous Bondage" compares the rhetoric of "the founding fathers of the Poe Society" to that of "pro-slavery ideologues" (180) and concludes with the claim that "Poe's racialized Gothicism . . . requires that we rethink the meaning of color and the making of monsters, as well as question the myths of the masters who still haunt the halls of the academy" (207). Such claims made overt the politics of interpretation, arguing what has since become a truism in the humanities, that to read a text "apolitically" is to take a political — specifically a reactionary — position.

The argument over "Poe and race" was made more contentious by the suggestion that the point of it all was to "out" Poe as a racist. As late as 2002, J. V. Ridgely frames his review of *Romancing the Shadow* with the question "How racist was Poe?" as if the purpose of all scholarship pertaining to Poe and race were to answer that single question. Although that question grossly oversimplifies the purposes of the collection he was reviewing, Ridgely had some grounds for believing that Poe's personal racism was what all the fuss was about. Ten years earlier he had written an essay at the request of the *Poe Studies Association Newsletter,* ostensibly a review of Dayan's "Romance and Race" and Dana Nelson's *The Word in Black and White,* but actually a discussion of the authorship of a review in the *Southern Literary Messenger* that Dayan had referred to as Poe's most authentic love poem, an attribution question that deserves some attention here. If Poe had written the review (of James Kirke Paulding's *Slavery in the United States* and William Drayton's anonymously published *The South Vindicated from the Treason and Fanaticism of the Northern Abolitionists*), it would have been his most direct statement on race and slavery. It *is* a kind of love poem, in part, since the *Messenger* reviewer argues that the word "patriarchal" isn't strong enough to describe the bonds of affection that form between master and slave: "That is an easy transition by which he who is taught to call the little negro 'his,' in this sense and *because he loves him,* shall love him *because he is his*" ("Slavery" 338). He concludes with thanks to the books' authors for their defense of the benevolent institution:

> Nothing is wanting but manly discussion to convince our own people at least, that in continuing to command the services of their slaves, they violate no law divine or human, and that in the faithful discharge of their reciprocal obligations lies their true duty. Let these be performed, and we believe (with our esteemed correspondent Professor Dew) that society in the South will derive much more of good than of evil from this much abused and partially-considered institution. ("Slavery" 339)

The review's unequivocal defense of slavery served as an entrance to larger discussions about Poe and race: Dayan, Rowe, and Nelson used it to dispel the notion that Poe didn't care about slavery and instead to establish, if only as a starting point, that Poe was categorically racist and pro-slavery. Even Marchand, back in 1934, had based his brief discussion of Poe's engagement with slavery on the "Paulding-Drayton review."

In fact, the review bounced in and out of the Poe canon throughout the twentieth century. James Harrison, in his 1903 edition of Poe's complete works, included it, but in a 1941 dissertation on the Poe canon, William Doyle Hull, citing a letter from Poe to pro-slavery novelist Beverly Tucker discussing an essay on slavery, attributed the review to Tucker. Bernard Rosenthal in a 1974 essay questioned the attribution to Tucker, essentially reopening the issue and making the review semi-fair territory for critics: one couldn't assume Poe's authorship, but one could use the controversy to set the terms for a discussion of Poe and race. In the 1992 *PSA Newsletter* essay cited earlier, Ridgely, a respected Poe scholar who was then at work on an edition of Poe's writings for the *Messenger,* offered detailed evidence supporting Hull's attribution to Tucker, concluding that Rosenthal's thesis was "deeply flawed" (6). Meanwhile, Terence Whalen, through a close examination of the *Messenger,* Poe's correspondence with Tucker, and Tucker's secessionist novel *The Partisan Leader,* supported Ridgely's conclusion, virtually proving Tucker's authorship in a 1994 article later revised and included in his book *Edgar Allan Poe and the Masses.*

While the controversy surrounding the "Paulding-Drayton Review" offers a good example for Bibliography-and-Research-Methods classes of the importance of old-fashioned literary sleuthing, most critics engaged in the debate have acknowledged all along that Poe cannot, and should not, be declared simply "innocent" or "guilty" of racism, particularly not on the basis of a single review. On one side of the issue, critics argue that Poe's association with the *Messenger* is far more important: as Rosenthal and Rowe have argued, Poe (for all intents and purposes) edited the magazine that propagated the review's pro-slavery sentiments. Rowe compares Poe's case to that of Paul de Man, the philosopher and literary critic who, posthumously, became a center of controversy for his contributions to pro-Nazi periodicals during the 1940s: "Wary as we should be of the dangers of charging 'guilt by association,' we must acknowledge that the association of publication in the same newspaper or journal can be the basis for a substantial case" ("Poe" 119). More specifically, Jared Gardner argues that while Poe did not write the "Paulding-Drayton Review," he certainly had a hand in editing it, but even more, "he wanted readers to believe the anonymous essay was by him" (133). Scattered evidence of Poe's support for slavery can be found outside the *Messenger* as well: for instance, he dedicated his *Tales of the Grotesque and Arabesque* to Drayton, the anonymous author of *The South Vindicated,* and he included support for abolition among his list of reasons to dislike Longfellow and Lowell when they were his enemies. Even Poe's defenders can claim only that the issue of slavery was relatively unimportant to him, not that he in any way opposed it or denounced the racism typical of his time.

On the other side, one can reasonably question the sincerity of Poe's alliance with the *Messenger's* pro-slavery contributors, considering how opportunistic he was generally and how desperate for employment he was at the time he worked at the *Messenger*. Whalen argues that trying to pin down Poe's position on slavery becomes more difficult the closer one looks at the *Messenger* during his tenure as review editor. According to Whalen, T. W. White, the *Messenger's* owner and nominal editor, tried to avoid being too closely associated with any political position: he published Tucker, but he also published a rebuttal to Tucker that argued for African colonization and gradual emancipation. As White's employee, Poe had to walk a fine line in trying not to offend anyone who might support or subscribe to the magazine. Whalen calls the position of Poe and his employer "average racism," which he points out "was not a sociological measurement of actual beliefs but rather a strategic construction designed to overcome political dissension in the emerging mass audience" (111–12).[6] J. Gerald Kennedy adds that Poe's "only public remarks about slavery per se during his stint with the *Messenger*" regard slavery as a necessary evil as opposed to the positive good claimed by its apologists (236) — not a heroic position (or one that we can assume reflected Poe's personal belief) but one that makes singling Poe out for his personal racism seem misguided or, at least, of limited use. His berating New England abolitionists, too, can be taken more as opposition to radicalism than explicit support for slavery (Whalen 137–38). Because Poe's racism does seem unexceptional in its antebellum context and because arguing for very long over just how racist he — or any individual, for that matter — was only obscures larger, more vital issues surrounding race, most recent critics have sought to shift the focus away from Poe's personal racism toward antebellum discourses of race as reflected and, in some cases, deconstructed in Poe's work.

The concern with race and region, especially in regard to *Pym*, gained momentum when Toni Morrison declared in her book *Playing in the Dark* (1992) that "No early American writer is more important to the concept of American Africanism than Poe. And no image is more telling than . . . the visualized but somehow closed and unknowable white form that rises from the mists at the end of [*Pym's*] journey" (32). Not only is race crucial to our understanding of Poe, but Poe is crucial to our understanding of race in American literature and history. Morri-

son's approach to blackness and whiteness inspired more nuanced readings of race in American literature and, along with Rowe's and Dayan's
provocative essays, encouraged scholars to go beyond the observations
of Fielder and Kaplan in regard to *Pym*. For instance, Dana Nelson argued that Pym's binary vision of "black" and "white" typify the ethno-
centrism of the colonizer, but that Poe's novel undermines Pym's
perception, effectively "decentering" his colonialist discourse. Nelson's
reading of *Pym* forecast some important trends: she used the language
of deconstruction to write about *Pym*'s relationship to the real world, she
discussed race in the context of exploration and colonialism along with
that of domestic slavery, and she argued that Poe's personal racism did
not prevent him from writing a novel that could be read as anti-racist.
Similarly, in *Gothic America,* Teresa Goddu argued that "even as *Pym*'s
color symbolism seems constantly to create difference, it elides that
difference while articulating a discourse of racial identity that is constructed, and hence vulnerable to change" (85).

Expanding considerably on Sidney Kaplan's argument, Sam Worley
in a 1994 article drew specific connections between Pym's representation
of the Tsalalians and descriptions of Africans in antebellum pro-slavery
writing. For most of the essay, Poe appears to be in league with William
Gilmore Simms and John C. Calhoun: "For Poe and the proslavery
writers, Blacks are understood as simultaneously cooperative and demonic. Their evil is simply exposed; it does not develop in response to
any stimulus" (232). And yet Worley concludes, similarly to Nelson, that
Poe also undermines the racist rhetoric his protagonist endorses: "We are
left with a work that both constructs and deconstructs social hierarchy
along the axis of language" (242). For Jared Gardner, Poe's interests in
race and in writing-as-code are inextricable; for instance, Poe reads auto-
graphs the way racialist phrenologists read skulls. Incorporating the
deconstructionist reading of *Pym* as a quest for the origin of writing,
Gardner sees the novel as simultaneously a quest for racial origins, a
voyage that affirms the theory of polygenesis in opposition to "the fantasy of an original whiteness, a world without racial difference, to which
the nation might somehow return" (134). As Kennedy had done a decade earlier in exploring the conjunction of death and writing in Poe,
Gardner stakes a claim for a symbiotic relationship between *race* and
writing at the end of *Pym*: "To attempt to escape a world of racial differ-

ence — to find a world where all is perfect whiteness — is, in the logic of this novel, to arrive at a point at which writing can no longer exist" (149). While Gardner is not primarily interested in Poe's personal beliefs about race, he reads the novel as affirming racist pseudoscience and envisioning a kind of national apocalypse of racial conflict.

Building on Nelson's insights, Paul Lyons maintains that the South Seas are a more important referent for the Tslalal episode than the southern United States.[7] In *Pym* as in many other antebellum texts, "the polar opposite of the 'civilized' white man appears, not as an African, but as the 'savage' South Seas islander found at the other end of the earth," Lyons explains, after investigating a number of those texts, including reports by explorers Charles Wilkes, J. N. Reynolds, and Benjamin Morrell (whose narrative Poe appropriated in composing *Pym*), as well as Wilkes's sailing orders, written by none other than James Kirke Paulding, then-Secretary of the Navy. Lyons demonstrates that the orientalist discourse of those writers pervades *Pym*, but he also suggests that Poe might have been trying to "out-herod Herod" in exaggerating the dark sensationalism of Morrell's largely fabricated (and ghost-written) text (313). Again, *Pym* seems simultaneously to endorse and challenge racist ideology: "Such a reading might find in *Pym* a series of profoundly ambivalent errors that, being 'graven' within the text, furnish a blueprint for a counter-reading that the text itself does not care to perform" (314).

A final twist on recent discussions of race and *Pym* is the suggestion that Poe identified with the racial Other as he wrote the novel. For Terence Whalen, the crew of the Jane Guy represents "capital's relentless quest for new information," and the Tsalians plot against this encroachment in a manner similar to Poe's plan for his own magazine: "Poe argued that nothing would change until a coalition of writers banded together to seize control of American letters" (191). Building on the coincidence of Poe and Frederick Douglass living in the same Baltimore neighborhood at the same time, Gerald Kennedy draws a number of parallels between Douglass's 1845 *Narrative* and Pym's *Narrative*. One semi-autobiographical reference is particularly intriguing: after referring to Poe's leave-taking letter to Allan, in which he rails against being subjected to "the complete authority of the blacks," Kennedy points out the irony of "the fictional Pym hiding like a runaway slave beneath the decks of the Grampus. . . . For Poe's break with Allan in 1827 [the same year

Pym takes flight] and his subsequent disinheritance effectively ended his prospect of becoming a Southern slaveholder and barred him from the genteel caste to which he aspired" (234). Moreover, both Pym and Douglass negotiate their way through worlds filled with deception and cruel irony while clinging to faith in a benevolent higher power. Kennedy offers a reading of *Pym*'s last pages that again suggests that Poe might have written a socially progressive text despite himself:

> For some critics, the novel's final image — of a colossal polar figure whose skin is "of the perfect whiteness of the snow" (*CW,* I:206) — identifies Poe as a Southern bigot in quest of racial purity. But the novel authorizes a contrary, subversive reading, for as Pym approaches his own textual vanishing point, this emissary of supposed enlightenment is literally in the same boat with a "savage" and a "half-breed Indian" (*CW,* I:55). That is, the American picaro cannot at last avoid the multicultural nature of social experience; the destiny of Pym, the white man, cannot be dissociated from that of the black and the red. (252)

Kennedy had previously referred to Pym as an "abyss of interpretation," and that phrase is as apt in the aftermath of "race" readings as it was when the novel was attracting post-structuralist approaches. Critics can regard it as an exploration of race, writing, spirit, or all of the above, but still no two interpretive maps of Pym's voyage look alike.

While *Pym* seemed like the obvious place to start examining Poe and race, critics have explored whiteness and blackness in a number of stories and poems. It seems unlikely that Poe self-consciously turned his attention to race in some stories and neglected it in others, and the prevailing assumption seems to be that race is always in the unconscious of his work, although it rises into clear view in a large handful of texts dealing with mastery, servitude, and revolt. In his contribution to *Romancing the Shadow*, Rowe discusses "The Journal of Julius Rodman" as an imperialist text, consistent with the orientalism of "A Tale of the Ragged Mountains" and the racism of "Murders in the Rue Morgue." As in his work on *Pym*, Rowe argues that critics must come to terms with the fact that Poe used his fiction to support human oppression: "It is thus not just the conventionality of Poe's racist and imperialist fantasies that we should condemn but also the extent to which Poe has employed his undisputed powers as a creative writer to weave such fantasies into what has for so long been appreciated for its aesthetic qualities" (95). James Livingston, in a 1993 Freudian analysis of Poe's fiction (and life), similarly focuses on Poe's personal racism, concluding that slavery played a major role in stunting his mental and artistic development. Slavery, like love in Poe's tales, presumes a relationship of "hypertrophy and atrophy of will" as opposed to a recognition of the humanity of the Other (191). (His argument resembles Dayan's description of the pro-slavery review as a love poem, and Livingston, too, assumes Poe's authorship of the review.)

However, as was the case with *Pym,* most recent critics have seen Poe's tales as complex and ambivalent on matters of race and slavery, and have been less interested than Rowe or Livingston in condemning Poe. Michael J. S. Williams, like Rowe, reads "A Tale of the Ragged Mountains" in the context of orientalism and U.S. imperialism, but he argues that Poe is exposing the perils of — rather than embracing — the nation's "imperial ambition" (58). Leland Person's essay in *Romancing the Shadow* uses the tropes of vitiligo and topsy-turvy dolls to describe Poe's "philosophy of amalgamation" in "The Black Cat," "The Murders in the Rue Morgue," and "Hop-Frog," as well as "Ligeia," and concludes with something close to a consensus view (as of 2001): "Coordinating embedded (it is tempting to say repressed) racial discourse with first-person narratives of psychopathology, Poe inevitably represented the fault lines of racist psychology." Citing Nelson's contention that *Pym* reflects Poe's racism even as it deconstructs racist ideology, Person refers to the four tales he discusses as "[d]econstructions of black essentialism" (221).

In a remarkable essay, Leslie Ginsberg links Southern newspaper reporting of Nat Turner's rebellion, popular magazines' representations of pet ownership and abuse, and Poe's "The Black Cat," demonstrating the way antebellum Americans — slavery apologists and abolitionists alike — associated pet ownership with slavery; thus, Ginsberg makes plausible the reading of the black cat as a figure for the abused slave. The fact that pro-slavery ideology likened Africans to beasts while promoting a familial model of slave-ownership comes as no surprise, but when combined with the lesser-known anxiety of some abolitionists over pet ownership because of its "uncomfortable echoes of slavery" (108) it supports a more complex cultural reading of Poe's story. Like Leslie Fiedler, Ginsberg recognizes a racial component to Poe's pre-Freudian expression of the uncanny: "if we accept that what often appears to be uncanny is really well known, the seemingly uncanny and compulsively repeated scenes of domestic violence throughout 'The Black Cat' reveal nothing less than that familiar story of familial abuse, a tale which has its double in the model of domestic slavery" (123). Person also sees the story tapping into a white collective unconscious. He contends that the white splotch that eventually forms a gallows on Pluto's breast "ironically thematizes the progress of vitiligo not as a sign of racial 'encroachment' or erasure but as a sign of white racial guilt and black revenge" ("Poe's Philosophy" 218).

The racist linkage between apes and Africans has provided the basis for provocative readings of "The Murders in the Rue Morgue" and "Hop-Frog" (originally published with the subtitle "or, The Eight Chained Orang-Outangs"). Both Rowe and Lindon Barrett point out that Georges Cuvier, who is "key to Dupin's comprehension of the baffling events in the apartments of Madame L'Espanaye" (Barrett 169), promoted a system of species classification that placed Africans between Caucasians and apes in the great chain of development (Rowe 97–98, Barrett 168–69). Barrett regards the fact that Dupin wins because he is both rational and capable of comprehending the irrationality of the killer ape as both an assertion of whiteness and a blurring of the correspondence between Reason and whiteness: "Dupin's triumph documents that the truly white person always looks necessarily and intently beyond Europe and whiteness" (175). In one of the most compelling essays yet written on Poe and race, Elise Lemire, like Barrett, recounts the pseudoscience that informs "Rue Morgue," but she makes more striking use of another set of cultural "texts" surrounding the predominance of Blacks as barbers in Philadelphia around the time Poe wrote his story there. Moving the discussion of Poe and race out of the South, Lemire points out that Poe's razor-wielding orangutan plays into a commonplace caricature — she cites, for instance, a Peale's Museum exhibit featuring stuffed monkeys as barbers — so that "by making a barbering razor the chief murder weapon, Poe draws on perceived similarities precisely to invoke the frightening and dangerous possibility of black upward mobility that black barbering signaled for so many whites" (186). Lemire then relates that fear to the fear of amalgamation (miscegenation) and the anger that fear fueled toward abolitionists who were thought to promote it: Poe "has the instrument of [upward] mobility for many free blacks, the barber's razor, serve as the means of violating the bodies of two cloistered white women" (198). Lemire and Ginsberg both succeed in demonstrating how much racial tensions and conflicts were part of the air Poe breathed by reading Poe's stories alongside texts he is likely to have read, illustrations and exhibits he is likely to have seen.[8] Both shed some light on "the mind of Poe," but tell us more about the racially charged America he inhabited.

These essays also accomplish what Teresa Goddu calls for in her essay "Rethinking Race and Slavery in Poe Studies," which appeared in a special "New Directions" issue of *Poe Studies* in 2000: "a more comprehensive and complex consideration of slavery and race in Poe's work would situate his texts within a larger sociocultural field and at the nexus of multiple cultural discourses" (15). Goddu achieves this goal herself in her contribution to *The Cambridge Companion to Edgar Allan Poe* (2002), in which she demonstrates the conventionality of Poe's racial caricature and sensationalism in "A Predicament," "The Pit and the Pendulum," and "Hop-Frog," arguing that Poe simultaneously employs and critiques those devices. Her analysis of these stories also evokes the best readings of race in *Pym*, which generally conclude that the text both embraces and undermines racial hierarchies. In the case of "A Predicament," "Poe may expose the contemptuous racial codes upon which [Psyche] Zenobia's story rests, but he continues to circulate their conventions" (104); having compared the tortures of "The Pit and the Pendulum" to the descriptions of suffering in anti-slavery tracts, she concludes that "Poe exposes the literary marketplace's taste for sensational scenes of horror even as his tale exploits that appetite for its own commercial success" (107). Goddu's fundamental point is vital: that we can't pretend to understand Poe's uses of race outside the literary marketplace and its discourse of sensationalism.

"Hop-Frog," which until the late 1990s had attracted little attention, has emerged as an important text, given its reversal of the master-slave relationship and the lynching image with which the story concludes, as eight men, ostensibly "masters" dressed as orangutans, are set ablaze by a servant who has been pushed too far. Goddu's claim parallels her reading of the other two stories, that "Hop-Frog's jest simultaneously performs the conventions of sensationalism and exposes their investments: that sensationalism depends upon slavery for its effects, that it embodies terror in the form of 'blackness,' and that it appeals to its audience's voyeurism"

(108). One of the basic interpretive problems the story presents is the fact that even as Hop-Frog "reveals" the bestial nature of the king and his ministers, he reveals his own monstrous cruelty — initially we are led to sympathize with him against his masters, but his revenge seems out of proportion to his mistreatment. Paul Christian Jones argues that in evoking sympathy for Hop-Frog and Tripetta, Poe is imitating the rhetoric of sentimental abolitionist literature; the point of this anti-abolitionist story is to recognize the danger of sympathizing with slaves. While Goddu and Jones read "Hop-Frog" in light of contemporary sensational and sentimental writing, Paul Gilmore sees the antebellum freak show — specifically, racialized exhibits questioning whether or not the subject was a "man" — as an important cultural intertext for Poe's story. Gilmore agrees that the story is about race, but he relates that concern to what critics *used to* think the story was about — Poe's personal fantasies of revenge against real and perceived literary enemies. Whereas Jones argues that Poe's ultimate aim is to demonize the insurgent slave, Gilmore contends that the story "reveals the supposed men [the king and his ministers] as monsters while demonstrating the more powerful manhood of the exotic, abnormal other through his subtle plan of revenge" (111). For Gilmore, the fierce but "fully individuated and complex" character of Hop-Frog becomes a version of Poe the avenging literatus: "Identifying himself with a figure of racial otherness . . . Poe satirizes both the racial politics of the antislavery Bostonian literary circles and the mass market in sensational literature in an attempt to establish himself in a position of literary authority" (124).

In making the case for Poe's self-identification as racial Other, Gilmore refers to an 1849 verse satire, A. J. H. Duganne's "A Mirror for Authors," which refers to "our literary Mohawk, Poe!" and is illustrated with a silhouette of a dancing Poe adorned with feathers, brandishing a tomahawk in one hand and a knife in the other. Leon Jackson, in a recent essay, explores the implications of the trope of critic-as-Native American and its persistence as a way of describing Poe, who more or less embraced that image early in his career but tried to escape it in the 1840s. Jackson's reading of "The Man That Was Used Up" suggests that constructions of American whiteness depend not just on the African-Americanist presence suggested by Toni Morrison but also the specter of the Native American: "General Smith's attempts to eradicate or displace the Natives evinces an obvious desire to create an American territory unsullied by racial difference; he is a celebrated Indian Killer. . . . Ironically, his attempts have not only failed to eradicate the Native Americans but have left him so thoroughly dismembered that he is compelled to rebuild himself using artificial materials" ("Behold" 19). Poe's ambivalence on racial issues — or, more specifically, his tendency to endorse white supremacy in his reviews and then undermine similar assertions in his fiction — surfaces again in regard to Native Americans: he ridicules them in "Used Up," referring to the "Bugaboo" tribe, for instance, even as he satirizes the Indian fighter; in other texts he depicts them as savages, and yet at times he relishes the role of "literary Mohawk." Jackson's essay, like those of Lyons and Rowe, reminds us that discussions of Poe and race should not be limited to his portrayal of African-Americans.

If gender has received less attention in Poe studies than race, it might be because a feminist response to Poe seems too obvious: the tellers of Poe's tales, who are nearly always men, idealize the women in their lives and sometimes kill them, perhaps because "the death . . . of a beautiful woman is unquestionably the most poetical topic in the world" (*Essays and Reviews* 19).[9] As early as 1920, psychoanalytic critic Lorine Pruette had noted that Poe's women "are never human" but are instead male fantasies. And yet Jay Hubbell's uncritical appraisal of these objectifications seems to have prevailed until at least the 1960s: "One finds in Poe . . . something akin to the Renaissance literary worship of woman as embodying the spirit of beauty and goodness. . . . Poe's notions about women were definitely Southern" (536). Before the 1980s, only a few scholars even bothered to broach the topic of the pervasive objectification of and violence against women in Poe's works, or to make the point that the tales of dying women and poems of female idolatry might register differently with women readers than with the men who made up the majority of Poe scholars. In her discussion of "The Murders in the Rue Morgue" in 1983, Judith Fetterly does just that, and asks a series of important questions: "why . . . are the victims women? And why is the beast male? And why has the sailor wished to keep in his closet a 'pet' of such 'intractable ferocity' and 'imitative propensities'? And why does Dupin choose this particular situation for the demonstration of his analytic powers?" (157) As Fetterly demonstrates, the story hinges on the victims being female, the ape and his owner male. In attacking the women, the ape is, after all, imitating in some form the behavior of his master; Dupin, who solves crimes by identifying with the perpetrator, "must recognize the existence of the beast in and as himself" (156), although he "collaborates in the sailor's illusion of innocence" (158). In a recent essay for the *Cambridge Companion to Poe,* Karen Weekes surveys the representations of women in Poe's fiction and poetry and concludes that Poe's feminine ideal can be found in "[g]entle, vulnerable, delicate females, such as Eleonora and Annabel Lee, [who] pose no sexual or intellectual threat" (160). Citing brief earlier comments by Nina Baym and Joseph Moldenhauer, Weekes writes, "It is hard to determine which repeated treatment of women is more demeaning: to see them as creatures in their own right, but ones who must die in order to serve a larger, androcentric purpose, or to utilize them as lifeless props for the purposes of the narrator's emotional excesses" (150).[10] One might counter Baym's and Weekes's point that Poe's women aren't real with the observation that Poe's men aren't exactly real either, but it remains true that even within the unrealistic, symbolic worlds of Poe's poetry and fiction, the women are for the most part props and projections of the men. The question remains where to position Poe in relation to his narrative and poetic personae.

A series of readings of "Ligeia" shows a range of interpretation similar to what we saw in regard to race in the Tsalal episode of *Pym.* In his 1969 book *The Romance in America,* Joel Porte argued that Ligeia is sexually oppressed by the story's narrator: "From Ligeia's point of view, the play is the tragedy 'Woman' and its hero the conquering male organ. The dark lady has been provisionally annihilated in the culmination of the narrator's erotic fantasy" (73). Ligeia does not return except as a fulfillment of the narrator's fantasy, "an orgy of necrophilic omnipotence" (74–75). Leland Person, almost twenty years later, interpreted the story as a prime example of Poe's career-long "illustrating and critiquing a male tendency to disembody women — the attempt to preserve, usually in the form of an art object or through some other act of the imagination, an image of woman which denies her human complexity and represses those very aspects of human being which the male would rather not face in himself" (*Aesthetic* 46). Like Porte, he sees the narrator as Ligeia's oppressor, but his reading gives Poe much more credit for envisioning female creativity and rebellion. In Person's reading, the story ends with Ligeia's triumph, not the narrator's: "He is unable, finally, to create the harmless art object he desires, and he must end his narrative at the precise point when the powerful Ligeia subverts it and threatens to take it over" (33–34). While Porte did not by any means conflate Poe with his narrator, he did not distance Poe's narrative strategies from the narrator's fantasies; Person, though, contends that Poe's purpose is to *expose* the narrator's control mechanisms and, through Ligeia, to challenge them. Gerald Kennedy's 1993 reading of the story also suggests that Poe's aim, whether he realized it or not, was to show the destructiveness of male fantasies. Kennedy links Ligeia with the women who inhabit Poe's poetry, women on whom the male personae of the poems are utterly dependent, and upon whose deaths they are emotionally devastated. The narrator psychologically tortures Rowena because she "inhabits the realm of prose," like any woman who is not Ligeia: "In this brilliant scene fusing the two wives into a beautiful, undying woman, Poe suggests that the idolatry of the poems and the loathing of the tales are reciprocal effects of a relationship to Woman based on dependency. . . . The pattern of violence against women throughout Poe's fiction repeatedly betrays the male protagonist's outrage at his own helplessness and insufficiency" (125, 126).

Also writing in 1993, Diane Price Herndl is less willing than the male critics just cited to position Poe against his narrator. She too believes Ligeia's rejuvenation is the result of her own strength, not the narrator's imagination, but that fact hardly redeems the story's ethos, since she uses her powerful will only "to become, again, [only] a body" (93). Cynthia Jordan (1989) also gives Poe less credit for exposing what Kennedy calls the "neurotic paradigm" of the narrator; the fact that the story ends in the narrator's silencing the woman's story seems to reflect Poe's own disposition. Jordan regards the last line of the story, in which the narrator shrieks the name "of the Lady — of the LADY LIGEIA," as "his last crime of omission, for the story Ligeia is obviously dying to tell, in her own words, is now lost" (139). And yet, like Person, Jordan makes the case for Poe's ability to give voice to the female "second story": "Ligeia" marks the first stage in a development she traces through "Usher" and then to the admirably "androgynous mind" of Dupin (149). Thus, in some way Person, Kennedy, and Jordan all complicate the equation of Poe with his misogynist narrators and even make the case that he defamiliarizes, and in so doing reveals, the ugly implications of his characters' misogyny.

Feminist readings of Poe have not been limited to "Ligeia," of course. Person, Kennedy, and Jordan all extend their claims to other stories, and, in a 1993 special issue of *Poe Studies* devoted to "Poe and Women," Jacqueline Doyle, Monika Elbert, and Joan Dayan also argue for some version of a "feminist Poe," going well beyond "Ligeia" to do so. Dayan makes perhaps the most compelling case that Poe deliberately undermined the conventional representations of women in sentimental poetry as well as Gothic fiction. The answer to the question with which she titled her essay, "Poe's Women: A Feminist Poe?" is, with surprisingly little qualification, yes. Focusing mostly on Poe's poetry, Dayan shows how frequently Poe's speakers render themselves passive, how possession becomes dispossession (9), even claiming that "Poe means to attack the subordination of women, and that we might see his preoccupation with 'love' as the more serious desire to dramatize how women struggle with the idea someone else has made of them" (8).[11] Poe's deconstruction of gender is, of course, part of a larger deconstructive project — "the ungendering that lurks beneath Poe's surface play on gothic ghosts and hauntings begins . . . with the unsettling of the subject" (9) — but "his treatments of women [are] key" to his larger social critique (11).

In "Poe's Women" as in other essays, Dayan recognizes, perhaps better than any other critic, the complexity of Poe-and-gender, particularly in her ability to see its connections with Poe-and-race. "[I]n Poe's writings how slippery, how easily reversed is the divide between human and brute, lady and slave," she wrote in "Romance and Race." In "Amorous Bondage," she elaborated considerably on this slippage:

> Poe demonstrates that just as justifications of slavery depended on making the black nonhuman and unnatural, women were also subject to the minds of men. Women would always remain on the side of the body, no matter how white, rarefied, and ethereal, or how black, earthy, and substantial. They can be hags or beauties, furies or angels. They are nothing but phantasms caught in the craw of civilization, and Poe's Gothicism literalizes the way in which racialist terminology — and the excesses of a system that depended on discourses of gender purity for its perpetuation — generated its own gods and monsters. (202)

As with race, addressing gender in Poe involves acknowledging his benighted thinking on the subject while also recognizing the ways he exposes the dangers of the dominant (sexist) ideology in his work. In his poetry and in the tales of dying and revenant women, "Ligeia" particularly, Poe enacts a master-slave reversal between the male subject and female object: "Without mentioning blacks, Poe applies the accepted argument on the 'nature' of Negroes and the 'spirit' of women — both feeling, not thinking, beings — to the white men usually excluded from such categorization" (189). Dayan's reading of "Ligeia" similarly disturbs both racial and gender hierarchies, as she argues convincingly that Poe's narrator describes Ligeia in terms that run very close to those of the "tragic mulatta" or "octoroon mistress" (200).

Dayan's work helps us to see better the complexity of Poe's "Southern face" — the fact that his attitudes toward race, gender, class, literature, you name it, can be traced to the hierarchies that aristocratic Southerners used to invent themselves, and yet, once again, Poe's writing often exposes and undermines those hierarchies. Richard Gray and David Leverenz have recently made the point that Poe, dedicated as he was to exposure of humbug, decipherment of codes, and all-purpose deconstruction, was just the man to critique the construction of the Southern gentleman he longed to be.[12] According to Gray, "Poe was perhaps never more of a Southerner than when he was imitating one: applying himself assiduously to the role of Virginia dandy, even when much of the historical evidence was against him" (Southern 6). And yet Gray makes probably the strongest case that has been made for regarding Poe as a Southern author. While acknowledging Poe's personal racism (even asserting in 2000 that, "the more convincing case, at the moment, belongs with those who claim he did" write the "Paulding-Drayton Review" [17]), he relates it to a larger conservative ethos associated with the South before and after the Civil War: "a sense of evil, a distrust of 'meddling' and change, a preoccupation with the past, a rejection of ideas of perfectibility and progress, a hatred of abstractions, and a belief in hierarchy" (15). That set of values informs a canon that fits rather cozily into the twentieth-century Southern literary tradition of (this is Gray's list) Faulkner, Tate, Robert Penn Warren, and William Styron (21), but the key text becomes not *Pym* but "The Fall of the House of Usher," the prototype of Southern Gothic fiction. None of this is terribly new or surprising; however, Gray takes the case a step further, arguing that Poe cultivated the combination of aristocratic bearing and cultural marginality consistent with the mythical Southern gentleman. According to Gray, Poe's "model of behavior . . . was one that Fredric Jameson would term a simulacrum: that is, a copy of something for which, in the culture in question, the original never existed" (13).

While Gray saw Poe playing the trumped-up role of Southern Gentleman, David Leverenz, in an earlier essay written for the influential collection *The American Face of Edgar Allan Poe* (1995), asserted that "Poe inhabits and undermines gentry fictions of mastery, not least by exposing the gentleman as a fiction" (212). Leverenz combines post-structuralist theory and social history to demonstrate, among other things, that Poe's classic tales "can be read not only as allegories of the male psyche's attempts to confront the inward female [as in the readings of "Ligeia" already discussed], but as deconstructions of how antebellum gentry culture produced the categories of 'gentleman' and 'lady' along with its production of the more starkly binary opposition, 'black' and 'white'" (223). His readings of "The Man of the Crowd" and "The Cask of Amontillado" particularly illustrate the ways Poe uses textuality to play "a trickster role at the alienated margin of gentry culture" (233). Leverenz extends that argument to a wide range of texts in an essay for the Oxford *Historical Guide to Poe* (2000), exploring "crossings" in Poe, mind-body transgressions, women-on-top, and master-slave reversals particularly. Like Dayan's work, Leverenz's opens up new avenues for more effectively historicizing race and gender in Poe's writing, and in demonstrating how stories that seem to have little if anything to do with race and gender actually say a great deal about the construction of whiteness and manhood, and about social identities generally.

Two more recent examples of this sort of work are Dana Nelson's essay relating "Some Words with a Mummy" to fraternal ritual and polygenesis (1997; later incorporated into *National Manhood,* 1998) and Robert Beuka's essay on Jacksonian manhood and race in "The Man That Was Used Up" (2002). "Some Words" had traditionally been read as one of Poe's clearest and most extended rants against "progress" and democracy, but Nelson shows how the story more specifically exposes the fictions upon which white fraternal organizations were built: "This story has a great deal of fun spinning out what the Other of white civilization, scientific progress, and representative order might say if only given a chance to respond" (*National* 208). Nelson's historicist reading complicates simple assertions that "Some Words" is an expression of Poe's deep conservatism: through the disruption of the fraternal ritual, Poe's Allamistakeo challenges a faith in progress that included a belief in polygenesis and depended on the subjection of women and "inferior" races. Beuka takes up a text that had traditionally been discussed as a satire on some specific political target (such as Richard M. Johnson, Van Buren's vice president; or General Winfield Scott) and as an exercise in literalizing the metaphor (and debunking the myth) of the self-made man. He builds on these earlier explications by considering the story in the context of Jacksonian Indian removal, which Poe drew attention to by having General John A. B. C. Smith "used up" by Kickapoo and "Bugaboo" Indians and by having Smith rebuilt by his black servant, Pompey.[13] For Beuka, "Smith's dismembered form suggests Poe's revisionary take on the evolving mystique of 'national manhood': The General is a representative figure after all, but a figure reflecting a union compromised by its own racial divisiveness, a vulnerable illusion of wholeness whose fragile stability is undercut by its own oppressive racial politics" (36). Focusing on both race and gender, as well as nation, these readings further Poe's "political rehabilitation," recontextualizing Poe's caricature of Native Americans and African Americans to argue that his real project, conscious or not, was to expose the hierarchies he so often seemed to endorse.

Nelson's and Beuka's readings don't rely on Poe's Southern background, and in that respect, too, they mark what I see as an advance in historicist Poe scholarship. A number of recent historicist critics have regarded Poe's involvement in the nascent American publishing industry as a more important field of investigation than his Southern upbringing; just as our understanding of race in Poe's work has been advanced by examinations of contemporary publications (see Lyons, Worley, Ginsberg, and Goddu, for instance), so too can a closer look at Poe's writing and publishing environment open up discussion of Poe and gender. Laura Saltz, for example, reads "The Mystery of Marie Roget" against the sensational newspaper reportage that surrounds it — the penny press's discussion of Mary Rogers's murder and the issue of abortion. There's no effort to redeem Poe here: "He subordinates Marie and her body's productions to his own literary production, attempting to secure his place in the market that so provokes him" (240). Eliza Richards's work on the shared influence and inspiration of Poe and popular women poets requires that we reappraise much nineteenth-century women's poetry and reconsider the value of originality as opposed to reproduction and refinement. In "The Poetess and Poe's Performance of the Feminine," she argues that, "[r]ather than rejecting the feminine, [as a poet] Poe becomes an expert in the field, out-feminizing the feminine in a masculine rendition that inverts female poetic practice" (8). But, as Richards shows, he also distances himself from what were thought to be feminine modes of expression in his critical essays. In an article focusing particularly on spiritualist women poets, Richards argues that Poe, as an impersonator of female poets and then as a posthumous "phantom voice" channeled by spiritualists such as Sarah Helen Whitman, was central to the development of an aesthetic of mimicry ("Lyric").

Of course, "old" historicists had detailed Poe's literary relations and struggles with the publishing world long before the advent of the politically oriented new historicism. In the 1950s and '60s, several important studies of Poe-as-magazinist provided a much fuller picture of his response to the sector of the American political and economic world he knew best. Perry Miller's *The Raven and the Whale* (1956) described Poe as a player among the scandal-mongering New York literati, while Sidney P. Moss's *Poe's Literary Battles* (1963) told the stories of Poe versus Lewis Gaylord Clark, Henry Wadsworth Longfellow, and Thomas Dunn English. Robert D. Jacobs gave a detailed account of Poe's career in *Poe: Journalist and Critic* (1969), and Michael Allen revealed the profound importance of *Blackwood's Edinburgh Magazine* on Poe's style and his conception of audience in *Poe and the British Magazine Tradition* (1969). Stuart Levine, in *Edgar Poe: Seer and Craftsman* (1972), offered subtle readings of Poe's stories with reference to their historical contexts, including slavery as well as the literary marketplace.

And yet, with the rise of history-of-the-book scholarship, along with various types of social criticism in the 1980s and '90s, literary historians and critics have taken this work in several new directions, in addition to those discussed above in relation to race and gender. Leon Jackson, for instance, discusses Poe's relationship with print — his tendency to dwell on the effects of typeface and paper quality in his reviews, the shoddy production of his own early books of poetry, and, most interestingly, his great hopes for anastatic printing, a process by which he believed writers could bypass compositors and reproduce their own hand-crafted pages.

As Jackson points out, Poe believed the anastatic process would give authors control over their own texts, "collaps[ing] the Gutenberg Galaxy" ("Italics" 20). Kevin Hayes's *Poe and the Printed Word* (2000) is a kind of mini-biography focusing on Poe's relationship with books and periodicals, providing a good deal of useful context.

One intriguing marketplace issue that Poe's work highlights is that of originality and plagiarism. Eliza Richards's aforementioned work continues a discussion that picked up steam with David Reynolds's milestone study *Beneath the American Renaissance* (1988), in which Reynolds demonstrated how conventional many of Poe's sensational devices actually were. But in contrast to the new historicists, who tend to be skeptical of the notion that great authors transcend the network of social and political texts that engage them, Reynolds argued that Poe, like the other writers in the Renaissance pantheon, exercised greater artistic control than his sensational contemporaries and made lasting art out of the materials of popular culture. He also exercised greater social control, ultimately rejecting the subversive tendencies of popular sensationalism by having his criminals confess or bringing on Dupin to restore order.

Of course, Poe's appropriations of other writers sometimes verged on plagiarism and other times tumbled right in. Stephen Rachman regards Poe's plagiarism as a deconstructive tool, for it enables Poe to speak in many voices and break down authorial unity: "Thus, Poe plagiarizes not simply to usurp another's authority, but to assert his own authority while questioning the tradition in which he asserts it" (83). After comparing passages from "The Man of the Crowd" to Dickens's sketch "The Gin Shops," Rachman uses Poe's character as a trope for the story that contains him, with implications for Poe's approach to authorship and textuality: the story "is a composite text, plagiarized and permeated with other texts; it is the text of the crowd" (74). In the first chapter of his book *Reading at the Social Limit*, Jonathan Elmer reads "The Man of the Crowd" and "William Wilson" as emblematic of Poe's anxiety over originality and plagiarism; indeed, anxiety seems to be the whole point of trying to detect plagiarism or establish its boundaries. For Poe, "[s]uch an anxiety is the anxiety of self-ownership, and it is also the undoing of all possibilities of ownership or possession" (92). This tension between individuality and the social self makes "William Wilson" an essential text for Elmer, whose study also explores sensationalism, senti-

mentalism, detective fiction, and hoaxes, all of which exemplify his notion of the "social limit," where the individual is figured into the mass or
the people and the mass or the people are reflected in the individual,
"simultaneously exposing the self as social, unnervingly plural, and the
social as self, uncannily singular" (20).

Other critics have zeroed in more on the confluence of literary politics
and national politics in recent years. Robert Con Davis-Undiano re-
examines the Montresor-Fortunato relationship, long thought to be a
reflection of Poe's literary battles, in light of a factional fight within Freemasonry, which in Poe's time retained considerable symbolic power. David
Long uses "Some Words with a Mummy" to argue that Poe's politics are
best understood in relation to, but not as a simple reflection of, the American Whig party. Once again, Poe's "position" is equivocal, undermining
its own surface meaning. Recognizing that Poe's "particular form of free
enterprise was to escape enslavement within a corrupt American literary
system by mastering the system itself" (7), Long argues along lines similar
to Terence Whalen's concept of "average racism": Poe "evolved (or simply
improvised) a politics of vacillation that served to qualify and to obscure
his ideological position" (7). The Whig party represented "hands-on
governmental control, moral accountability among the masses, and formal
unity among disparate factions" (8), all values that would resonate with
Poe, whose fiction and literary theory were similarly oriented toward
control, moral accountability, and formal unity. And yet, Poe's politics
adhere to no party program, at least partly because of Poe's dim view of
"progress" and collective action. Long argues that "Poe testified to the
reality of the Whigs' worst nightmare: the violation of the natural order by
human nature in all its perversity" (18).

This correspondence between literary and national politics may seem
trivial — it's not as if Poe influenced the outcome of any election or
changed the direction of a reform movement — but even compared to
the volatile atmosphere of cultural warfare that prevails today, in the
1830s and 1840s the political and literary realms often coalesced —
Hawthorne's political appointment to and removal from the Salem Custom House was no fluke. Poe, after all, wrote "Some Words" for the
Whigs' party organ, the *American Whig Review,* and years earlier actively
sought (and, of course, sabotaged his efforts to win) an appointment in
the Tyler administration. But more generally, to be an American writer

in Poe's time was to be part of a debate over literary nationalism. Meredith L. McGill, in her contribution to *The American Face of Edgar Allan Poe* and her book *American Literature and the Culture of Reprinting, 1834–1853*, rewrites the story of Poe's involvement with Young America, a group of writers associated with the Democratic party, devoted to promoting a national literature of "American themes" (an effort Poe had ridiculed in his days with the *Southern Literary Messenger*) and lobbying for international copyright protection. McGill examines Poe's appropriation by Young America through James Russell Lowell's article-length biography of Poe, arguing that "Poe did not abandon his critical ideals so much as he lost control over them as they were translated into the literary nationalist idiom" ("Poe" 275). In her chapter "Unauthorized Poe," McGill describes Poe's involvement in reprint culture, demonstrating that some of Poe's stylistic trademarks — allusiveness to British literary tradition, spatial and temporal dislocation, and eclecticism (*American* 151) — helped his works circulate by meeting generic expectations of the period. Thus, McGill significantly revises the traditional view of Poe's place in antebellum literary culture: "Most often invoked as the victim of a literary marketplace that undervalued American authors' labor, Poe is both subject to and seeks to benefit from the peculiar structure of this market" (*American* 150). Pointing out that Poe made a decided shift toward American settings for his tales in 1843, Gerald Kennedy, like McGill, analyzes Poe's motives for affiliating with Young America despite his considerable qualms about their project (*American Turn*).[14] Both argue that Poe is a central figure in the shaping of literary nationalism, yet another reversal of a traditional view.

As of this writing, the fullest treatment of Poe's relation to antebellum politics and economics is Terence Whalen's *Edgar Allan Poe and the Masses* (1999). Whalen demonstrates Poe's deep engagement with the literary marketplace and what he referred to as "the horrid laws of political economy," thoroughly debunking the old image of Poe as detached from the American scene. While Poe tried repeatedly and desperately to triumph over those horrid laws, or to work them to his advantage by, for instance, controlling his own magazine, capital remained "the enemy that would haunt Poe throughout his career as a commercial writer" (57). The point that Whalen made in regard to Poe's "average racism" applies generally to his analysis, which describes the various ways Poe wrote to the market.

Whether inflating subscription figures of the *Southern Literary Messenger,* cheering on the anastatic printing process, or trying to turn "codes" (and by extension the ability to decipher them) into gold, Poe spent his career trying, with little success, to manipulate the system to his advantage, or to undermine it — as always, Poe's response is bifurcated.

In Whalen's explicitly Marxist reading, as in other recent studies of Poe as an actor in the antebellum sociopolitical arena, Poe's significance depends more on what makes him typical than what makes him exceptional. That's not to say that these critics flatten Poe's writing and experience or try to present him as "just another writer"; instead, they treat Poe as a point of entry to issues in American culture that are not restricted to literary study. Whalen, for instance, "uses" Poe to demonstrate the extent to which information became a commodity in the 1830s, just as Worley and Lyons use *Pym* to gain insight into nineteenth-century pro-slavery arguments and orientalism. A recent American Studies reader includes a section on "The Man of the Crowd" as an expression of the fears and fascination surrounding American cities, despite the fact that the story is set in London. A skeptic might see that claim of displacement as a wishful imaginative leap — why talk about American urbanization via a story set in London? Likewise, one might question claims that "The Black Cat" and "Ligeia," which make no direct reference to Africa, America, or slavery, are informed by racialist discourse. But therein lies the attraction. As with psychoanalytic criticism, as well as New-Critical close reading, the goal of most cultural-studies work is to uncover latent content, to bring what's buried to the surface. And as we have seen, what surfaces is often in ironic opposition to what appeared on first glance — the Poe who angers or disappoints us by reinforcing racist and sexist stereotypes is also subverting the logic of those stereotypes. Of course, it all depends on how convincing the evidence is — to paraphrase Freud, sometimes a black cat is just a black cat — but most of the critics I've referred to in this chapter make reasonable, if debatable, arguments that Poe's work becomes even more compelling when read in terms of antebellum social and political issues.

I began this chapter describing the readings that historicize Poe's work by addressing political and social issues as the "real challenge" to traditional Poe scholarship. I would like to close the chapter by reiterating that the larger, ongoing challenge is to read Poe through multiple perspectives. As Leland Person acknowledges, "[r]ecognizing an 'Africanist presence' in Poe's tales means reading race and racism in deeply encoded symbolism that obviously signifies on many other levels" (220–21). I think his comment applies to reading gender and reading capital or class as well, and most critics who have argued for Poe's political significance would agree with Person that their work is not meant to cancel out the other levels on which Poe's stories have traditionally been read. Indeed, readings of Poe in relation to national manhood or the rise of modern capitalism are more likely to complement ahistorical symbolic readings than to tear them down.

"The Black Cat," for instance, exemplifies one of Poe's central out-of-place-and-time concerns, namely the imp of the perverse, the instinct for self-destruction; in Joseph Moldenhauer's reading of "Poe's aesthetics, psychology, and moral vision," the perverse sadism in that story and others ironically is a positive good for the narrator, because self-destruction is "a route to the aesthetic heaven of death" (297). Christopher Benfey offers a contrasting reading (cited in the last chapter) within the same traditional set of concerns, that the twin fears of love and isolation, "[t]aken to extremes . . . both lead to disaster: One cat avoids us and is blinded, another cat follows us and is killed" (43) — note the powerful use of the universalizing "us" in his conclusion. I believe those readings are enhanced by, for instance, considering that the story also reads like a temperance tract — that in Poe's time, a reform movement seeking to limit that particular form of self-destruction had gained such momentum that his first readers would have immediately recognized in it the conventions of temperance literature — so that what Moldenhauer and many other readers regard as an amoral tale came in a moralizing package, another ironic twist to a thoroughly ironic story.[15] Similarly, Leslie Ginsberg's research into the politics of pet ownership in relation to slavery deepens our understanding of how the narrator's perverse abuse of the cat would have resonated with magazine readers in 1843, who knew the conventions of abolitionist fiction just as they knew those of temperance fiction. Of course, the story is not just about any murder, but about a husband's murder of his wife, and so the questions Judith Fetterly asked about the significance of gender in "Rue Morgue" apply here also. Can Benfey's "us" mean men *and* women, when it's not just "one cat" that gets killed but one wife? That's a challenge, to be sure; but it's the same kind of challenge Benfey's ahistorical reading offers to Moldenhauer's, that any new reading presents to all the old ones. While there are some interpretations that simply defy others, that require "choosing sides," most of the readings I've surveyed in the last three chapters, somewhat surprisingly, work together well to convey the complexity of Poe's work and his world. Accordingly, the best new work on Poe has tended to revise, without rejecting, the conclusions of previous generations of scholars.

Notes

[1] John Carlos Rowe included a revised version of this essay in his book *At Emerson's Tomb: The Politics of Classic American Literature* (New York: Columbia UP, 1997).

[2] Campbell also recurrently uses the word "darky" in the essay, which elicited this comment from Toni Morrison: "Although I know this sentence [containing "darky"] represents the polite parlance of the day, that 'darky' was understood to be a term more acceptable than 'nigger,' the grimace I made upon reading it was followed by an alarmed distrust of the scholar's abilities. If it seems unfair to reach back to the thirties for samples of the kind of lapse that can occur when certain manners of polite repression are waived, let me assure you equally egregious representations of the phenomenon are still common" (*Playing in the Dark: Whiteness in the Literary Imagination* [Cambridge, MA: Harvard UP, 1992], 10–11).

[3] See also H. Marshall McLuhan, "Edgar Poe's Tradition," *Sewanee Review* 12 (1944): 24–33, in which he defines Poe in opposition to the New England tradition and, oddly enough, claims that "In his own fashion . . . Poe had as great a working faith in civilization as Thomas Jefferson" (33). The most extended late-twentieth-century appraisals of Poe as Southerner not discussed in this chapter are G. R. Thompson, "Edgar Allan Poe and the Writers of the Old South," in *Columbia Literary History of the United States,* ed. Emory Elliott, 262–77 (New York: Columbia UP, 1988); Robert D. Jacobs, "Edgar Allan Poe," in *The History of Southern Literature,* ed. Louis D. Rubin et al., 127–35 (Baton Rouge and London: Louisiana State UP, 1985); and Louis D. Rubin's chapter on Poe in *The Edge of the Swamp: A Study in the Literature and Society of the Old South* (Baton Rouge and London: Louisiana State UP, 1989), 127–89.

[4] The few commentaries on race in *Pym* during this period include Eric Mottram, "Poe's Pym and the American Social Imagination," in *Artful Thunder: Versions of the Romantic Tradition, in Honor of P. Vincent,* ed. Robert J. DeMott and Sanford E. Marovitz, 25–53 (Kent, OH: Kent State UP, 1975), and Harold Beaver's introduction to *The Narrative of Arthur Gordon Pym of Nantucket,* by Edgar Allan Poe, 7–30 (Harmondsworth: Penguin, 1975).

[5] See Joan Dayan, "Amorous Bondage: Poe, Ladies and Slaves," in *The American Face of Edgar Allan Poe,* ed. Shawn Rosenheim and Stephen Rachman, 179–209 (Baltimore and London: Johns Hopkins UP, 1995), for her account of the reaction her work received from the Poe Society of Baltimore (179–80).

[6] Leslie Ginsberg also points out that *Graham's,* the Philadelphia magazine Poe edited in the 1840s, published both abolitionist sympathizers and slavery apologists, including Paulding ("Slavery and the Gothic Horror of Poe's 'The Black Cat,'" in *American Gothic: New Intervention in a National Narrative,* ed. Robert K. Martin and Eric Savoy [Iowa City: U of Iowa P, 1998], 110).

[7] Terence Whalen argues similarly that "organized treachery by South Sea natives was standard fare in exploration narratives" (*Edgar Allan Poe and the Masses* [Princeton, NJ: Princeton UP, 1999], 178).

[8] Compare Lemire's project to that of a more traditional Poe scholar. Richard Kopley, in *Poe and the Philadelphia Saturday News* (Baltimore: Enoch Pratt Free Library, Edgar Allan Poe Society, and the Library of the University of Baltimore, 1991), points to an 1838 news item, which Poe almost certainly would have seen, of an African American man who killed his wife with a razor (8–10), as well as an article in the same publication that refers to a "hideous Negro with an ourang-outang face" (14). But Kopley's essay is concerned with uncovering Poe's sources, not with analyzing representations of race. He acknowledges that the linkage of orangutang and black man is "unarguably racist" (10) yet asserts that Poe's intention was not to espouse racism but to emphasize "the unhumanness of the orangoutang" (14).

[9] See Joel Porte, *The Romance in America: Studies in Cooper, Poe, Hawthorne, Melville, and James* (Middletown, CT: Wesleyan UP, 1969), 74: "Like so many of Poe's heroes, the narrator [of "Ligeia"] seems to prefer his women dead or cataleptic, so that he can use their bodies in his favorite fashion — as raw materials for his erotic fantasies." See also Barbara Cantalupo, "Poe's Female Narrators," *Southern Quarterly* 39.4 (2001): 49–57.

[10] Nina Baym devotes three paragraphs to Poe in her survey, "Portrayal of Women in American Literature, 1790–1870," in *What Manner of Woman: Essays on English and American Life and Literature,* ed. Marlene Springer, 211–34 (New York: New York UP, 1977); Moldenhauer ("Murder as a Fine Art: Basic Connections Between Poe's Aesthetics, Psychology, and Moral Vision," *PMLA* 83 [1968]: 284–97) refers to Poe as "symbolically, a killer of beautiful women" (294), but makes little of that insight, since his interest is in murder as part of Poe's aesthetic. See also Paula Kot's survey of feminist readings of Poe ("Feminist 'Re-Visioning' of the Tales of Women," in *A Companion to Poe Studies,* ed. Eric W. Carlson, 388–402 (Westport, CT, and London: Greenwood, 1996), and Kot's essay "Painful Erasures: Excising the Wild Eye from 'The Oval Portrait,'" *Poe Studies* 28 (1995): 1–6.

[11] See also Leland S. Person, "Poe's Poetics of Desire: 'Th'Expanding Eye to the Loved Object,'" *Poe Studies* 32 (1999): 1–7, on the passive condition of Poe's poetic subjects.

[12] Richard Gray's chapter on Poe in *Southern Aberrations: Writers of the American South and the Problems of Regionalism* (Baton Rouge: Louisiana State UP, 2000) is a substantially revised version of his essay "'I Am a Virginian': Edgar Allan Poe and the South," in *Edgar Allan Poe: The Design of Order*, ed. A. Robert Lee, 182–201 (London: Vision; Totowa, NJ: Barnes & Noble, 1987).

[13] See also David Haven Blake's "'The Man That Was Used Up': Edgar Allan Poe and the Ends of Captivity," *Nineteenth-Century Literature* 57 (2002): 323–49, which also argues for a broader satirical target than previous scholars had recognized. Blake reads the story in the context of captivity narratives as well as images of cyborgs in American culture: "By presenting the Indian threat as a bugaboo or as nonexistent, Poe's story leads us to wonder whether the cyborg's ultimate mission is not so much to defeat an enemy society as to conquer its own" (330).

[14] See also Claude Richard, "Poe and 'Young America,'" *Studies in Bibliography* 21 (1968): 25–58.

[15] See T. J. Matheson, "Poe's 'The Black Cat' as a Critique of Temperance Literature," *Mosaic* 19 (1986): 69–81.

5: Lionizing: Poe as Cultural Signifier

Examining the Meisterstück Edgar Allan Poe, the ingenious structure of clean proportions and mysterious depth is revealed. As in Poe's works, where logic and mysticism are interlinked in an unparalleled manner, every detail reveals profound aesthetics. With the Meisterstück Edgar Allan Poe this great American writer has found extraordinary and stylish recognition.
— Brochure produced by Montblanc, 1998

NOT LONG AFTER my book *Edgar Allan Poe Revisited* was published, the manager of a Montblanc boutique contacted me about giving a talk to tie in with their new Meisterstück Edgar Allan Poe writing instrument. Eager to promote my book and secretly hoping for a deep discount, I gave her a copy to use as part of a window display and spent a half hour telling her about Poe's interest in autography, his own meticulous penmanship, his dreams of anastatic printing allowing writers to self-publish without typesetting, the implications of Poe's titling his prospective magazine first the *Penn,* then the *Stylus,* and so on. The relationship never got past that meeting: my hopes of owning a Montblanc pen were unrealized, the manager kept a copy of my book but never displayed it, and there was no public lecture on Poe and pens. More recently, a middle school teacher asked if I would come talk to two hundred seventh graders about Poe; after discussing a few possible dates, we settled on October 31. Then she asked if I generally dressed up as Poe for these occasions.

I mention these incidents not to emphasize the distance between the academic Poe and the pop-culture Poe, but to help make the case that the two are in close proximity. It is easy to imagine a bearded, bespectacled English professor — me, for instance — sarcastically dismissing, say, Michael Jackson's ambition of playing Poe. But that same professor might also find himself talking seriously about how Poe scholarship might help sell ridiculously expensive pens or wondering if Michael Jackson still needs a consultant. And while I did not portray Poe for the seventh grade, I did take along a bag of visual aids and hand props; after my presentation, I joined my host's home room to watch *The Simpsons'* rendition of "The Raven." It is true that the current popular image of Poe — drug abuser as well as alcoholic, lunatic, and Gothicist to the exclusion of all else — is at odds with most of the academic writing I have described in the last three chapters. At the same time, the Poe whose caricature decorates Barnes & Noble shopping bags has always drawn students to his work, helped keep him in print, made publishers a little more interested even in academic writing about him. But beyond that, scholars in recent years have been paying more attention to what might be called "the Poe effect," the creation and maintenance of Poe's image, the various ways this image interacts with popular culture and with Poe's writing. As Mark Neimeyer puts it, "the popular exploitation of Poe can be seen as adding another dimension to the element of the uncanny already present in the author's writings since these productions are all strangely Poe and not Poe at the same time" (222).

This recent interest in the Poe effect has occurred largely because of the trends discussed in the previous chapter. Research emphasizing the "cultural work" of fiction and poetry has helped blur the boundaries between high and middle and low brow, between literary text and subliterary context; for example, although many more academic essays continue to be written on Poe's "The Fall of the House of Usher," serious scholarly attention is also paid to Roger Corman's low-budget film adaptations of "Usher" and other Poe tales.[1] Don G. Smith's *The Poe Cinema* attests not only to the popularity of Poe's mystique as a source for films but also interest in the films themselves. And websites such as Peter Forrest's *House of Usher* and *The Poe Decoder* combine emphasis on academic scholarship and sightings of Poe in the broader cultural landscape.[2] At the 2002 International Poe Conference sponsored by the Poe Studies Association, panelists presented work on Poe's connections to the World Wrestling Federation, hard-boiled detective fiction, Dario Argento's slasher films, and Bob Dylan.

At the same conference, guest speaker E. L. Doctorow angered much of the audience by referring to Poe as "our best bad writer." Many must have feared that the old battle over Poe's "place" would have to be fought yet again — even our *best* bad writer would not rank in the top ten, or even top thirty. But this characterization, echoing as it does the earlier assessments by T. S. Eliot and Allen Tate, deserves serious consideration, however much one admires Poe's writing. I believe Doctorow was attempting to explain Poe in terms other than literary greatness as usually conceived. Perhaps his point was not to demote Poe to a lower tier of the pantheon but to try to get at why Poe's writing defies the usual assessments of literary merit, making him impossible to rank; to try to understand why, despite his frequent technical clumsiness, Poe sticks with so many readers, particularly readers who happen to be writers, graphic artists, musicians, film makers, and so on. The cultural-studies Poe scholars share that interest: why is Poe so adaptable, and in what surprising forms do his work and image appear? More specifically, how is Poe reinterpreted by Vincent Price or Lou Reed? Why does Poe appear in mainstream culture as a misunderstood Southern Romantic Poet in the 1900s and as the godfather of slasher films half a century later? If, as Allen Ginsberg claimed, "Everything leads to Poe," the paths connecting Poe to everything must be worth exploring (Willner).

I can explore only a fraction of those paths in this chapter — a full history of Poe's posthumous echoes, influences, and image outside literary criticism would require a book much longer than this one — so I would like to recommend several works that survey various parts of the field. *Poe and Our Times,* a 1986 collection of essays mostly on Poe's influence but also addressing reputation and modern scholarship, is a good place to start. A less academic starting point would be Paul Haining's *Edgar Allan Poe Scrapbook,* a loosely organized but rich collection of illustrations, documents, and commentary. J. Gerald Kennedy's introduction to the Oxford *Historical Guide* explores why Poe remains vital at the turn of the twenty-first century, the various ways his writing is disarmingly conversant with our own era. John E. Reilly's 1965 dissertation and his later essays (for *Poe and Our Times* and *A Companion to Poe Studies)* document an impressive number of poems, novels, plays, and films that either pay tribute to Poe or exploit him in some way. Neimeyer's "Poe and Popular Culture" in *The Cambridge Companion to Edgar Allan Poe* provides a good brief survey along with insight into Poe's continuing popularity as a cultural referent, while Kevin Hayes's "One Man Modernist" (in the same collection) does the same for Poe's influence on modernist visual art. Ronald Smith's *Poe in the Media,* although already somewhat dated, is an impressive descriptive bibliography. The already noted *Poe Cinema* provides summaries, production, and marketing histories, and reviews of over seventy-five Poe-related films. Tony Magistrale and Sidney Poger analyze a number of Poe's literary inheritors from Arthur Conan Doyle to Stephen King (and also include a chapter on film) in their book *Poe's Children*. An extremely useful volume edited by Lois Vines, *Poe Abroad*, traces Poe's posthumous international influence. Benjamin F. Fisher has compiled three (to date) annotated bibliographies of "Poe and Detection" as well as several lists of fugitive Poe references. And Burton Pollin, in his catalogue *Images of Poe's Works*, in his essay on art, music, opera, and dance for *A Companion to Poe Studies*, as well as in numerous articles and checklists on those subjects, has added much to our understanding of the extent of Poe's presence in popular culture as well as his continuing influence.

At about the same time when scholars such as C. Alphonso Smith and Oliver Huckel claimed Poe as a Southerner (see chapter 1), several remarkably similar plays about Poe's life were written and performed in the United States. Although he had remained a popular writer throughout the nineteenth century, these plays represented something new: middle-brow entertainment derived from Poe. The most striking feature of these plays is their sameness, starting with the titles: *The Raven: A Play in Four Acts and a Tableau* by George Hazelton, Jr. (1895, revised several times and novelized in 1909), *The Raven* by Olive Dargan (1904), and *The Raven: A Play in Five Acts* by Arthur Ketchum (n.d.). One other, *The Raven: A Poetic Drama* (1913), by James Vila Blake, is based on the poem but does not include Poe as a character.[3] The *Raven* plays demonstrate that in the early part of the twentieth century scholarly orators were not the only ones conceiving a Southern Poe. Each play emphasizes the contrast between North and South; all three transplant Virginia Clemm from Baltimore to Richmond or Charlottesville so that she assumes the full symbolic force of her name, depicting her as a belle who faithfully follows Poe to New York, which of course proves an inhospitable environment to them both.

All three *Raven*s accentuate the antebellum Southern setting of the early acts with gratuitous minstrel/slave characters. The stage directions for Hazelton's opening scene include "Negroes heard singing in the distance" as part of a landscape that also includes a "colonial" house, "Rustic seat in front of tree," "rustic bench," "rustic table," "rocking chair," and Mr. and Mrs. Allan "drinking tea under trees." Thus the Allans' urban mansion is converted to something more pastoral, like a plantation, complete with singing slaves. The featured "darky" character is named Erebus, whose blackness is emphasized not only by his name but by remarks from Poe, who praises him for his "good . . . heart under your black skin" (26) and Poe's friend Tony, who at one point greets him, "And Erebus, too! Black as ever!" (27). Erebus, who complements Virginia as a symbol of the old South, has also followed Edgar to New York, where he recognizes the incongruity of the Southern household in the cold Northern climate: "I don' like dis yar New York State fo nothin'," he proclaims to Virginia. "Gib me ole Virginiah!" When young Virginia asks why, he replies, "Fo' de Lord, honey, it pears like up yah dars nine months ob winter and free months ob damn late fall" (22). A few moments later, Poe relates the cold climate to his reception in New York — "Jack Frost seems the only reliable patron of the poets" (27) — and in the same scene, Muddy reports having failed in her efforts to sell Poe's poems in the city.

Dargan's primary slave character, Mum Zurie, is, like Erebus, faithful to Edgar, although she doesn't accompany the Poes to New York. She and her children Tat (short for Tatermally) and Bony (short for Bonaparte?) are mainly vehicles of local color and comic relief, but Zurie is onstage for much of the first three acts, often providing exposition and choral insight. At one point, just after Virginia has escaped the clutches of the treacherous Neilson Poe to marry Edgar (prior to moving north), Zurie confides in soliloquy:

> Fo' de Lawd, fo' de Lawd! Bress dem two babies! O, de signs am all wrong! Miss Babylam' come back when she done start away! . . . Wha' make Mas Nelson come fo' babylam'? O, fo de Lawd, fo' de Lawd! (Tat and Bony stare at their mother in terror as she proceeds) I see de brack hawk what flies outen de dead swamp! OOO! I see knives drippin' and guns poppin'! OOOO! I see de coffin — de coffin — an' it's all dark night . . . (27)

While Edgar and Virginia are of course headed for trouble, Zurie's vision exceeds anything that happens in the play and, like the use of slave characters itself, is completely unnecessary to the plot. Later, Zurie demonstrates her devotion to Poe along with her ignorance of the world of publishing and commerce, telling a friend of Virginia's that if "Mas Edgah want to be rich . . . All he got to do jes scribble, scribble on a bit o' papah an' de gol' come rollin' down de chimney!" (38) Like Erebus in Hazelton's play, Zurie joins with Virginia and Muddy in a trio of subservient characters who believe in Poe but cannot save him from his fate.

Ketchum's faithful slave character, Mose (the minor slave characters are Pluto and Cato), takes the opposite view of Poe's ability to turn scribbling into gold, although his essentially accurate assessment is also couched in his ignorance of the profession of authorship:

> MOSE: Fortune! How you gwine make your fortune?
>
> POE: (Indicating mss.) With these; these are the wings that I must fly with, who knows how high or far.
>
> MOSE: Land Marse Poe, why them is jes' those potries dat you write. You don't think you gwine make your fortune with them.
>
> POE: Sure of it Mose, with them and those that will come after them. . . .
>
> MOSE: For the land sakes Marse Poe, do folkses pay money for them, real true money? (II.1)

Despite his skepticism of Poe's potential earning power, Mose volunteers to accompany him north but must settle for Poe's promise to return for him when he has made his fortune. Mose follows the pattern not only of the contented slave but of the naive-but-wise observer of events taking place on the white main stage. At his moment of greatest insight, Mose even drops his dialect — as rendered in the script — to condemn the practice of dueling: "Honor! I don't see where the honor is for two young gentlemen to shoot each other!" (II.2)

The use of racist plantation humor, along with the foregrounding of setting in Poe's life tragedy — too ambitious to stay in the South, too pure and lofty-minded to survive in the North — can be seen as part of the Southernizing trend I discussed in chapter 1. These plays continue what was already a longstanding tradition of regarding the South as the locus of the nation's past way of life, innocent, agrarian, idealistic, and unchanging, where slavery is represented by innocent clowns and sages (often the same character) and the North is icy in spirit as well as climate. As in the centenary tributes, in these plays Poe is depicted as a refined Southerner to explain and underscore his innocent, ethereal nature, rather than, for instance, characterizing him as the pugnacious publishing insider he quickly became as editor of the *Southern Literary Messenger* (before moving on to *Burton's* and *Graham's* in Philadelphia), more a representative of a volatile and complex publishing world than a displaced Ashley Wilkes.

The three *Ravens* offer a range of representations of Poe's creative dysfunction, but they all elevate his failures to the realm of tragedy, and in so doing deflect the blame from Poe to either a hostile environment or fate itself. As Virginia lies dying, Poe upbraids himself: "I brought her to this land of ice and snow!" Muddy responds, "No. Destiny brought her" (Dargan 58). Casting Poe as a tragic hero would be nearly inevitable in these plays, which depict him as both besieged by enemies and undone by hubris. Both the jealousies and the hero's Icarian spirit stem from the fact that Poe is decidedly a *poet*. None of these plays mention specific tales; in fact, Dargan has Poe reproach himself at one point for "Selling myself to that devil of prose that I may bring in that fool's litter — money — money — money!" (45). Poems arise directly from the events depicted in the plays, particularly Virginia's death. For instance, in the Dargan play, while grieving for Virginia, Poe composes "The Conqueror Worm" but is interrupted by a raven that flies in through the window; Ketchum ends his play with Virginia dying as Poe recites "The Raven."

Hazelton's Poe is the most stable of the three: although his drinking prompts Allan to kick him out of the house and he poisons himself in the last scene, Poe never actually appears drunk or delusional onstage. Dargan and Ketchum, while clearly sympathetic to Poe, both show him intoxicated and depict manic-depressive mood swings. More than Hazelton, they present Baudelairian images of Poe, in whom genius and madness are inseparable. Ketchum even alludes to the appeal of this romantic persona when a female fan says to Poe's partner (also the play's villain) John Bisco, "I utterly refuse to have him less wicked then [sic] dear Lord Bryon [sic] at the least, tell me he isn't and I'll never read his poetry again" (IV.2). When Bisco plies him with drink, Poe declares himself "with the gods, beyond all good and evil" (IV.5). By the end of Dargan's play, Poe is reduced to proposing marriage to his uncomprehending landlady, then proceeding to a bar where he becomes so manic that other patrons insist on having him thrown out. And yet the play endorses Poe's proclamation of his own angelic nature:

> I know this place. It is the poet's house of dream that all my life I've
> sought to reach. I am dying now, and they let me in, because I have
> been true and never surrendered! The master will read it in my face. I
> have not eaten of the flesh-pots! I have beggared my body, but I have
> not beggared my soul! (70)

When offered money for a bed, he retorts, "I dare not touch it, sir, lest
I be infected, for the angels that look upon us know that I shall be in
health when disease sits in your jaundiced lips and pestilence flaps her
wings in your blood!" (71). Finally, Poe "looks back at the men who are
gazing at him intently, and speaks slowly, erect and godlike" the play's
last words: "In His own Image created He man!" (72) It is as if Dargan
and Ketchum are dramatizing Baudelaire's poem "The Albatross," in
which, like the captured bird, the poet is "Exiled to the ground amid the
jeering pack, / His giant wings will not let him walk" (ll. 15–16). Poe's
schizophrenia and his alcoholism, then, are of a piece with his role as a
displaced Southerner and an angel of the imagination. Indeed, as a
Southern angel the Poe of these three melodramas fits perfectly the
description offered by Baudelaire half a century earlier:

> [F]or Poe, the United States [specifically, the modern, industrial U.S.
> represented in these plays by New York] was nothing more than a vast
> prison through which he wandered with the feverish unrest of one who
> was born to breathe the air of a purer world — a great and barbarous
> gas-lit nightmare — and that his inner spiritual life, as a poet or even as
> a drunkard, was but one perpetual effort to flee the influence of this
> hostile milieu. (*Edgar Poe* 80)

Sophie Treadwell's 1936 play *Plumes in the Dust* revived some of the
conventions of the *Raven* plays, but on the whole Treadwell's handling
of dialogue and character is more subtle and her use of biographical
material somewhat more responsible than her predecessors'. For instance, the first scene takes place in Richmond, with the slave character
Miranda telling Fanny Allan "they's one of them Yankee peddlers at the
back doah" (I.1.1), but black characters are not deployed for laughs or
prophecy — which is to say, they aren't used much at all. Moreover,
unlike the earlier plays, this one includes scenes in Baltimore, as well as
a return to Richmond, in contrast to the simple South-to-North movement of the *Raven*s. In fact, John Allan's villainous treatment of Poe,

present but barely explained in the earlier plays, here is linked to class anxiety, as Allan hypocritically fawns over a debauched, irresponsible friend of Poe's from the University because he is a "gentleman," clearly revealing in the process his awkwardness as a socially ambitious merchant. Treadwell makes Allan's hypocrisy all the more stark by concocting an illegitimate birth for Poe. Allan uses Poe's bastardy to justify his mistreatment of him, including his obstruction of Poe's courtship of Elmira Royster, while Allan himself has just fathered a child with a slave. Thus Treadwell makes this inevitable villain, John Allan, a symbol of Southern dishonor and self-contradiction, and in doing so complicates the earlier identification of Poe's South as a paradise lost.

Similarly, Treadwell invokes but dampens the Baudelarian image of Poe. In act 2, John P. Kennedy informs Poe that while both his poetry and fiction were judged to be the best by the *Saturday Visiter,* he is being awarded the $50 prize for fiction rather than the $25 for poetry. Poe is indignant at not being awarded both and insists on taking the $25 prize instead of the $50, despite his family's poverty: "But, sir, I am a poet! — naturally I want recognition for what I am giving my life to — not for something I do just in the hope of earning some money" (I.2.48). Later, at an ill-fated soiree in New York, he declares (adopting the language of an actual letter written by Poe), "With me, poetry has not been a purpose, but a passion; and the passion — to the few who love me and whom I love . . . to the dreamers and those who put faith in dreams as the only realities . . ." (II.2.32), before someone interrupts, asking him to recite "The Raven." Not only are these statements less melodramatic than similar instances in the earlier plays, but Treadwell makes the demonic, self-destructive side of Poe's character less romantic than her predecessors by showing how his reputation for drunkenness and dishonesty hindered him. Before Poe's arrival at the aforementioned party, the New York literati gossip about his drinking and lack of integrity, and he validates their depictions by showing up drunk and belligerent, verbally attacking Griswold and N. P. Willis; the scene ends when Muddy arrives to tell Poe that Virginia has died. In the last act, Poe visits Elmira Royster, who in this play is the true love of his life, but her suspicions of his motives prevent a happy ending. Moreover, her suspicions are justified: Poe's mixed motives do include gaining financial support for his magazine, and Elmira has been warned that he will try to get her money.

While Treadwell's play strays far from the historical record, her best scenes — the confrontations with John Allan in act 1 and the literati in act 2, and the attempted reunion with Elmira in act 3 — show how a fictionalized life of Poe might be rendered realistically and with emotional force. But at the same time, her striving for realism and complexity creates thematic discontinuity; we see Poe in more places, coming in contact with more people, but the scenes don't build effectively on each other. Supporting characters go undeveloped, and Poe himself remains an enigma. Perhaps for these reasons, audiences found the play unsatisfying, as it closed after a two-week run on Broadway. Still, when read in light of the biographical plays produced earlier in the century, *Plumes in the Dust* is an admirable, though flawed, attempt to correct an overly romanticized version of Poe.

By the time *Plumes in the Dust* was produced, Poe's image was shifting decisively from the tortured romantic poet to the godfather of the macabre, thanks largely to a trio of Universal films starring Bela Lugosi and Boris Karloff: *The Murders in the Rue Morgue* (1932), *The Black Cat* (1934), and *The Raven* (1935). About two dozen Poe-related films had been made by the early 1930s, but these Hollywood blockbusters, produced during the first golden age of horror films, cemented Poe's place in modern pop culture. None of the three had much in common with the works from which they took their titles, but, particularly in the case of *The Raven*, they did much to reshape Poe's image.

Their most notable American predecessor is D. W. Griffiths's *The Avenging Conscience* (1915), a film that weaves together several Poe stories, primarily "The Tell-Tale Heart," into a cautionary tale in which a young man apparently murders his uncle/guardian to clear the way for marriage and freedom.[4] But luckily for the young man, his crime, as well as his eventual exposure, the suicide of his would-be bride Annabel, and the frightening visions of devils who torment him in retribution, all turn out to be a dream; he awakens grateful and hopeful of a bright future. *The Avenging Conscience* is ahead of its time in its emphasis on Poe's macabre fiction, but to the extent that it creates any image of Poe, it is that of a moralist: murder and hellish retribution are contained within the dream, employed strictly as a warning. At the end of the film, we are surprised not only to learn that most of the action has been a dream but that the dreamer is in fact Poe, and this Poe is after all a romantic poet: he is last seen lying by a river, reading lines from "Annabel Lee" to his future wife.

In contrast, Universal's *The Raven,* directed by Louis Friedlander, interprets both the title poem and Poe's fiction as if its creator were the Marquis de Sade. Lugosi plays Dr. Richard Vollin, a mad genius whose twin obsessions are Poe and torture. He first appears in the film reciting "The Raven" as the camera moves back from the image of a gigantic shadow on the wall cast by the statuette of a raven on his desk. "The raven," he tells a visitor, "is my talisman." Later, he interprets the poem for a group of guests, some of whom he plans to torture and kill (with the help of Karloff's character, Edmund Bateman). He explains that the raven represents Poe's torment over being deprived of the love of his life, but he strays somewhat from the text: "When a man of genius is denied of his great love, he goes mad. His brain . . . is tortured. So he begins to think of torture — torture for those who have tortured him."

Of course, this is just what he has in mind for Judge Thatcher, who is trying to protect his daughter from Vollin, as well as the daughter's fiancé and the daughter herself. To help with the dirty work, he has entrapped Bateman, an escaped convict, who poses as his servant until the guests retire and the mayhem begins. Vollin explains Bateman's hideous appearance to his guests: during the war, "Arab bandits . . . mutilated him and tortured him. They have a genius for devising torture. It's almost the equal of Edgar Allan Poe." But in fact Vollin himself has mutilated Bateman, and he seeks to replicate Poe's tortures in his vengeful scheme. Since there is actually little torture in Poe's plots, Vollin draws inspiration from only one story, "The Pit and the Pendulum." The father gets the pendulum, while the lovers are to be crushed in a room with enclosing walls (there is no pit, however). At the height of his maniacal glee, Vollin declares, "Poe conceived it. I have done it, Bateman! Poe, you are avenged!" Vollin thinks the spirit of Poe lives in him, and the film does nothing to contradict that belief. No one points out, for instance, that the other torture devices scattered around Vollin's basement have no relation to anything in Poe's fiction, much less Poe's personal desires. At this moment, though, Poe becomes a byword for gothic horror among moviegoers. As Neimeyer observes, *The Raven* is not only about a kind of Poe-esque madness but perhaps "just as much about a latter-day popular obsession with Poe, a sort of metafictional comment on Hollywood's and, more generally, popular culture's focus on and exploitation of frequently distorted views of the writer and his works" (217). Indeed, filmmakers, playwrights, graphic artists, and teachers have followed Dr. Vollin's lead in making "Poe" signify torture, murder, insanity, and perversity.

Especially filmmakers — and especially those at American International Pictures, which made thirteen Poe-inspired films between 1960 and 1971, most of them directed by Roger Corman and starring Vincent Price.[5] Universal had used Poe's name to market the Lugosi films in the 1930s, but by the 1960s, Poe's reputation was sufficiently gothicized that AIP made his association with horror the primary focus of their ad campaigns. The trailer for *The Masque of the Red Death* promises "A Masquerade of the Macabre / An Orgy of Savage Lusts / Conceived by the Master Designer of Evil Desires / Edgar Allan Poe." The *Premature Burial* trailer explains, "Only Edgar Allan Poe, who knew intimately the tortures of madness, could create such ever-increasing suspense." Some of the films deviate considerably from the plots of Poe's stories, while others ignore them altogether, as the series solidified the false impression of Poe as a writer of narrow range: the macabre, savage lusts, evil desires. AIP even published novelizations of the screenplays, so that Poe's new fans could buy and read *The Pit and the Pendulum* by Lee Sheridan and Richard Matheson.

While the AIP films were consistently unfaithful to their literary source material, they were faithful to their own advertising. In *Masque of the Red Death,* Price's Prospero casually orders the torture of prisoners, shoots an arrow into the neck of a nobleman who begs entrance into his castle, commands revelers to imitate the animals he thinks they resemble, and so on. (The savage lusts are more implied than depicted, thanks to the production code prohibiting onscreen sex or nudity.) The titillation of sex and torture also drive Corman's *The Pit and the Pendulum,* in which one of Price's characters (he plays both father and son) tortures and kills his wife and brother for committing adultery. In Corman's films, torture epitomizes the broader presence of "evil," a word Poe generally stayed away from. Prospero's Satan-worship, for instance, plays a large part in Corman's *Masque,* although Poe makes no reference to it. Roderick Usher, standing in a room hung with portraits of his ancestors, tells his visitor, "Evil is not just a word. It is a reality. . . . It can be created, it was created by these people." As is never the case in Poe's fiction, "evil" is its own explanation.

As much as these films distort the stories and play to the lowest common gothic denominators, they remain popular even among academics. As Neimeyer argues, Corman and Price's work "is one of the highpoints in the commodification of Poe, imposing a theatrically gothic aspect on the writings, much in the tradition of Victorian illustrations, and making him a favorite to a wide range of audiences" (218). Price's charismatic performances often transcend the clumsy scripts, and Corman certainly knew how to make a visual impact despite modest budgets. The films are always colorful but claustrophobic: they might not follow Poe's plots or his intellectual or psychological twists and turns, but the best ones do *look* like Poe stories. Indeed, the ambitious yet low-budget feel of the Poe series (and the rest of Corman's oeuvre) anticipated the aesthetic of much independent film of the late twentieth and early twenty-first centuries. Perhaps for that reason, Corman's work has inspired a number of scholarly books, articles, and dissertations, again demonstrating the dissolving of boundaries between academic and popular cultures. Despite their availability on VHS and DVD, these films that provided shared cultural (semi-)literacy for baby boomers are little-known to high school and college students of the twenty-first century; even so, they fueled Poe's continued popularity and shaped an enduring, if somewhat misleading, image of his works. In its second and third generations, this image has taken the form of Eric Draven (played by Brandon Lee) in the 1994 film *The Crow*, the WWF star known as Raven, and the Baltimore NFL team, all of which, like the 1934 film, transform a poem about "mournful and neverending remembrance" (as Poe described it) into a sinister, violent figure (albeit one you might want to root for).[6] It shows up in countless productions — stage, screen, website, and print — throughout the world. (To give one example, I saw a lavish Catalan musical entitled *Poe* in Barcelona in 2002, based loosely on "The Fall of the House of Usher" but, with its employment of demons, a dream sequence, torture chamber, and sexual content, clearly inspired by Poe-related films more than by Poe's writing.)

At about the same time Poe became a staple of B-movie horror, he found another pop-culture niche in comic books ranging from *Classics Illustrated* to *Tales from the Crypt*. Poe's tales were ideally suited to the former publication, which attempted to attract young readers to classic literature; *CI* adapted "The Pit and the Pendulum," "Hans Pfaall," and "Usher" in the August 1947 number and "The Gold-Bug," "The Tell-Tale Heart," and "The Cask of Amontillado" in June 1951.[7] Poe became a favorite of the less staid, more graphically compelling horror comics in the 1950s and 1960s: *The Haunt of Fear, Nightmare, Chilling Tales, Creepy, Eerie, Chamber of Darkness,* and so on (Inge 8–13). Thomas Inge argues that "[w]ithout Poe, the entire horror genre of the comic book might not have developed as it did" (8), but the corollary could also be argued — that without horror comics, Poe's late-twentieth-century image might not have developed as it did. While slightly more faithful to Poe's plots than films tended to be, the horror comics' artists played up the sex and violence more than even Corman did. Popular magazine fiction from this period reinforced Poe's gothic image: in Manly Wade Wellman's "When It Was Moonlight" (published in the fantasy magazine *Unknown* in 1940), Poe investigates a case of premature burial only to discover — and vanquish — a female vampire, while Michael Avallone's "The Man Who Thought He Was Poe" (*Tales of the Frightened,* 1957) features a Poe aficionado who plots his wife's murder, only to be tricked by her and entombed in a refrigerator.

Comic and graphic artists, as well as popular fiction writers, continue to gravitate toward Poe. "The Raven and Other Poems" relaunched *Classics Illustrated* in 1990, with "The Fall of the House of Usher" appearing later that year. Jason Asala began a Poe comics serial in 1996, using Poe as a fictional main character whose adventures allude to Poe stories (Inge 15–16), and in 1997 Maxon Crumb released a book of his interpretations of seven stories and poems. More recently, *Rosebud Graphic Classics* devoted its first issue (2001) to Poe, with illustrations by Crumb, Rick Geary, Gahan Wilson, and others. The illustrations range from deliberately silly to sinister, but, in a departure from earlier comic book practice, nearly all accompany original Poe text.[8]

A more outlandish recent descendent of the horror comics, the graphic novel *In the Shadow of Edgar Allan Poe* (2002) literalizes the commonplace assertion that Poe was "haunted by demons." The story, by Jonathan Scott Fuqua, seems more improvised than plotted. In 1831 the ghost of Poe's father convinces him to cast his lot with demons who will inspire his best writing but wreck his personal life. Fuqua resurrects the Griswoldian rumor that Poe had a sexual relationship with his aunt Maria Clemm, making the incestuous love triangle the story's other focal point. The novel tries to generate tension and mystery from the question of how much of Poe's self-destruction and misfortune is caused by the demons and how much by himself, but the result is mostly confusion, as if the demons can't decide what sort of creatures they are. The graphics, on the other hand, are striking: the combination of photography and digital illustration (by Stephen John Phillips and Steven Parke) and multiple images conveying a single event on each page generates more intensity than the text. At the same time, its scenario unifies the academic and pop-culture Poes: Poe's story of incest and demonic possession comes in the form of a recently discovered diary that has been given to a professor, himself a grieving, heavy-drinking widower. In most respects Fuqua observes the chronology of Poe's career carefully; the professor even comments on how the diary matches up with the known facts of Poe's life, creating the potential for metatextual commentary on the construction of Poe biography and Poe myths. That potential goes unfulfilled, however, and this artistically innovative book presents Poe in the depraved yet romanticized terms of the nineteenth century.

By the middle of the twentieth century "Poe" had become synonymous with literary detection as well as gothic horror. Arthur Conan Doyle acknowledged the debt of all detective fiction writers to Poe in 1908: "Each may find some little development of his own, but his main art must trace back to those admirable stories of Monsieur Dupin, so wonderful in their masterful force, their reticence, their quick dramatic point" (117–18). Since then, Poe has been cited repeatedly as the father of modern mystery and detective fiction by novelists and scholars,[9] and the Mystery Writers of America named their annual award the "Edgar" in Poe's honor in 1946. It is not surprising, then, that mystery writers often build their plots around Poe, either by making some piece of Poeana the stolen article or devising crimes based on Poe stories or by writing Poe in as a character.

An early, impressive example of the first strategy is Amelia Reynolds Long's novel *Death Looks Down* (1945), which revolves around a series of murders related to the theft of a rare "Ulalume" manuscript from a university library. Long's narrator, graduate student Katherine "Peter" Piper, helps the ingenious detective Ted Trelawney unravel the plot and identify the culprit, who turns out to be a graduate student who discovered the manuscript, sold it for less than its market value to the university, and then conspired to steal it back. Long invokes Poe throughout the novel, as each murder alludes to a short story (a motif that becomes truly ridiculous only with the fourth and final murder, based on "Metzengerstein"). The relationship between Piper and the pipe-smoking Trelawney resembles the relationship between Poe's narrator and Dupin; Piper is more helpful than Poe's narrator, but like him she marvels at the detective's analytic ability and insight into character and motive. Moreover, the "Ulalume" manuscript recalls the purloined letter, as it is stolen, replaced with a replica, then hidden in plain sight (by being returned to the display case in place of the forgery when the thief fears detection). In the last chapter, Trelawney outwits the murderer by "borrow[ing] a page from [the murderer] Woodring's own book" and entrapping him with an adaptation of "The Fall of the House of Usher" in which a student impersonates a murder victim risen-from-the-dead to shock the culprit into confession.

Death Looks Down reflects Poe's popularity as a cultural signifier at mid-century, linking his stories to the fictional murders; but at the same time, Long places Poe on a scholarly pedestal — or at least the novel's students and professors do. At one point a police sergeant learns from Dr. Rourke, a Poe specialist, that the university paid ten thousand dollars for the "Ulalume" manuscript:

> "Ten grand!" The sergeant was impressed. "Say, this guy, Poe, must be good! He oughtta write for Hollywood."
>
> For a minute it was even money whether Dr. Rourke would explode or merely pass out quietly in a faint.
>
> "Edgar Allan Poe," he said in the voice that he reserved for those who were beyond redemption, "died in 1849. He was one of America's greatest poets — if not *the* greatest."
>
> The sergeant looked annoyed at the implied rebuke.
>
> "Oh, yeah?" he said argumentatively. "What'd he have that Eddie Guest ain't got?"
>
> "I'm afraid I must decline to answer that question," Dr. Rourke replied, and his tone would have frozen Niagara Falls solid. "It would require more time than either of us can spare just now." (32)

The two characters live in different worlds as far as literature is concerned: Long gently lampoons the low-brow police sergeant for not knowing who

Poe is (in contrast to the more erudite Detective Trelawney), and at the same time contributes to her caricature of Dr. Rourke as a snooty intellectual, unwilling or unable to talk outside his academic cocoon. The exchange seems unrealistic for 1945, by which time Poe's name would have been recognized by almost any American adult with a high school education; meanwhile, the academic tide had shifted toward recognizing Poe's short stories as his most important accomplishment, at the expense of the poems Dr. Rourke admires. Long seems to be aiming for the middle-brow reader who would distance herself from the ignorance of the sergeant and the pretentiousness of the professor — and yet that same reader might be drawn to Poe because he offers both academic legitimacy and entertainment value, as the professor and the sergeant demonstrate. Fittingly, both are willing to measure Poe's greatness in monetary terms: the sergeant concludes that Poe must be great if his poem can fetch ten thousand dollars, while scholars like Dr. Rourke create the market for such manuscripts by maintaining Poe's reputation. Dr. Rourke also reminds us that although Long herself is using Poe's sensational fiction as a motif throughout her middle-brow mystery, Poe remains not a schlockmeister but "one of America's greatest poets." Anticipating a number of Poe-related mysteries, Long's book exemplifies the convergence of sensationalism — Poe's and his interpreters' — and "great literature."

Published over fifty years later, Joanne Dobson's *The Raven and the Nightingale* might be read as an updated *Death Looks Down*: it takes place in and around a college, is narrated by a woman — this time a professor, not a student — who helps a professional male detective solve the crime, and revolves around the theft of Poe-related documents. Here, too, Poe stories are playfully woven into the plot: motifs from "Usher" and "Ligeia," references to doppelgängers, and a denouement that parallels "The Purloined Letter." However, Dobson, an American literature professor herself, is far more concerned with academic — particularly gender — politics, understandably, since she wrote the book amidst the culture wars of the 1990s. Her murderer is a desperate, ambitious adjunct professor, a woman who kills her male thesis director for appropriating her trendy, jargon-laden thesis on Poe into a career-making academic book. The thesis director, both villain and victim, parallels Poe, who, according to the newly discovered diaries of the fictional "poetess" Emmeline Foster, stole the concept and refrain of "The Raven" from Foster's poem "The Bird of the Dream." Thus Dobson pays tribute to Poe by referencing his stories but creates a subplot in which Poe's dishonesty implicates him in a young woman's death.

Other mystery writers, such as William Hjortsberg and Harold Schecter, have taken the risk of writing Poe into their plots as a character. In *Nevermore* (1994), Hjortsberg has Poe's ghost repeatedly visit Arthur Conan Doyle as Doyle and Harry Houdini pursue a serial killer in New York in 1923. Poe is rather unremarkable for a ghost: he has little to say to Doyle beyond revealing that he is unaware of his own death and thinks *Doyle* is the one haunting *him*. (Indeed, Poe seems to be reliving his life: when Doyle encounters him in Washington, he is sick from his fateful drinking binge in that city in 1843.) Even so, Hjortsberg's resurrection of Poe in a novel featuring Doyle and Houdini makes sense in light of the three men's shared fascination with the possibility of communicating with the dead. Houdini spent much of his career debunking spiritualists but was drawn to them largely because he longed for contact with his deceased mother; at the same time, his escapes imitated resurrection from the grave, crossing boundaries of life and death in a manner reminiscent of "Loss of Breath" and "The Fall of the House of Usher."[10] In *Nevermore*, his skepticism is shaken when a mystic speaks to him in his mother's voice. Meanwhile, Doyle, most famous for his creation of the ultra-rationalist detective Sherlock Holmes, devoted much of his career to promoting spiritualism, writing books, giving lectures, and, in 1920, debating Houdini on the topic. Hjortsberg could have made even more of this struggle between rationalism and detection on one hand and faith or longing for a transcendence of death on the other, as this struggle plays such an important role in Poe's work; but then again, *Nevermore* makes no pretense of being a novel of ideas. At least Hjortsberg integrates the three men's common obsession into a mystery that also honors the genre's lineage.

Hjortsberg also employs the device of having the criminal model his crimes on Poe stories. Like Clyde Woodring, the killer of *Death Looks Down*, and Lugosi's Dr. Vollin in *The Raven*, Hjortsberg's killer takes inspiration from Poe, burying a victim alive in one of Houdini's coffins, dressing up as an ape to throw another out of a window, attempting to wall up Doyle with only a bottle of wine to drink, and so on. The ghost of Poe is amused by all this, suggesting that he relished the macabre murders he wrote: "the ghost opened wide his moonbeam mouth in a caterwaul of chilling laughter. And as he laughed, he slowly dissolved, whirling away like the wisps of smoke in an icy wind until nothing remained but the disembodied laughter, a terrifying echo seeming to resound from the very bowels of hell itself" (145). He tells Doyle, "It's one thing to write about murder in the abstract, to invent a blood-drenched fiction is a fine fancy. But, how much more sublime to populate a narrative with actual corpses and render the scene in crimson gore instead of printer's ink" (145). Hjortsberg's novel provides a snapshot of Poe's public image at the end of the twentieth century: father of the detective story, a ghost whose presence is felt by other writers like Doyle, but most of all still the master of the macabre. Buried (alive) underneath these images is the more philosophical Poe who wrestled with his own rationalism over the possibility of life after death.

Like Hjortsberg's *Nevermore,* Harold Schecter's novel of the same title presents a serial-killer mystery solved by a duo of historical figures not known as detectives: Poe himself and, believe it or not, Davy Crockett. It's an intriguing partnership: Poe and Crockett were, after all, contemporaries; Crockett was a publishing phenomenon at the time Poe was immersed in print culture. (In the *Southern Literary Messenger* in 1835, Poe wrote a brief, harsh notice of *An Account of Colonel Crockett's Tour to the North and Down East* and alluded to Crockett's famous grin in his review of Theodore S. Fay's *Norman Leslie.*) Schecter sets them up, as one would expect, as a classic odd couple who speak completely different brands of English, argue constantly, and yet ultimately work well together, a perfect combination of brains and brawn. But fleshing out Poe's character, even to the point of having him narrate the novel, proves problematic. Schecter's rendering of Poe's speech — and Crockett's, for that matter — is awkward and constantly distracting. At one point, speaking to a boy who wants to know why he has a handkerchief around his mouth as he sorts through old newspapers, Poe replies, "As you are perhaps unaware . . . the pleural membranes of the human lung are, in many cases, unusually susceptible to certain varieties of airborne mold commonly found in houses which — " before being interrupted by the boy. His narration is similarly overdone — for instance, as he describes that same interruption: "Before I could elucidate further, the walleyed youth — whose upbringing had clearly been sadly deficient in matters of rudimentary etiquette — abruptly turned to Crockett and asked: 'What are you doing here, Davy?'" (358).

In Schecter's novel the murders do not imitate Poe's fiction, but the plot self-consciously — and cleverly — combines motifs from Poe's tales and biography. The murderer, whose trademark is scrawling the word "Nevermore" in the victim's blood at crime scenes, turns out to be Poe's female doppelgänger. His half-sister Lenore, unknown to Poe and the rest of the world, is determined to avenge their father David Poe's humiliation at being hooted off the stage by a Baltimore audience in 1810 by tracking down and killing the audience members a quarter century after the fact. About two thirds of the way through the novel, Poe believes that *he* may be the killer, so disturbed is he by the glimpses he gets of his double. As absurd as it all sounds, this Poe-esque maneuver does create some much-needed suspense in the second half of the novel. Combined with recurring references to Poe's fiction — the narration includes a number of lines he would later use in his tales, at one point he narrowly escapes from a burning house owned by a man named Roger Asher, and so on — this playfulness redeems the book considerably. In fact, the self-reflexiveness suggests that the breakneck plot twists, extreme predicaments (which include Poe being buried alive by thugs), and strained humor might be a tribute to the Poe who simultaneously imitated and lampooned the gothic style of his day.[11]

While the horror and detective genres have tended to repeat themselves in their use of Poe, a wide range of artists in various media have taken Poe's inspiration in more original directions. Poe's influence on modernism and postmodernism is impossible to measure or summarize, but it seems reasonable to claim that Poe's greatest contribution to arts and literature, popular or otherwise, has been delivered through artists who refer to or interpret him as they challenge established forms, a list that would include poets Charles Baudelaire, Stéphane Mallarmé, Paul Valéry, Wallace Stevens, Allen Ginsberg, and Richard Wilbur; filmmakers Jean Epstein, Luis Buñel, and Alfred Hitchcock; visual artists Édouard Manet, Odilon Redon, Aubrey Beardsley, and René Magritte; composer/musicians Claude Debussy, Philip Glass, and Lou Reed; fiction writers Fyodor Dostoyevsky, Guy de Maupassant, J. D. Salinger, Vladimir Nabokov, Jorge Luis Borges, Carlos Fuentes, Ishmael Reed, Paul

Auster, Richard Powers, Don DeLillo, Joyce Carol Oates, John Barth, and Margaret Atwood.

If, as Borges claims, every writer creates his own precursors (*Labyrinths* xi), then certainly Poe has been recreated in a number of different forms by the writers and other artists in the list above. Nabokov, for example, rewrote "Poe" as an avatar of Humbert Humbert, alerting readers to his own appropriation of Poe-esque techniques and themes in *Lolita*. Borges, as John Irwin demonstrates in *The Mystery to a Solution,* reinvented the analytic detective story in the spirit of Poe. Irwin asks a fundamental question, how is *literary* detective fiction possible — that is, "How does one present both the analytic solution of a mystery and at the same time conserve the sense of the mysterious on which analysis is based?" (2). His answer traces seemingly innumerable paths, but essentially he finds that both Poe and Borges have it both ways by evoking labyrinthine networks of allusion and intellectual play. Indeed, as the contributors to Patricia Merivale and Susan Elizabeth Sweeney's collection *Detecting Texts* make clear, Poe's influence on detective fiction is particularly strong in the subgenre known as the metaphysical or postmodern detective story, a tradition that can be traced through numerous twentieth-century writers but epitomized by Paul Auster.

Since the early 1980s Auster has developed a postmodern detective fiction that, unlike that of Poe and Borges, avoids solution altogether as a way of conserving the sense of the mysterious. In his novella *City of Glass* (1985), Auster, like Nabokov and Borges before him, references Poe, at a moment when the writer/detective Quinn tracks Peter Stillman Sr. to "a knobby outcrop at 84th Street known as Mount Tom. On this same spot, in the summers of 1843 and 1844, Edgar Allan Poe had spent many long hours gazing out at the Hudson. Quinn knew this because he made it his business to know such things. As it turned out, he had often sat there himself" (100). By this point, late in the novella, the allusion comes as no surprise, as Auster has already created a fun-house of authorial reflection (one implication of the book's title). Quinn writes mysteries under the name William Wilson, which is also a pseudonym in Poe's story of that title. Like Poe's "William Wilson," *City of Glass* examines the construction and destruction of identity: from the beginning, Quinn's personality is split not two ways but three, with the help of Wilson's detective character Max Work: "In the triad of selves that

Quinn had become, Wilson served as a kind of ventriloquist, Quinn himself was the dummy, and Work was the animated voice that gave purpose to the enterprise" (6). Quinn splits his personality yet again when he gets a phone call asking for the Paul Auster Detective Agency and, on a whim, identifies himself as Auster and takes the job. Later he looks up Paul Auster in the phone book, only to find a writer, not a detective. Thus the novelist Auster toys with the implications of authorship (or Austership) much as Poe did in *The Narrative of Arthur Gordon Pym,* in which, for instance, the fictional Pym discusses his relationship with "Mr. Poe" in the preface to the narrative, which contains several other autobiographical references.

Instances of doubling pile up in *City of Glass* more quickly than they do even in "The Fall of the House of Usher," as Quinn/Auster reflects both the man who hires him and the man he's hired to follow, who are themselves son and father, Peter Stillman Junior and Senior. Stillman Jr., who hires Quinn, was tortured as a child by his father, who, in a maniacal attempt to recover "natural language" by isolating his son, kept him in a dark room and beat him when he tried to speak. During their only interview, the still childlike Stillman (whose wife, incidentally, is named Virginia) repeatedly tells Quinn/Auster that Peter Stillman "is not my real name." Later, reflecting on the case, Quinn imitates Stillman's syntax in his narration: "All I can say is this: listen to me. My name is Paul Auster. That is not my real name" (49). When Quinn first sees Peter Stillman's father, he sees two men who match his photograph of Stillman so closely that he does not know which one to follow. Purely by chance, he follows the right Stillman, and eventually nearly becomes the man he shadows ("As it turned out, he often sat there himself"). But by the story's end, Quinn, who in his obsession with the case has thrown away all vestiges of his old, tripartite identity, nearly replicates the condition of the isolated younger Peter Stillman, lying alone in a dark room in Stillman's vacated apartment for a long but indefinite period of time.

Like Poe, Auster uses the doubling motif to probe the nature of individual identity — how it is formed, how "unique" any one person can claim to be, whether a person can remake himself, how schools and cities alter individual consciousness, and so on. Although he at one point quotes Dupin ("An identification of the reasoner's intellect with that of his opponent," again creating a double), Quinn more closely resembles the accidental detective of "The Man of the Crowd," who, even as he doubles the old man, concludes that the other is "a book that will not permit itself to be read."[12] Like Pym analyzing the chasms of Tsalal, Quinn attempts to read the elder Stillman's walks through the city after noting the resemblance of his unpredictable routes to letters of the alphabet, but the question of whether their "author" — Stillman — intended them as letters remains open. At the end of the novella, the unnamed narrator is no more able to read Quinn than Quinn was able to read Stillman. He has been basing his own narrative on Quinn's red notebook, which, not surprisingly, matched the notebook carried by the elder Stillman. "There were moments when the text was difficult to decipher," he tells us, "but I have done my best with it and have refrained from any interpretation. The red notebook, of course, is only half the story, as any sensitive reader will understand" (158). Indeed, although we learn that the elder Stillman has committed suicide by the end of the novel, that fact provides no closure, and we are left with a sense of unresolved mystery, a story only half-written, again much like *Pym* or "The Man of the Crowd." In its defiance of interpretation and its foregrounding of the uncertainties of language and identity, *City of Glass* amplifies the postmodern tendencies of Poe's fiction.

Just as Nabokov, Borges, Auster, and other fiction writers paid homage to Poe without having murderers reproduce scenes from his stories, innovative filmmakers throughout the century have created a countertradition to the films that brandish Poe's name simply to conjure images of horror. Jean Epstein's 1928 *La Chute de la Maison Usher* moves slowly through a plot derived from "The Oval Portrait" as well as "Usher," but Epstein's emphasis is not on action, certainly not on horror, but on the interplay of moving images, many of which have no necessary relation to the story: curtains billowing along a corridor, leafless trees silhouetted against a gray sky, frogs mating. Epstein's ending may be even less faithful to Poe's story than anything in Corman's work, but it barely matters in a film that draws the viewer's attention away from plot. Epstein explained that "[i]n preparing a film from Poe, the primary aim is to put together (not without difficulty) an immense and singular technique. Having achieved this, and with the images on hand to be given sense, it can be seen that, as well as for Poe, technique today can lie almost entirely in the relation between images" (liner notes to DVD). Epstein, then, seems to have drawn inspiration more from Poe's aesthetic theory than from his sensational plot devices.

Alfred Hitchcock, who, like Poe, was a serious, multi-dimensional artist with a one-dimensional popular reputation, expressed his admiration of Poe in a 1960 article: "[I]t's because I liked Edgar Allan Poe's stories so much that I began to make suspense films. Without wanting to seem immodest, I can't help but compare what I try to put into my films with what Poe put in his stories; a perfectly unbelievable story recounted to readers with such a hallucinatory logic that one has the impression that this same story can happen to you tomorrow" (qtd. in Davidson, 4). In a recent article comparing Hitchcock and Nabokov, James A. Davidson discusses Poe as their most significant common literary influence. While Davidson does not explicitly link Poe to the other commonalities he sees in Hitchcock and Nabokov — game theory, cameo appearances and self-reference, use of the doppelgänger and unreliable narrator — they are all prominent in Poe's work as well. Davidson points out that in *Marnie*, Hitchcock alludes to Poe by giving the title character the last name of Edgar (a change from the book on which the film is based) and sets the action in three cities and one state in which Poe lived: Baltimore, New York, Philadelphia, and Virginia. Perhaps Hitchcock also had Poe biography in mind when he chose a story in which childhood trauma (an assault on the mother, as opposed to Poe's mother's death) creates psychological disorders in the adult Marnie Edgar. Otherwise, despite the Poe allusions, *Marnie* is less Poe-esque than, for instance, *Psycho*, which places Norman Bates in a role similar to the narrators of "The Tell-Tale Heart" and "The Black Cat," or *Vertigo*, with its emphasis on obsession, doubling, and the fantasy of a woman returning from the dead.

Another intriguing instance of an experimental filmmaker explicitly referencing Poe is Federico Fellini's short film "Toby Dammitt," the last of the trilogy making up *Histoires Extraordinaires* (1967; released in the U.S. as *Spirits of the Dead*). The first two films, Roger Vadim's "Metzengerstein" and Louis Malle's "William Wilson," are relatively faithful to Poe's stories, although both are more sexually provocative than anything in Poe. "Toby Dammitt," as indicated in the film's titles, is "liberally adapted from 'Don't Wager Your Head to the Devil,'" which is itself a translation of a translation of Poe's title "Never Bet the Devil Your Head." Like Poe's story, Fellini's film ends with a man named Toby

Dammit being decapitated by a hidden cable as he attempts a daring stunt; and in both, the devil walks off with the head. Fellini's Toby (Terence Stamp), however, is a hedonistic, alcoholic young actor just arrived in Rome to work on a film, a "Catholic western" in which he will presumably play Christ. After being hounded by photographers at the airport, then interviewed on an inane television show and honored at a nightmarish parody of an awards ceremony (the Italian Oscars, or "Golden She-Wolves"), Dammit races out of town in a new Ferrari. He ends up at a bridge that has been partially washed away, creating a chasm, and on the other side he sees a young girl dressed in white and playing with a large white ball. He had seen this vision before, on his arrival at the airport, and had told the TV interviewer that "for me, the devil is friendly and joyful. He's a little girl." He tries to jump the chasm but of course doesn't see the cable stretched across it.

Although Fellini seems concerned primarily with satirizing the movie industry and celebrity culture, he also evokes sympathy for Dammit, a Shakespearean actor on the skids who is victimized by fawning but demanding show-business people as well as his own demons. During the awards ceremony, a beautiful, mysterious woman approaches him and immediately pledges herself to him: "I'll take care of you always. . . . You won't be alone anymore because I'll be with you always. Whenever you put out your hand, you will find my hand." Although he nods off as she finishes this speech (Was she a dream all along? A dream within a dream?), he clearly longs for the stability she spoke of: "A wonderful woman . . . she took my hand. She stroked my hand. She said, 'I'm here for you. I'm the woman of your dreams.' But I'm not waiting for you." Dammit fits the romantic artist role that Poe himself tried to appropriate from Byron and that Baudelaire successfully promoted after Poe's death. Already an old story by 1967, it has become even more familiar after the premature deaths of self-destructive visionary rock stars, Jim Morrison and Kurt Cobain in particular: a young, hedonistic, world-weary male artist, uncomfortable with celebrity, pursued by demons, in desperate need of a nurturing woman, kills himself rather than witness his own decline. Don G. Smith rightly observes that "the image of the pale, silver-haired, red-lipped child as Satan will haunt viewers for a very long time," but equally haunting is the long sequence leading up to that final frame, in which Dammit's face and maniacal laughter reveal his total desperation: having been a zombie throughout the film, he comes to life only as he races toward his death.

Although I have tried to distinguish what I see as more creative uses of Poe from the generally formulaic works of melodramatic stage biographies, horror movies, and mystery novels, I still contend that no rigid line can be drawn between the pop-culture Poe and the academic or avant-garde Poe. For instance, as popular as Fellini is, he is regarded as an art-film director today, especially in the U.S., yet when "Toby Dammit" was marketed as part of *Spirits of the Dead,* American International, its U.S. distributor, billed the trilogy as another in the series of titillating B-movies: "Edgar Allan Poe's Ultimate Orgy. An adventure in terror beyond your wildest nightmares" (Smith 186). Other examples are easy to find. Dario Argento's film *Opera* (1987), which not only alludes to Poe's fiction but, according to film critic Michael Sevastakis, "reaches a visual equivalent of Poe's elegantly wrought prose style," combines the aesthetics of low-budget slasher films with surrealism and Hitchcockian symbolism.[13] *The Simpsons'* interpretation of "The Raven" (1990) with James Earl Jones has probably been watched by more people than any other adaptation of a Poe work, and yet some of its biggest fans are professors who relish, for instance, the postmodern humor of Homer-as-narrator reading a book entitled "Forgotten Lore." One could argue that Matt Groening's parodic treatment of the poem is appropriate to its almost comically overwrought style (and yet it still scares Homer). Lou Reed and Robert Wilson's *POEtry* (2001), a rock opera based on Poe's life and works, has one foot in the avant-garde and one foot in mainstream rock and roll, like much of Reed's work. On *The Raven* (2003), the double-CD spinoff of *POEtry,* Reed adapts Poe to his personal mythology, emphasizing self-destructive impulses, the unleashing of repressed desires, and the guilt that follows. The rewrites of Poe poems and stories (including "The Raven") are for the most part bathetic, but some of Reed's original songs with thematic links to Poe work better. On "Guilty," Reed declaims over a tight rock groove and Ornette Coleman's beautifully off-kilter saxophone: "Guilty / I'm paralyzed with guilt / It runs through me like rain through silk / Guilty / My mind won't leave me alone / My teeth rot and my lips start to foam / 'Cause I'm so guilty . . . What did I say? What did I do? / Did I ever do it to you? / Don't turn your back / I can't look you in the eye / I — I — I — I guess I'm guilty as charged." Unfortunately, despite Reed's obviously sincere identification with Poe, most of *The Raven* is as pretentious and shallow as the previous grand attempt at a Poe-rock concept album, the Alan Parsons Project's *Tales of Mystery and Imagination* (1976).[14]

One final example, returning to the 2002 International Poe Conference: the night before E. L. Doctorow's talk, the conference participants attended a performance of "Three Tales by Poe" ("MS. Found in a Bottle," "The Man of the Crowd," and "The Tell-Tale Heart") presented by Puppetsweat Theater, a group that combines shadow puppetry with video, original soundtracks, and live narration. Their performance was rigidly faithful to the texts and easily accessible — they would have been a hit at the middle school where I struggled with my hand props. But at the same time, their interpretations of the stories were original and visually compelling in the manner of expressionist cinema. The cutouts used to cast shadows on a large screen were held by dancers who created various effects with the positioning of the props and with the motions of their bodies. The direction emphasized the long periods of inactivity and waiting in "The Man of the Crowd" and "The Tell-Tale Heart," creating palpable suspense. "The Man of the Crowd" featured the disconcerting image of a throng of men in bowler hats walking down a city street, each of them with Poe's face superimposed on their own. Meanwhile, in a long period without narration, the soundtrack consisted of almost whispered, rhythmic vocal sounds that turned out to be the recorded text of the story with the vowels removed from the speaker's voice. This combination of effects captured perfectly the disconcerting, claustrophobic feel of Poe's story.

As this chapter suggests, there are as many pop-culture Poes as there are lit-crit Poes, as his image and his works have accommodated — or been forced to accommodate — changing times and a variety of approaches. Why has Poe proved so resilient, so present, over 150 years after his death? Gerald Kennedy suggests that Poe, writing "at the historical moment when public education and a secular, capitalistic mass culture had begun to supplant organized religion as the principal influences of thought and belief," simply anticipated a number of the predicaments and preoccupations of modern culture (Introduction 14), including dislocation from history, spiritual uncertainty and death anxiety, and a fascination with science, exploration, and information. Shawn Rosenheim's book *The Cryptographic Imagination: From Edgar Poe to the Internet* (1997) places

Poe at the center of a history of encoding and decoding, with clear implications for his current academic importance and wider popularity: "Detective fiction and science fiction are among the most popular literary forms of the last three centuries; by tracing their origins back to the cryptographic values encoded in their formation, we discover specific links among cryptography, Poe's innovations in genre, and the effects of technology on literature" (3). In short, Poe continues to fascinate a wide range of readers and popular culture continues to reinvent him because Poe's work took off in so many directions, which is why "everything leads to Poe." Strictly as an icon, Poe is a marketer's dream, especially after Lugosi and Price: his name, even his face, simultaneously signifies the thrill of a campfire ghost story and the erudition of great literature (Neimeyer 206). If that pairing seems paradoxical, the paradox is fitting for a writer who, in his literary theory and ambitions as a magazinist sought to unite elite literary taste with bad taste, which he saw as crucial to mass circulation. In 1835, Poe defended the horrific conclusion of his story "Berenice" to his prudent future employer T. W. White, owner of the *Southern Literary Messenger*: "[T]o be appreciated you must be read, and these things are invariably sought after with avidity" (Letters 1:58). Over a century and a half later, they still are.

Notes

1 See, for instance, Cyndy Hendershot, "Domesticity and Horror in *House of Usher* and *Village of the Damned*," *Quarterly Review of Film and Video* 17 (2000): 221–27, and Maren Longbella's M.A. thesis "Poe, Corman, Todorov: The Fantastic from Literature to Film" (U of North Dakota, 1990), as well as Don G. Smith's discussions of Corman's films in *The Poe Cinema: A Critical Filmography of Theatrical Releases Based on the Works of Edgar Allan Poe* (Jefferson, NC, and London: McFarland, 1999).

2 As of this writing, the best clearing house for Poe websites is Heyward Ehrlich's "A Poe Webliography: Edgar Allan Poe on the Internet," http://andromeda.rutgers.edu/~ehrlich/poesites.html#A.

3 Hazelton's play opened in Baltimore in 1895 and was performed in Richmond and Washington as well, but it was not received well by newspaper critics, according to N. Bryllion Fagin, *The Histrionic Mr. Poe* (Baltimore: Johns Hopkins UP, 1949), 227. John E. Reilly discusses Hazelton's play in "Poe in American Drama: Versions of the Man," in *Poe and Our Times*, ed. Benjamin F. Fisher (Baltimore: Edgar Allan Poe Society, 1986), 18–19. I cite the typescript of Dargan's play, but it was also published

under the title *The Poet* in Dargan's collection *Semiramis and Other Plays* (New York: Brentano's, 1904). I have found no records of performances of the plays by Dargan, Ketchum, or Blake. Reilly discusses another early biographical play, *Edgar Allan Poe: A Character Study,* by Catherine Chisolm Cushing, which played for a single night in New York in 1925, and Fagin notes another play, *Edgar Allan Poe* by B. Iden Payne and Thomas Wood Stevens, which had a brief run at the University of South Carolina in 1933 (230). According to Reilly, Cushing's play depicts Poe as a rebellious youth to appeal to a "Roaring Twenties" audience (19–22).

[4] Griffith directed the first Poe biopic, the one-reel *Edgar Allan Poe,* in 1909, in which Poe writes "The Raven" after a raven flies into his room, then hurries out to sell the poem to buy food and medicine for the dying Virginia (Smith, *The Poe Cinema* 8).

[5] Corman directed eight of the AIP Poe films; Price starred in eleven of them, including seven of the eight directed by Corman (Mark Neimeyer, "Poe and Popular Culture," in *The Cambridge Companion to Edgar Allan Poe,* ed. Kevin J. Hayes [Cambridge and New York: Cambridge UP, 2002], n. 224).

[6] At Maryland Public Television's impressive "Knowing Poe" website, one can watch a video of members of the Baltimore Ravens reciting "Quoth the raven, 'Nevermore.'" http://knowingpoe.thinkport.org/library/news/ravens.asp.

[7] Earlier, in 1944, "Annabel Lee," "The Bells," and "The Murders in the Rue Morge" had appeared in separate issues. See M. Thomas Inge, "Poe and the Comics Connection," *Edgar Allan Poe Review* 2.1 (2001): 5.

[8] The exceptions are Geary's "Tell-Tale Heart," which excerpts Poe's story, Spain Rodriguez's "The Inheritance of Rufus Griswold," and Clive Barker and Mark A. Nelson's "New Murders in the Rue Morgue," with text originally published by Barker in 1984. The most notable inheritor of the pulp-Poe tradition is Stephen King, who, for instance, reworked "The Cask of Amontillado" as "Dolan's Cadillac" (1989). On popular fiction that refers to or is obviously indebted to Poe, see Tony Magistrale and Sidney Poger, *Poe's Children* (New York: Peter Lang, 1999), as well as John E. Reilly's "Poe and Imaginative Literature" and his essays, "Poe in American Drama: Versions of the Man," in *Poe and Our Times,* ed. Bejamin F. Fisher (Baltimore: Edgar Allan Poe Society, 1986), 18–31, and "Poe in Literature and Popular Culture," in *A Companion to Poe Studies,* ed. Eric W. Carlson (Westport, CT: Greenwood, 1996), 471–93.

[9] See Thomas Joswick, "Moods of Mind: The Tales of Detection, Crime, and Punishment," in *A Companion to Poe Studies,* ed. Eric W. Carlson (Westport, CT: Greenwood, 1996), 238.

[10] See Kenneth Silverman, *Houdini!!!* (New York: HarperCollins, 1996), esp. 279–84. Silverman, who also wrote an excellent Poe biography (*Edgar A. Poe: Mournful and Never-ending Remembrance* [New York: HarperCollins, 1991]), refers to Houdini's interest in Poe several times in *Houdini!!!,* noting, for instance, that

Houdini once purchased a writing desk believed to have belonged to Poe (210) and that he at one point considered making a film based on some of Poe's tales (263).

[11] Schecter has since published another novel with Poe as detective, this time teaming up with P. T. Barnum in *The Hum Bug* (2001). Reilly mentions several more books featuring Poe as a major character ("Poe in Literature and Popular Culture," 482–83).

[12] See Patricia Merivale, "Gumshoe Gothics," in Patricia Merivale and Susan Elizabeth Sweeney, eds., *Detecting Texts: The Metaphysical Detective Story from Poe to Postmodernism* (Philadelphia: U of Pennsylvania P, 1999). *Detecting Texts* includes three other essays that discuss *City of Glass* (or the entire *New York Trilogy*), all of which acknowledge Poe's presence in Auster's novella.

[13] Michael Sevastakis, "A Dangerous Mind: Dario Argento's *Opera* (1987)." *Kinoeye*, 24 June 2002. 28 paragraphs. Accessed 16 May 2003. http://www.kinoeye.org/02/12/sevastakis12.html. Sevastakis notes that Argento "has always felt 'a great affinity with Poe,' saying 'I understand his pain.' His notorious declaration, 'I like women, especially beautiful ones . . . being murdered . . . ,' has been coupled with Poe's infamous dictum, 'The death of a beautiful woman is, unquestionably, the most poetical topic in the world.'" I am also indebted to John Rocco's presentation, "The Origin of All Horror: Poe and Narrative Film from Griffith to Hitchcock to Argento," International Edgar Allan Poe Conference, Towson, MD, 4 October 2002.

[14] A more successful Poe project by contemporary musicians and actors is *Closed on Account of Rabies* (Paris/Mouth Almighty/Mercury Records, 1997), produced by Hal Willner, who also produced Reed's *The Raven*. Most of the double-CD consists of unabridged readings of Poe's works with musical settings. Readers include Iggy Pop, Marianne Faithfull, Dr. John, and Christopher Walken.

Afterword:
Loss of Breath: Writing Poe's Last Days

HAVING BEGUN THIS study with a newspaper notice of Poe's death, I would like to return to the events leading up to that moment, the week before the beginning of Poe's afterlife. On September 27, 1849, Poe boarded a steamer in Richmond bound for Baltimore, the first leg of his journey home to New York. On October 3 in Baltimore, Joseph Walker wrote to Joseph E. Snodgrass that Poe was at Ryan's 4th Ward polls, "rather worse for the wear . . . in great distress," and "in need of immediate assistance." Poe was taken to Washington College Hospital, where he was attended by Dr. John J. Moran and died on October 7. Other than this information gleaned from the memoirs of Snodgrass, Moran, and Neilson Poe, almost nothing else is known about the last ten days of Poe's life.[1] Had Poe known that his life, writing, and image would generate so much interest — over three dozen biographies, thousands of pages of literary criticism, over seventy films, countless middle-school projects, a Montblanc pen — he might well have planned just this sort of disappearance, a gaping hole in his life narrative, an unreadable conclusion.

Poe's cause of death is a perfect mystery: we know enough to invite speculation, and Poe's cult status has inspired a series of passionate theorists, but the body of evidence remains too slender for a definitive solution.[2] Poe was almost certainly debilitated by alcohol when Walker found him on October 3. That Walker's phrase "worse for the wear" indicates drunkenness is supported by Snodgrass's memoir as well as several contemporary, albeit indirect, sources such as John P. Kennedy and John R. Thompson, not to mention the fact that "Ryan's 4th Ward Polls" was a tavern known as Gunner's Hall (*Poe Log* 844). However, it is impossible to separate the fatal effects of this episode of heavy drinking from other health problems. Poe had been ill frequently in the last two years of his life, but instead of anything like modern medical records, we have, again, memoirs and letters that often blur the results of binge drinking with depression and other illnesses.[3] Working from this scanty information, doctors, historians, and amateur sleuths have at various times suggested tuberculosis, epilepsy, diabetes, and encephalitis as underlying if not primary causes of Poe's death. Two of the more sensational diagnoses have appeared in the last decade: rabies (1996) and carbon monoxide poisoning (1999). The former received enough media coverage to inspire the title of Hal Willner's Poe tribute CD, *Closed on Account of Rabies*, but the symptoms on which the diagnosis was based were partial and unreliable, coming from Dr. Moran's second and third versions of Poe's death, both written over twenty-five years after the fact and, because of contradictions and implausibilities, generally discredited by scholars. Albert Donnay, a public health researcher, argued in a 1999 conference paper, more recently adapted as a one-act play, that Poe died from carbon monoxide poisoning, having described its symptoms in his fiction, particularly in his description of Roderick Usher. Here, too, most Poe scholars were skeptical, objecting to a clinical reading of Poe's fiction and questioning whether the symptoms of carbon monoxide poisoning — headache, fatigue, muscle aches, nausea, diarrhea, confusion, dizziness, etc. — were not also consistent with ailments already associated with Poe (such as alcoholism). Whether it killed him or not, Poe has become a posthumous spokesman for carbon monoxide-poisoning awareness, just as he has served as an antidrug spokesman at the Philadelphia Poe Historic Site, where, in the late 1980s, a banner with Poe's likeness and the words "Poe says 'Just Say No to Drugs'" hung from the ceiling of a lecture hall.

Assuming that Poe's death was caused by an episode of heavy drinking combined with some preexisting condition that rendered him frail, the real mystery remains, what happened between September 27 and October 3? If he had drinking companions, who were they and why did they abandon him? Was he in Baltimore for the entire period, or did he make it to Philadelphia and then return to Baltimore instead of proceeding home to New York? Why, when Walker found him, was he wearing shabby, ill-fitting clothes unlike anything he usually wore? One time-honored but still unproven explanation has Poe victimized by a gang of thugs who plied him with alcohol, beat him, and forced him to vote repeatedly at various polls for the same candidate. The evidence for this theory includes the facts that this practice, known as "cooping," was common in Baltimore at the time, that Poe was drunk, and, again, that the tavern where he was found was also a polling place. It also explains the change of clothes, since some effort might have been made to alter the cooping victims' appearances. What makes the cooping theory difficult to accept is the fact that no one mentioned it until about twenty years after Poe's death, at a time when biographers were trying to rehabilitate his reputation.[4]

In 1998 John Evangelist Walsh published a book arguing that Poe had been the victim not of a cooping but of Elmira Royster Shelton's three brothers. Determined to prevent Poe from marrying into the family, the Royster brothers followed Poe to Philadelphia to threaten him, warning him to return to New York and never to see their sister again — but Poe escaped and headed south to Baltimore, where the brothers found him and, knowing his weakness, forced him to drink and left him at Gunner's Hall, helpless and disgraced. To his credit, Walsh gathers an impressive body of information relating to Poe's disappearance, and he argues the case for a violent Royster intervention as well as it could be argued; but, like cooping and carbon monoxide poisoning, his theory is at best only plausible, not probable.

Poe's many biographers generally respect the silence of the historical record concerning the period between September 27 and October 3, but Poe's death scene at Washington College Hospital in Baltimore, extended over four days, is too crucial to the closure of any Poe biography to leave blank. Dr. Moran, the physician who attended Poe, provided the "facts" for virtually every Poe biographer in a letter he wrote to Maria Clemm a month after Poe's death, in which he describes Poe as being initially "unconscious of his condition," then experiencing a "busy, but not violent or active delirium — constant talking — and vacant converse with spectral and imaginary objects on the walls" (Quinn and Hart 32). According to Moran, Poe became somewhat more coherent on his second day in the hospital but was severely depressed. When Moran mentioned the possibility of Poe's being visited by friends, his patient "broke out with much energy, and said the best thing his best friend could do would be to blow out his brains with a pistol" (33). Moran then describes Poe's death, which occurred two days later:

[H]e commenced calling for one "Reynolds," which he did through the night up to *three* on Sunday morning. At this time a very decided change began to affect him. Having become enfeebled from exertion he became quiet and seemed to rest for a short time, then gently moving his head, he said "*Lord help my poor Soul*" and expired! (33)

As W. T. Bandy points out, Moran proved an unreliable witness; for instance, he contradicted the calling out for "Reynolds" in two later accounts (29, 32–33). But since those later accounts, written in 1875 and 1885, are in other respects even less trustworthy than the 1849 letter, biographers have relied on this one document as the basis for their death scenes, which usually integrate references to Poe's poetry and fiction with the information provided by Moran.[5]

Most common are references to *Arthur Gordon Pym*'s final scene, suggested by linking "Reynolds" to the Antarctic explorer Jeremiah Reynolds, whose reports provided Poe with source material. Edward Shanks (1937), Marie Bonaparte (1939), Arthur Hobson Quinn (1941), Philip Lindsay (1953), Frances Winwar (1959), David Sinclair (1977), Wolf Mankowitz (1978), and Jeffrey Meyers (1992) all refer to or quote *Pym*, a book Poe wrote twelve years before his death, in describing his last thoughts. "And when, on the last night of all, he so strangely called for Reynolds — as it seemed to those about him — was this not as dying men call on the mother," asks Bonaparte rhetorically, "for had not Reynolds, like Arthur Gordon Pym, striven to conquer the South Pole, that white symbol of the frozen-in-death mother?" Bonaparte then paraphrases a line from "For Annie," quoted nearly as often as *Pym* (understandably so) in reference to Poe's death: "The 'danger,' the 'crisis,' were over at last, now that the 'fever called living' was past" (206). Arthur Hobson Quinn speculates that on the conscious level at least Poe's deathbed thoughts turned to stories in which sea exploration led to knowledge of a new dimension:

> Perhaps to his dim and tortured brain, he seemed to be on the brink of a great descending circle sweeping down like the phantom-ship in the "Manuscript found in a Bottle" into "darkness and the distance." In that first published story, Poe had written, "It is evident that we are hurrying onward to some exciting knowledge — some never to be imparted secret, whose attainment is destruction." (640)

Quinn then shifts Poe's thoughts to *Pym* and through *Pym* to Jeremiah Reynolds. Similarly, Winwar imagines Poe's mind "wandering to the unknown seas which Reynolds had sailed, and from them to the grandeur of his own vision of ultimate extinction, as the chasm threw itself open to receive him and there arose that 'shrouded human figure, very far larger . . . than any dweller among men. And the hue of the skin of the figure was of the perfect whiteness of the snow'" (376). Edward Shanks invokes *Pym* without mentioning Reynolds and offers a slightly different interpretation: "His death-cries recalled the most agonising episode in *Arthur Gordon Pym*: it seemed to him that he was dying of thirst" (78).

While about half of Poe's biographers have cited *Pym* in their depictions of his death, nearly all find some emblematic reference to Poe's poetry or fiction at that crucial moment. William Bittner describes Poe as "irrevocably in the Maelström" as he calls out for Reynolds. Mary Newton Stanard, in her highly romanticized biography *The Dreamer* (1925), quotes "To One in Paradise," "Bridal Ballad," "Annabel Lee," and "The Conqueror Worm" in her last four pages, in which the cause of Poe's death seems to be his "swallow[ing] the draught . . . that would free his spirit" (380). And Jeffrey Meyers, like Winwar, Sinclair, and Mankowitz, quotes the last lines of *Pym*, but also speculates that the room in which Poe died "resembled the grim cells, chambers, vaults and tombs of his most lurid stories" (254).

My point is not that these biographers are falsifying Poe, since a basic assumption behind this study is that there are many posthumous Poes, constructed according to the demands of academe, publishing, and the film industry. And within the realm of traditional narrative biography, some effort to make sense of Poe's death, if only by speculating about his last thoughts and connecting those thoughts to his fiction or poetry, would seem nearly inevitable: literary biography that scrupulously avoided linking the life to the works would almost certainly fail to produce any real insight. One could perhaps write a Poe biography with multiple endings or in some other way foreground the unreliability of the evidence surrounding his death, highlighting the fact that we don't know Poe so much as we know the documentary evidence related to his life. *The Poe Log: A Documentary Life of Edgar Allan Poe, 1809–1849* nearly does just that by providing edited documentary evidence and leaving the speculations to readers. But for the most part, Poe biographies tend by their very nature (as stories that end with the protagonist's death) to endorse the idea that Poe was fated to live the kind of life he lived and to die as he did. William Gill in 1878 set the tone for future biographers: "From the moment of [Poe's] wife's death, he waged an unequal battle with a relentless fate" (240). Susan Archer Talley Weiss (1907) titles her chapter on Poe's death "The Mystery of Fate," and Arthur Hobson Quinn calls his postmortem chapter "The Recoil of Fate." Noting that toward the end Poe's paranoid fears were fixed not on Baltimore but on Philadelphia, Frances Winwar remarks, "Fate, alas, has seldom been known to come where it leaves its most conspicuous calling card" (372). Hervey Allen (1926) foreshadows Poe's "fate" throughout his biography, remarking that "all accidents with him were weirdly consistent" (667). Marie Bonaparte's reading of Poe's death is similarly deterministic: the inevitable return to the mother is a Freudian variation on Baudelaire's bold, early assessment that Poe's death was "almost a suicide, — a suicide prepared for a long time" (101).

The image of Poe experiencing the sensations of his own fiction, as if in fulfillment of his destiny, might sound like a device borrowed from the many plays based on his life — and, in fact, it is. *Plumes in the Dust* (discussed in chapter 5) ends with Moran and his wife attending to Poe and praying while he deliriously quotes from his several of his works, concluding with "The Conqueror Worm" and "The Premature Burial." Dominic Argento's opera *The Voyage of Edgar Allan Poe* (1976) represents Poe's last hours as a hallucinatory journey through painful memories, spiked with allusions to his poetry and fiction, and presided over by Rufus Griswold.[6] A more recent play, Julian Wiles's *Nevermore! Edgar Allan Poe: The Final Mystery* (1995), subjects Poe to the torment of his own stories' terror after boarding what turns out to be a death ship.[7] Although *Nevermore!* presents a highly romanticized Poe and contains a number of ridiculous moments, Wiles cleverly makes his audience guess throughout the play whether Poe is hallucinating or actually transported to a nether region where he must bargain for his soul. Jeremiah Reynolds has a large role as Poe's friend who double-crosses him, delivering him into the hands of the Satanic Captain Nimrod. In a trick ending, taking place at Poe's funeral, Poe appears in the guise of his own gravedigger and is reunited with his true love, Annabel Lee:

ANNABEL: Can this really be happening? Can it really be true?

POE: We must make our own truth, remember . . .

ANNABEL: I remember, but how — ?

POE: I wrote a new ending . . .

(They kiss passionately. Lights crossfade leaving them in silhouette. At the same time, lights rise D on the coffin, drawing our attention to it. The sound of splintering wood is heard and a hand appears out of the top of the coffin. From the glove on its hand, we know it is REYNOLDS. The hand becomes more and more desperate, its owner slowly suffocating, and then, as death comes, the hand is stilled.)

While the macabre sensationalism of the final image is worthy of American International Pictures and *Tales from the Crypt,* this ending is also wonderfully Poe-esque, calling attention to Wiles's manipulation of the audience with the last line, "I wrote a new ending." Poe, meanwhile, as if speaking for his own biographers and mythmakers, reminds us that "we must make our own truth."

As a final example of this remaking, George Egon Hatvary's detective novel *The Murder of Edgar Allan Poe* (1997) features Dupin, here a personal friend and, in many respects, double of Poe, traveling from Paris to the Northeast Corridor of the U.S. to uncover foul play in the weeks following Poe's death. He succeeds, of course: the culprit turns out to be not Griswold, not Elmira Royster's brothers, but "Reynolds," which is a pseudonym for the fictitious W. H. Tyler.[8] Hatvary's Poe plagiarized some of his marginalia items from a book by "Reynolds"; more significantly, he used a series of Reynolds's brief plot outlines as the basis for his major tales. The egomaniacal Tyler/Reynolds poisons Poe to avenge these literary thefts; then, as Dupin begins to close in on him, the villain subjects him to a "Pit and the Pendulum"-derived imprisonment but fails to kill the great detective. Although Hatvary brings in numerous historical figures associated with Poe — including Dr. Moran, who helps Dupin exhume Poe and performs an autopsy — he makes few concessions to plausibility. Dupin's physical resemblance to Poe makes him irresistible to Elmira Royster, setting up a rather disconcerting sex scene. But as with other Poe-related mystery novels, *The Murder of Edgar Allan Poe* does not set out to be realistic so much as to evoke various Poe myths and motifs. Here the doubling of Poe with his fictional detective — an identification Poe himself was happy to exploit[9] — is literalized, to the point of having Poe's character sleep with Poe's would-be bride. The novel also literalizes the commonplace that the author lives on through his characters, enabling him, as Poe says in *Nevermore!*, to write a different ending.

In Poe's early satire "Loss of Breath" (1832) the narrator, Mr. Lackobreath, finds himself in the unlikely position of being both dead and alive, being unable to breathe and yet retaining consciousness and, at times, movement. The story can be read as a burlesque of what would be a predominant concern in much of Poe's fiction and poetry: in what sense, if any, does life continue after death? Mr. Lackobreath (or his corpse) is stuffed into a coach, thrown out of a tavern, experimented on by doctors, maimed by a cat, mistaken for a thief and executed, and finally buried — alive, as far as he is concerned — in a vault where he encounters another unfortunate soul, Mr. Windenough. Together they make themselves heard by two newspaper men:

> The united strength of our resuscitated voices was soon sufficiently apparent. Scissors, the Whig Editor, republished a treatise upon "the nature and origin of subterranean noises." A reply — rejoinder — confutation — and justification — followed in the columns of a Democratic Gazette. It was not until the opening of the vault to decide the controversy, that the appearance of Mr. Windenough and myself proved both parties to have been decidedly in the wrong. (*CW* II:74)

I, too, find it irresistible to link Poe's death, and afterlife, with his fiction: like the resurrected Lackobreath, Poe — that is, his writing — still insists on being heard, but it is largely the curiosity of other writers, eager to settle or create a controversy, that resurrects Poe again and again. The open space at the end of his biography and continuing debates over his cause of death create an uncanny tribute to a writer whose work sometimes expressed faith in some sort of postmortem transcendence or reincarnation but at other times mocked that belief, as in "Loss of Breath." Poe's dead don't stay buried, but do they return on their own power, or only through the will of those who keep them alive through mourning (or who exhume them to settle an argument)? And what form do the dead take as they become objects of fascination to those who recreate them again and again? Poe had more than one answer to those questions, so it is only fitting that there have been so many answers, not just to the questions surrounding his death, but to those surrounding his life and works.

Notes

[1] See Dwight Thomas and David K. Jackson, *The Poe Log: A Documentary Life of Edgar Allan Poe* (Boston: G. K. Hall, 1987), 843–46; Arthur Hobson Quinn, *Edgar Allan Poe: A Critical Biography* (1941; reprint, New York: Cooper Square, 1969), 637–41; Kenneth Silverman, *Edgar A. Poe: Mournful and Never-ending Remembrance* (New York: HarperCollins, 1991), 433–36. The best summary of what is known and what has been conjectured about Poe's death can be found at the Edgar Allan Poe Society of Baltimore website, www.eapoe.org/geninfo/poedeath.htm. John Evangelist Walsh's book *Midnight Dreary: The Mysterious Death of Edgar Allan Poe* (New Brunswick, NJ, and London: Rutgers UP, 1998) contains a wealth of information regarding Poe's disappearance and death, but unlike the sources listed above, Walsh presents the facts in support of his own theory as to the cause of Poe's death.

[2] See Arno Karlen's chapter on Poe's medical condition in *Napoleon's Glands and Other Ventures in Biohistory* (Boston and Toronto: Little, Brown, 1984), as well as the Poe Society of Baltimore website. I asked Jeffrey Savoy of the Poe Society if anyone had suggested exhuming Poe to try to determine cause of death. He replied, "The chief problem with the idea of exhuming Poe's remains for testing is that they are, as I understand it, in a box directly beneath the monument. Although the monument is made of marble, it has grown rather brittle over the years and I doubt that permission to move it could be obtained, especially since the condition of Poe's remains is unknown. There is probably little or no tissue left" (personal e-mail, 28 Jan. 2003).

[3] See, for instance, Poe to George Eveleth, 4 Jan. 1848 (*The Letters of Edgar Allan Poe*, ed. John Ward Ostrom [New York: Gordion, 1966], 2:356); Poe to Maria Clemm, 7 July 1849 (*Letters*, 2:452); and Mary Louise Shew's recollection to John H. Ingram (Thomas and Jackson, *The Poe Log*, 694).

[4] Quinn, in his careful and detailed 1941 biography (*Edgar Allan Poe*), notes the cooping theory but gives it little credence (639). Silverman, in the definitive post-Quinn Poe biography (*Edgar A. Poe*), does not even mention it.

[5] In *A Defense of Edgar Allan Poe: Life, Character, and Dying Declarations of the Poet* (Washington, DC: William F. Boogher, 1885), John J. Moran claims that Poe was not intoxicated while under his care, but reduces the period of his care to sixteen hours. His revised account of Poe's dying words is more dramatic than anything later biographers attempted:

> I then said, "Mr. Poe, I must tell you that you are near your end. Have you any wish or word for friends?
>
> He said, "Nevermore."
>
> At length he exclaimed: "O God! Is there no ransom for the deathless spirit?"
>
> I said, "Yes, look to your Saviour; there is mercy for you and all mankind. God is love and the gift is free."

The dying man then said impressively, "He who arched the heavens and upholds the universe, has His decrees legibly written upon the frontlet of every human being, and upon demons incarnate." (72)

[6] A synopsis, reprinted from the original program, of *The Voyage of Edgar Allan Poe* is available at the Minnesota Public Radio webpage: http://music.mpr.org/features/0210_argento/poe_synopsis.shtml. See also John E. Reilly, "Poe in American Drama: Versions of the Man," in *Poe and Our Times,* ed. Bejamin F. Fisher (Baltimore: Edgar Allan Poe Society, 1986), 26–27; Reilly also reports on a play from the 1980s by Ted Davis entitled *Poe: A Gathering Storm,* which was also built around hallucinations suffered by Poe during his last hours (27–28). A 1928 short story, "In Which an Author and His Character Are Well Met," by Vincent Starrett (in *The Man Who Called Himself Poe,* ed. Sam Moskowitz [Garden City, NY: Doubleday, 1969] 67–85), uses a similar plot device to depict Poe's death.

[7] *Nevermore!* has been produced twice by Charleston Stage Company, Charleston, SC, and performed (to full houses) at the Dock Street Theatre, which was already in operation when Poe was stationed near Charleston in 1827–28. The play invokes a Charlestonian myth that "Annabel Lee" was inspired by Poe's memory of a Charleston belle, most often identified as Annabel Lee Ravenel.

[8] Hatvary's choice of the name W. H. Tyler is intriguing. When Poe was solving cryptograms in the pages of *Graham's* in 1841, he left unsolved two cryptograms submitted by W. B. Tyler. One was solved finally in the early 1990s, the other in 2000. Some Poe scholars have speculated that Poe was W. B. Tyler, but the evidence is inconclusive. See Stephen Rachman, "Poe, Secret Writing, and Magazine Culture: In Search of W. B. Tyler," paper presented at the Modern Language Association Annual Meeting, New Orleans, LA, 27 Dec. 2001.

[9] See Poe's letter to Philip Pendleton Cooke, in which he admits that "people think [the tales of ratiocination] are more ingenious than they are" and that "The reader is made to confound the ingenuity of the suppositious Dupin with that of the writer of the story" (*Letters,* 2:328).

A Selected List of Works by Poe

Books by Poe Published During His Lifetime

Tamerlane and Other Poems. Boston: Calvin F. S. Thomas, 1827.

Al Aaraaf, Tamerlane and Minor Poems. Baltimore: Hatch and Dunning, 1829.

Poems by Edgar A. Poe . . . Second Edition. New York: Elam Bliss, 1831.

The Narrative of Arthur Gordon Pym. New York: Harper and Brothers, 1838.

The Conchologist's First Book. [By Thomas Wyatt.] Philadelphia: Haswell, Barrington, and Haswell, 1839.

Tales of the Grotesque and Arabesque. Philadelphia: Lea and Blanchard, 1840.

The Prose Romances of Edgar A. Poe. Philadelphia: William H. Graham, 1843.

Tales. New York: Wiley and Putman, 1845.

The Raven and Other Poems. New York: Wiley and Putman, 1845.

Eureka: A Prose Poem. New York: Putnam, 1848.

Selected Posthumous Editions

Baudelaire, Charles, trans. *Histoires Extraordinaires. Nouvelles Histoires Extraordinaires. Aventures d'Arthur Gordon Pym. Eureka. Histoires Grotesques and Sérieuses*. Paris: Michel Lévy, 1856–65.

Benton, Richard P., ed. *Eureka*. Hartford, CT: Transcendental Books, 1974.

Griswold, Rufus Wilmot, ed. *The Works of the Late Edgar Allan Poe*. 4 vols. New York: J. S. Redfield, 1850–56.

Harrison, James A., ed. *The Complete Works of Edgar Allan Poe*. New York: Thomas Y. Crowell, 1902–3. Reprint, New York: AMS Press, 1965, 1979.

Levine, Stuart, and Susan Levine, eds. *The Short Fiction of Edgar Allan Poe: An Annotated Edition*. Indianapolis: Bobbs-Merrill, 1976. Reprint, Champaign: U of Illinois P, 1990.

Mabbott, Thomas Ollive, ed. *The Collected Works of Edgar Allan Poe*. 3 vols. Cambridge, MA: Harvard UP, 1969–78. Reprint, Urbana and Chicago: U of Illinois P, 2000.

Ostrom, John Ward, ed. *The Letters of Edgar Allan Poe*. 2 vols. Cambridge, MA: Harvard UP, 1848. Reprint, New York: Gordian, 1966.

Pollin, Burton R., ed. *The Collected Writings of Edgar Allan Poe*. 5 vols. New York: Gordian, 1981–97.

Quinn, Patrick F., ed. *Poetry and Tales*. New York: Library of America, 1984.

Quinn, Patrick F., and G. R. Thompson, eds. *Poetry, Tales, and Selected Essays*. New York: Library of America, 1996.

Stedman, Edmund Clarence, and George Edward Woodberry, eds. *The Works of Edgar Allan Poe*. Chicago: Stone and Kimball, 1895. Reprint, New York: Scribner's, 1914.

Thompson, G. R., ed. *Essays and Reviews*. New York: Library of America, 1984.

Varner, John Grier, ed. *Edgar Allan Poe and the Philadelphia* Saturday Courier. Charlottesville: U of Virginia, 1933.

Wilbur, Richard, ed. *Poe: Complete Poems*. New York: Dell, 1959.

Works Cited

Abel, Darrel. "A Key to the House of Usher." *University of Toronto Quarterly* 18 (1949): 176–85.

Alan Parsons Project. *Tales of Mystery and Imagination: Edgar Allan Poe*. Poly-Gram, 1976.

Allen, Hervey. *Israfel: The Life and Times of Edgar Allan Poe*. 1926. Rev. ed. New York: Farrar and Rinehart, 1934.

Allen, Michael. *Poe and the British Magazine Tradition*. New York: Oxford UP, 1969.

Appignanesi, Lisa, and John Forrester. *Freud's Women*. New York: Basic Books, 1992.

Auerbach, Jonathan. *The Romance of Failure: First-Person Fictions of Poe, Hawthorne, and James*. New York: Oxford UP, 1989.

Auster, Paul. *City of Glass*. 1985. *The New York Trilogy*. New York, Penguin, 1990.

Avallone, Michael. "The Man Who Thought He Was Poe." In *The Man Who Called Himself Poe*, ed. Sam Moskowitz, 123–38. Garden City, NY: Doubleday, 1969.

Babener, Liahna Klenman. "'The Shadow's Shadow': The Motif of the Double in Edgar Allan Poe's 'The Purloined Letter.'" *Mystery and Detection Annual* 1972: 21–32. Reprinted in *The Purloined Poe: Lacan, Derrida, and Psychoanalytic Reading*, ed. John P. Muller, and William J. Richardson, 323–34. Baltimore and London: Johns Hopkins UP, 1988.

Bandy, W. T. "Dr. Moran and the Poe-Reynolds Myth." In *Myths and Reality: The Mysterious Mr. Poe*, ed. Bejamin F. Fisher, 26–36. Baltimore: Edgar Allan Poe Society, 1987.

Barrett, Lindon. "Presence of Mind: Detection and Racialization in 'The Murders in the Rue Morgue.'" In *Romancing the Shadow: Poe and Race*, ed. J. Gerald Kennedy and Liliane Weissberg, 157–76. New York: Oxford UP, 2001.

Baudelaire, Charles. *Baudelaire on Poe*. Trans. and ed. Lois Hyslop and Francis E. Hyslop, Jr. State College, PA: Bald Eagle, 1952.

Baym, Nina. "Portrayal of Women in American Literature, 1790–1870." In *What Manner of Woman: Essays on English and American Life and Literature,* ed. Marlene Springer, 211–34. New York: New York UP, 1977.

Beatty, Richmond Croom, et al., eds. *The Literature of the South.* Chicago: Scott Foresman, 1952.

Beaver, Harold. Introduction to *The Narrative of Arthur Gordon Pym of Nantucket,* by Edgar Allan Poe, 7–30. Harmondsworth: Penguin, 1975.

Benfey, Christopher. "Poe and the Unreadable: 'The Black Cat' and 'The Tell-Tale Heart.'" In *New Essays on Poe's Major Tales,* ed. Kenneth Silverman, 27–44. Cambridge and New York: Cambridge UP, 1993.

Benton, Richard P. "Is Poe's 'The Assignation' a Hoax?" *Nineteenth-Century Fiction* 18 (1963): 193–97.

Bertin, Celia. *Marie Bonaparte: A Life.* New York: Harcourt Brace Jovanovich, 1982.

Beuka, Robert A. "Jacksonian Man of Parts: Dismemberment, Manhood, and Race in 'The Man That Was Used Up.'" *Edgar Allan Poe Review* 3.1 (2002): 27–44.

Bittner, William. *Poe: A Biography.* Boston: Little, Brown, 1962.

Blake, David Haven. "'The Man That Was Used Up': Edgar Allan Poe and the Ends of Captivity." *Nineteenth-Century Literature* 57 (2002): 323–49.

Bloom, Clive. *Reading Poe Reading Freud: The Romantic Imagination in Crisis.* New York: St. Martin's, 1988.

Bonaparte, Marie. *The Life and Works of Edgar Allan Poe: A Psychoanalytical Interpretation.* Trans. John Rodker. London: Imago, 1949.

Borges, Jorge Luis. *Labyrinths.* New York: New Directions, 1964.

Boyd, Ernest. *Literary Blasphemies.* 1927. New York: Greenwood, 1969.

Briggs, Charles F. "The Personality of Poe." *The Independent* (13 Dec. 1877): 1–2.

Bronfen, Elisabeth. "Risky Resemblances: On Repetition, Mourning, and Representation." In *Death and Representation,* ed. Sarah Webster Goodwin and Elisabeth Bronfen, 103–129. Baltimore and London: Johns Hopkins UP, 1993.

Bronson, Walter C. *A Short History of American Literature.* Boston: Heath, 1900.

Brooks, Cleanth. *The Well-Wrought Urn: Studies in the Structure of Poetry.* New York: Harcourt, Brace and World, 1947.

Brooks, Cleanth, and Robert Penn Warren. *Understanding Fiction.* Englewood Cliffs, NJ: Prentice Hall, 1946.

————. *Understanding Poetry*. New York: Henry Holt, 1938.

Brooks, Peter. "The Idea of a Psychoanalytic Literary Criticism." In *Discourse in Psychoanalysis and Literature*, ed. Shlomith Rimmon-Kenan, 1–18. London and New York: Methuen, 1987.

Burwick, Frederick L. "Edgar Allan Poe: The Sublime and the Grotesque." *Prisms: Essays in Romanticism* 8 (2000): 67–123.

Butler, David W. "Hypochondriasis: Mental Alienation and Romantic Idealism in Poe's Gothic Tales." *American Literature* 48 (1976): 1–12.

Cagliero, Roberto. "Poe's Interiors: The Theme of Usurpation in 'The Cask of Amontillado.'" *Edgar Allan Poe Review* 2 (Spring 2001): 30–36.

Campbell, Killis. *The Mind of Poe and Other Studies*. 1933. Reprint, New York: Russell and Russell, 1962.

————. "Poe's Treatment of the Negro and of the Negro Dialect." *[University of Texas] Studies in English* 16 (1936): 106–114.

Cantalupo, Barbara. "Poe's Female Narrators." *Southern Quarterly* 39.4 (2001): 49–57.

Carlson, Eric W., ed. *A Companion to Poe Studies.* Westport, CT: Greenwood, 1996.

————, ed. *The Recognition of Edgar Allan Poe*. Ann Arbor: U of Michigan P, 1966.

Casper, Scott E. *Constructing American Lives: Biography and Culture in Nineteenth Century America*. Chapel Hill: U of North Carolina P, 1999.

Cooke, Alice L. "The Popular Conception of Poe, 1850–1890." *University of Texas Studies in English* 22 (1942): 145–70.

Corman, Roger, dir. *The Fall of the House of Usher*. Perf. Vincent Price, Mark Damon, Myrna Fahey. American International, 1960.

————. *The Masque of the Red Death*. Perf. Vincent Price, Hazel Court, Jane Asher. American International, 1964.

————. *The Pit and the Pendulum*. Perf. Vincent Price, John Kerr, Barbara Steele. American International, 1961.

Cox, James M. "Edgar Poe: Style as Pose." *Virginia Quarterly Review* 44 (1968): 67–89.

Cuddon, J. A. *The Penguin Dictionary of Literary Terms and Literary Theory*. 4th ed. London and New York: Penguin, 1999.

Dargan, Olive. *The Raven*. Typescript. 1904. Library of Congress.

Dauber, Kenneth. *The Idea of Authorship in America: Democratic Poetics from Franklin to Melville.* Madison: U of Wisconsin P, 1990.

Davidson, Edward H. *Poe: A Critical Study.* Cambridge, MA: Harvard UP, 1957.

Davidson, J. W. "Edgar A. Poe." *Russell's Magazine* 2 (1857): 163.

Davidson, James A. "Some Thoughts on Alfred Hitchcock and Vladimir Nabokov." *Images* 3 (May 1997): 4 pp. 17 Jan. 2003. http://www.imagesjournal.com/issue03/features/hitchnab1.htm.

Davis-Undiano, Robert Con. "Poe and the American Affiliation with Freemasonry." *symploke* 7 (1999): 119–38.

Dayan, Joan. "Amorous Bondage: Poe, Ladies and Slaves." In *The American Face of Edgar Allan Poe,* ed. Shawn Rosenheim and Stephen Rachman, 179–209. Baltimore and London: Johns Hopkins UP, 1995.

———. *Fables of Mind: An Inquiry into Poe's Fiction.* New York: Oxford UP, 1987.

———. "Poe's Women: A Feminist Poe?" *Poe Studies/Dark Romanticism* 26 (1993): 1–12.

———. "Romance and Race." In *The Columbia History of the American Novel,* ed. Emory Elliott. New York: Columbia UP, 1991.

Derby, James C. *Fifty Years Among Author, Books, and Publishers.* New York: Carleton, 1884.

Derrida, Jacques. "The Purveyor of Truth." Trans. Alan Bass. In *The Purloined Poe: Lacan, Derrida, and Psychoanalytic Reading,* ed. John P. Muller, and William J. Richardson, 173–212. Baltimore and London: Johns Hopkins UP, 1988.

DeVoto, Bernard. "At the Canon's Mouth." *Saturday Review,* 3 April 1937: 8.

Dobson, Joanne. *The Raven and the Nightingale.* 1999. New York: Bantam, 2000.

Doctorow, E. L. Address to the International Poe Conference, Goucher College, Towson, MD, 5 Oct. 2002.

Donnay, Albert. "Poisoned Poe: Evidence that Poe May Have Suffered from Neurasthenia (aka Multiple Chemical Sensitivity and Chronic Fatigue Syndrome) as a Result of Exposure to Illuminating Gas." Paper presented at the International Edgar Allan Poe Conference, Richmond, VA, 9 Oct. 1999.

Doyle, Arthur Conan. *Through the Magic Door.* Garden City and New York: Doubleday, Page, 1915.

Doyle, Jacqueline. "(Dis)Figuring Woman: Edgar Allan Poe's 'Berenice.'" *Poe Studies* 26 (1993): 13–21.

[Duganne, A. J. H.] "A Mirror for Authors." *Holden's Dollar Magazine* 3 (1849): 22.

Dumenil, Lynn. *The Modern Temper: American Culture and Society in the 1920s.* New York: Hill and Wang, 1995.

Eddings, Dennis, ed. *The Naiad Voice: Essays on Poe's Satiric Hoaxing.* Port Washington, NY: Associated Faculty, 1983.

"Edgar A. Poe." *The Eclectic* 25 (May 1852): 115–19.

"Edgar Allan Poe." *Graham's Magazine* (Feb. 1854): 219, 220.

"Edgar Allan Poe and the Hall of Fame." *Current Literature* 39 (1905): 613–14.

Elbert, Monika. "Poe's Gothic Mother and the Incubation of Language." *Poe Studies* 26 (1993): 22–33.

Eliot, T. S. "From Poe to Valéry." *Hudson Review* 2 (1949): 327– 42. Reprinted in *The Recognition of Edgar Allan Poe,* ed. Eric W. Carlson, 205–220. Ann Arbor: U of Michigan P, 1966.

Elmer, Jonathan. *Reading at the Social Limit: Affect, Mass Culture, and Edgar Allan Poe.* Stanford, CA: Stanford UP, 1995.

Elton, William. *A Glossary of the New Criticism.* Chicago: Modern Poetry Association, 1949.

English, Thomas Dunn. "Reminiscences of Poe (IV)." *The Independent* (5 Nov. 1896): 4–5.

Epstein, Jean, dir. *La Chute de la Maison Usher.* Jean Epstein Films, 1928.

Fagin, N. Bryllion. *The Histrionic Mr. Poe.* Baltimore: Johns Hopkins UP, 1949.

Fairchild, Francis. "A Mad Man of Letters," *Scribner's* (Oct. 1875): 690–99.

Faulkner, William. *The Portable Faulkner.* Ed. Malcolm Cowley. New York; Penguin, 1977.

Feidelson, Charles, Jr. *Symbolism and American Literature.* Chicago and London: U of Chicago P, 1953.

Fellini, Federico, dir. "Toby Dammit." In *Histoires Extraordinaires,* aka *Spirits of the Dead.* Dir. Roger Vadim, Louis Malle, and Federico Fellini. Perf. Terence Stamp, Jane Fonda, Alain Delon, Brigitte Bardot. Films Marceau/ Concinor/Pea Cinematografica, 1967.

Felman, Shoshana. "On Reading Poetry: Reflections on the Limits and Possibilities of Psychoanalytical Approaches." In *The Purloined Poe: Lacan, Derrida, and Psychoanalytic Reading,* ed. John P. Muller, and William J. Richardson, 133–56. Baltimore and London: Johns Hopkins UP, 1988. Reprint of "The Case of Poe: Applications — Implications of Psychoanalysis." In *The Literary Freud,* ed. Joseph H. Smith. New Haven: Yale UP, 1980.

Fetterly, Judith. "Reading about Reading: 'A Jury of Her Peers,' 'The Murders in the Rue Morgue,' and 'The Yellow Wallpaper.'" In *Gender and Reading: Essays on Readers, Texts, and Contexts,* ed. Elizabeth A. Flynn and Patrocinio P. Schweickart, 147–64. Baltimore and London: Johns Hopkins UP, 1986.

Fiedler, Leslie. *Love and Death in the American Novel.* 1960. Rev. ed. New York: Stein and Day, 1966.

Fisher, Bejamin F. IV. "Fugitive Poe References: A Bibliography." *Poe Studies* 14.2 (1981): 25–30; 15.1 (1982): 18– 22; 16.1 (1983): 7–12; 17.1 (1984): 11–21.

———. "Poe and Detection." *PSA Newsletter* 24.1 (1996): 4–7; 24.2 (1996): 3–6.

———. "Poe and Detection [Again]." *Edgar Allan Poe Review* 1.1 (2000): 17–23.

———, ed. *Myths and Reality: The Mysterious Mr. Poe.* Baltimore: Edgar Allan Poe Society, 1987.

———, ed. *Poe and Our Times.* Baltimore: Edgar Allan Poe Society, 1986.

Forclaz, Roger. "Psychoanalysis and Edgar Allan Poe: A Critique of the Bonaparte Thesis." In *Critical Essays on Edgar Allan Poe,* ed. Eric W. Carlson, 187–95. Boston: G. K. Hall, 1987.

Forrest, William Mentzel. *Biblical Allusions in Poe.* New York: Macmillan, 1928.

Freedman, William. "Poe's Oval Portrait of 'The Oval Portrait.'" *Poe Studies* 34 (2001): 7–12.

Friedlander, Louis, dir. *The Raven.* Perf. Bela Lugosi, Boris Karloff. Universal, 1935.

Fuqua, Jonathan Scott, Steven Parke, and Stephen John Phillips. *In the Shadow of Edgar Allan Poe.* New York: Vertigo/DC Comics, 2002.

Gallop, Jane. *Reading Lacan.* Ithaca and London: Cornell UP, 1985.

Gardner, Jared. *Master Plots: Race and the Founding of American Literature, 1787–1845.* Baltimore and London: Johns Hopkins UP, 1998.

Gargano, James W. "Poe's 'Ligeia': Dream and Destruction." *College English* 23 (1962): 337–42.

———. "The Question of Poe's Narrators." *College English* 25 (1963): 177–81.

Gilfillan, George. "Edgar Allan Poe." *Galleries of Literary Portraits*. Vol. 1. Edinburgh: Hogg, 1856.

Gill, William F. *The Life and Times of Edgar Allan Poe*. London: Chatto and Windus, 1878.

Gilmore, Paul. *The Genuine Article: Race, Mass Culture, and American Literary Manhood*. Durham, NC, and London: Duke UP, 2001.

Ginsberg, Lesley. "Slavery and the Gothic Horror of Poe's 'The Black Cat.'" In *American Gothic: New Intervention in a National Narrative*, ed. Robert K. Martin and Eric Savoy, 99–128. Iowa City: U of Iowa P, 1998. 99–128.

Glasgow, Ellen. *A Certain Measure: An Interpretation of Prose Fiction*. New York: Harcourt, Brace, 1943.

Goddu, Teresa. *Gothic America: Narrative, History, and Nation*. New York: Columbia UP, 1997.

———. "Poe, Sensationalism, and Slavery." In *The Cambridge Companion to Edgar Allan Poe*, ed. Kevin J. Hayes, 92–112. Cambridge and New York: Cambridge UP, 2002.

———. "Rethinking Race and Slavery in Poe Studies." *Poe Studies* 33.1–2 (2000): 15–18.

"The Graduate." *Northern Exposure*. CBS. 8 March 1995. (#104)

Graham, George Rex. "The Genius and Characteristics of the Late Edgar Allan Poe." *Graham's Magazine* (Feb. 1854): 216–25.

Gray, Richard. "'I Am a Virginian': Edgar Allan Poe and the South." In *Edgar Allan Poe: The Design of Order*, ed. A. Robert Lee, 182– 201. London: Vision; Totowa, NJ: Barnes & Noble, 1987.

———. *Southern Aberrations: Writers of the American South and the Problems of Regionalism*. Baton Rouge: Louisiana State UP, 2000.

Griffith, Clark. "Poe's 'Ligeia' and the English Romantics." *University of Toronto Quarterly* 24 (1954): 8–25.

Griffith, D. W., dir. *The Avenging Conscience*. Perf. Henry B. Walthall, Spottiswoode Aiken, Blanche Sweet. Essanay, 1914.

Griswold, Rufus Wilmot. "Death of Edgar Allan Poe." New York *Daily Tribune* 9 Oct. 1849. Reprinted in *Edgar Allan Poe: The Critical Heritage*, ed. Ian Walker. London and New York: Routledge, 1986.

Guerin, Wilfred L., et al., eds. *A Handbook of Critical Approaches to Literature*. 4th ed. New York: Oxford UP, 1999.

Haining, Paul, ed. *The Edgar Allan Poe Scrapbook*. London: New English Library, 1977.

Halleck, Reuben Post. *History of American Literature*. New York: American Book, 1911.

Halliburton, David. *Edgar Allan Poe: A Phenomenological View*. Princeton, NJ: Princeton UP, 1973.

Hart, James. *The Popular Book: A History of America's Literary Taste*. Berkeley: U of California P, 1961.

Harvey, Irene. "Structures of Exemplarity in Poe, Freud, Lacan, and Derrida." In *The Purloined Poe: Lacan, Derrida, and Psychoanalytic Reading*, ed. John P. Muller, and William J. Richardson, 252–67. Baltimore and London: Johns Hopkins UP, 1988.

Hatvary, George Egon. *The Murder of Edgar Allan Poe*. New York: Carroll and Graf, 1997.

Hawthorne, Julian. "My Adventure with Edgar Allan Poe." *Lippincott's Magazine* 48 (1891): 240–46. Reprinted in *The Man Who Called Himself Poe*, ed. Sam Moskowitz, 54–66. Garden City, NY: Doubleday, 1969.

Hayes, Kevin J. "One-Man Modernist." In *The Cambridge Companion to Edgar Allan Poe*, ed. Kevin J. Hayes, 225–40. Cambridge and New York: Cambridge UP, 2002.

———. *Poe and the Printed Word*. Cambridge and New York: Cambridge UP, 2000.

———, ed. *The Cambridge Companion to Edgar Allan Poe*. Cambridge and New York: Cambridge UP, 2002.

Hazelton, George, Jr. *The Raven: A Play in Four Acts and a Tableau*. 1895. New York: n.p., 1903.

Hemingway, Ernest. *Green Hills of Africa*. New York: Scribners, 1935.

Hendershot, Cyndy. "Domesticity and Horror in the *House of Usher* and *Village of the Damned*." *Quarterly Review of Film and Video* 17 (2000): 221–27.

Herndl, Diane Price. *Invalid Women: Figuring Feminine Illness in American Fiction and Culture, 1840–1940*. Chapel Hill and London: U of North Carolina P, 1993.

Hervey, John L. "Is Poe 'Rejected' in America?" *The Dial* (Feb. 1899): 73.

Hirsch, David H. "The Pit and the Apocalypse." *Sewanee Review* 76 (1968): 632–52.

Hjortsberg, William. *Nevermore*. 1994. New York: St. Martin's, 1996.

Hoffman, Daniel. *Poe Poe Poe Poe Poe Poe Poe*. 1972. Reprint, Baton Rouge and London: Louisiana State UP, 1998.

Hoffman, Stephen K. "Sailing into the Self: Jung, Poe, and 'MS. Found in a Bottle'" *Tennessee Studies in Literature* 26 (1981): 66–74.

Holland, Norman N. "Re-covering 'The Purloined Letter': Reading as a Personal Transaction." In *The Reader in the Text: Essays on Audience and Interpretation*, ed. Susan R. Suleiman and Inge Crossman, 350–70. Princeton, NJ: Princeton UP, 1980. Reprinted in *The Purloined Poe: Lacan, Derrida, and Psychoanalytic Reading*, ed. John P. Muller, and William J. Richardson, 307–22. Baltimore and London: Johns Hopkins UP, 1988.

Hopkins, Frederick M. "Shall We Preserve the Poe Cottage at Fordham?" *Review of Reviews* 13 (1896): 458–62.

Howells, William Dean. *Literary Friends and Acquaintance: A Personal Retrospect of American Authorship*. Ed. David F. Hiatt and Edwin H. Cady. Bloomington and London: Indiana UP, 1968.

Hubbell, Jay B. *The South in American Literature, 1607–1900*. Durham, NC: Duke UP, 1954.

———. *Who Are the Major American Writers?* Durham, NC: Duke UP, 1972.

Hubbell, Jay B., et. al. *Eight American Authors: A Review of Research and Criticism*. New York: Modern Language Association, 1956.

Hubbs, Valentine C. "The Struggle of Wills in Poe's 'William Wilson.'" *Studies in American Fiction* 11 (1983): 73–79.

Huckel, Oliver. "The Unique Genius of Poe's Poetry." In *Edgar Allan Poe: A Centenary Tribute* (1909), ed. Heinrich Ewald Buchholz, 45–54. London: Folcraft Library, 1972.

Hull, William Doyle II. "A Canon of the Critical Works of Edgar Allan Poe with a Study of Poe as Editor and Reviewer." Ph.D. dissertation. University of Virginia, 1941.

Hutcherson, Dudley R. "Poe's Reputation in England and America, 1850–1909." *American Literature* 14 (1942): 211–33.

Huxley, Aldous. "Vulgarity in Literature." *Saturday Review of Literature* (27 Sept. 1930): 158–59. Reprinted in *The Recognition of Edgar Allan Poe*, ed. Eric W. Carlson, 160–67. Ann Arbor: U of Michigan P, 1966.

Hyneman, Esther F. *Edgar Allan Poe: An Annotated Bibliography of Books and Articles in English, 1827–1973*. Boston: G. K. Hall, 1974.

Inge, M. Thomas. "Poe and the Comics Connection." *Edgar Allan Poe Review* 2.1 (2001): 2–29.

Ingram, John Henry. *Edgar Allan Poe: His Life, Letters and Opinions.* London: Hagg, 1880.

Irwin, John T. *American Hieroglyphics: The Symbol of Egyptian Hieroglyphics in the American Renaissance.* New Haven and London: Yale UP, 1980.

———. *The Mystery to a Solution: Poe, Borges, and the Analytic Detective Story.* Baltimore and London: Johns Hopkins UP, 1994.

Jackson, Leon. "'Behold Our Literary Mohawk, Poe': Literary Nationalism and the 'Indianation' of Antebellum American Culture." Forthcoming in *ESQ.*

———. "'The Italics Are Mine': Edgar Allan Poe and the Semiotics of Print." In *Illuminating Letters: Typography and Literary Interpretation*, eds. Megan Benton and Paul Gutjahr, 139–61. Amherst: U of Massachusetts P, 2001.

Jacobs, Robert D. "Edgar Allan Poe." In *The History of Southern Literature*, ed. Louis D. Rubin et al., 127–35. Baton Rouge and London: Louisiana State UP, 1985.

———. *Poe, Journalist and Critic.* Baton Rouge and London: Louisiana State UP, 1969.

Jirgens, Karl E. "Lacan, Jacques-Marie Emile." In *Encyclopedia of Contemporary Literary Theory*, ed. Irena R. Makaryk, 396–98. Toronto: U of Toronto P, 1993.

Johnson, Barbara. "The Frame of Reference: Poe, Lacan, Derrida." In *The Purloined Poe: Lacan, Derrida, and Psychoanalytic Reading*, ed. John P. Muller and William J. Richardson, 213–51. Baltimore and London: Johns Hopkins UP, 1988. Reprint of "Literature and Psychoanalysis: The Question of Reading — Otherwise." *Yale French Studies* 55–56 (1977): 457–505.

Jones, Paul Christian. "The Danger of Sympathy: Edgar Allan Poe's 'Hop-Frog' and the Abolitionist Rhetoric of Pathos." *Journal of American Studies* 35 (2001): 239–54.

Jordan, Cynthia S. *Second Stories: The Politics of Language, Form, and Gender in Early American Fiction.* Chapel Hill and London: U of North Carolina P, 1989.

Joswick, Thomas. "Moods of Mind: The Tales of Detection, Crime, and Punishment." In *A Companion to Poe Studies*, ed. Eric W. Carlson, 236–56. Westport, CT: Greenwood, 1996.

Kammen, Michael. *Mystic Chords of Memory: The Transformation of Tradition in American Culture.* New York: Vintage, 1993.

Kaplan, Charles, and William Anderson. *Criticism: Major Statements.* Boston: Bedford, 2000.

Kaplan, Morton, and Robert Kloss. *The Unspoken Motive: A Guide to Psychoanalytic Criticism.* New York: Free Press, 1973.

Kaplan, Sidney. Introduction to *The Narrative of Arthur Gordon Pym of Nantucket,* by Edgar Allan Poe. New York: Hill and Wang, 1960.

Karlen, Arno. *Napoleon's Glands and Other Ventures in Biohistory.* Boston and Toronto: Little, Brown, 1984.

Kennedy, J. Gerald. *The American Turn of Edgar Allan Poe.* Baltimore: Edgar Allan Poe Society and the Library of the University of Baltimore, 2001.

———. Introduction to *Arthur Gordon Pym and Related Tales,* by Edgar Allan Poe. Oxford World's Classics. New York: Oxford UP, 1994.

———. Introduction to *A Historical Guide to Edgar Allan Poe.* Ed. J. Gerald Kennedy. New York: Oxford UP, 2001. 3–17.

———. "The Limits of Reason: Poe's Deluded Detectives." *American Literature* 47 (1975): 184–96.

———. *"The Narrative of Arthur Gordon Pym" and the Abyss of Interpretation.* New York: Twayne, 1995.

———. *Poe, Death, and the Life of Writing.* New Haven and London: Yale UP, 1987.

———. "Poe, 'Ligeia,' and the Problem of Dying Women." In *New Essays on Poe's Major Tales,* ed. Kenneth Silverman, 113–29. Cambridge and New York: Cambridge UP, 1993.

———. "'Trust No Man': Poe, Douglass, and the Culture of Slavery." In *Romancing the Shadow: Poe and Race,* ed. J. Gerald Kennedy and Liliane Weissberg, 225–57. New York: Oxford UP, 2001.

———, ed. *A Historical Guide to Edgar Allan Poe.* New York: Oxford UP, 2001.

Kennedy, J. Gerald, and Liliane Weissberg, eds. *Romancing the Shadow: Poe and Race.* New York: Oxford UP, 2001.

Kent, Charles W., ed. *The Unveiling of the Bust of Edgar Allan Poe in the Library of the University of Virginia.* Lynchburg, VA: J. P. Bell, 1901.

Kent, Charles W., and John S. Patton. *The Book of the Poe Centenary.* Charlottesville: UP of Virginia, 1909.

Ketchum, Arthur. *The Raven: A Play in Five Acts.* Typescript. Library of Congress.

Ketterer, David. *The Rationale of Deception in Poe*. Baton Rouge and London: Louisiana State UP, 1979.

"Knowing Poe." 2002. Maryland Public Television. 16 May 2003. http:// knowingpoe.thinkport.org/library/news/ravens.asp.

Kopley, Richard. "The Hidden Journey of Arthur Gordon Pym." In *Studies in the American Renaissance* 1982, ed. Joel Myerson, 29–51. Charlottesville: UP of Virginia, 1982.

———. Introduction to *The Narrative of Arthur Gordon Pym of Nantucket*, by Edgar Allan Poe. Penguin Classics. New York: Penguin, 1999.

———. *Poe and the Philadelphia Saturday News*. Baltimore: Enoch Pratt Free Library, Edgar Allan Poe Society, and the Library of the University of Baltimore, 1991.

———. "The '*Very* Profound Under-current' of *Arthur Gordon Pym*." *Studies in the American Renaissance* 1987, ed. Joel Myerson, 143–75. Charlottesville: UP of Virginia, 1987.

———, ed. *Poe's "Pym": Critical Explorations*. Durham, NC: Duke UP, 1992.

Kot, Paula. "Feminist 'Re-Visioning' of the Tales of Women." In *A Companion to Poe Studies*, ed. Eric W. Carlson, 388–402. Westport, CT, and London: Greenwood, 1996.

———. "Painful Erasures: Excising the Wild Eye from 'The Oval Portrait.'" *Poe Studies* 28 (1995): 1–6.

Krainik, Clifford. "The Sir Moses Ezekiel Statue of Edgar Allan Poe in Baltimore." In *Myths and Reality: The Mysterious Mr. Poe*, ed. Bejamin F. Fisher, 48–58. Baltimore: Edgar Allan Poe Society, 1987.

Krutch, Joseph Wood. *Edgar Allan Poe: A Study in Genius*. New York: Knopf, 1926.

Lacan, Jacques. "Seminar on 'The Purloined Letter.'" Trans. Jeffrey Mehlman. *Yale French Studies* 48 (1972): 39–72. Reprinted in *The Purloined Poe: Lacan, Derrida, and Psychoanalytic Reading*, ed. John P. Muller and William J. Richardson, 28–54. Baltimore and London: Johns Hopkins UP, 1988.

Laplanche, Jean, and Jean-Baptiste Pontalis, *Vocabulaire de la psychoanalyse*. Paris: PUF, 1967.

Lathrop, G. P. "Poe, Irving, Hawthorne." *Scribner's* (Apr. 1876): 799–808.

Lawrence, D. H. *Studies in Classic American Literature*. 1923. Reprint, London and New York: Penguin, 1977.

Lemire, Elise. "'The Murders in the Rue Morgue': Amalgamation Discourses and the Race Riots of 1838 in Poe's Philadelphia.'" In *Romancing the Shadow: Poe and Race,* ed. J. Gerald Kennedy and Liliane Weissberg, 177–204. New York: Oxford UP, 2001.

Leverenz, David. "Poe and Gentry Virginia." In *The American Face of Edgar Allan Poe,* ed. Shawn Rosenheim and Stephen Rachman, 210–36. Baltimore and London: Johns Hopkins UP, 1995.

———. "Spanking the Master: Mind-Crossings in Poe's Sensationalism." In *A Historical Guide to Edgar Allan Poe,* ed. J. Gerald Kennedy, 95–127. New York: Oxford UP, 2001.

Levin, Harry. *The Power of Blackness.* New York: Knopf, 1958.

Levine, Stuart. *Edgar Poe: Seer and Craftsman.* Deland, FL: Everett/Edwards, 1972.

Lewisohn, Ludwig. *Expression in America.* New York: Harper and Brothers, 1932.

"The Life and Poetry of Edgar Allan Poe." *Chambers's Edinburgh Journal* 19 (1853): 138.

Lindsay, Philip. *The Haunted Man: A Portrait of Edgar Allan Poe.* London: Hutchinson, 1953.

Livingston, James. "Subjectivity and Slavery in Poe's Autobiography of Ambitious Love." *Psychohistory Review* 21 (1993): 175–96.

Loewen, James W. *Lies Across America: What Our Historical Sites Get Wrong.* New York: New Press, 1999.

Long, Amelia Reynolds. *Death Looks Down.* Chicago and New York: Ziff Davis, 1945.

Long, David. "Poe's Political Identity: A Mummy Unswathed." *Poe Studies* 23 (1990): 1–22.

Longbella, Maren. "Poe, Corman, Todorov: The Fantastic from Literature to Film." M.A. Thesis. U of North Dakota, 1990.

Lowell, James Russell. *Lowell's Complete Poems.* New York: Houghton, 1898.

Lynen, John. *The Design of the Present: Essays on Time and Form in American Literature.* New Haven and London: Yale UP, 1969.

Lyons, Paul. "Opening Accounts in the South Seas: Poe's Pym and American Pacific Orientalism." *ESQ* 42 (1996): 291–326.

Mabie, Hamilton Wright. "Poe's Place in American Literature." *Atlantic* (Dec. 1899): 733–45.

Macy, John. *The Spirit of American Literature.* 1908. New York: Modern Library, 1913.

Magistrale, Tony, and Sidney Poger. *Poe's Children.* New York: Peter Lang, 1999.

Mankowitz, Wolf. *The Extraordinary Mr. Poe.* New York: Summit, 1978.

Marchand, Ernest. "Poe as Social Critic." *American Literature* 6 (1934): 28–43.

Matheson, T. J. "Poe's 'The Black Cat' as a Critique of Temperance Literature." *Mosaic* 19 (1986): 69–81.

Matthiessen, F. O. *American Renaissance.* New York and London: Oxford UP, 1941.

———. "Edgar Allan Poe." In *Literary History of the United States,* ed. Robert E. Spiller and Willard Thorp, 321–42. New York: Macmillan, 1948.

McGill, Meredith L. "Poe, Literary Nationalism, and Authorial Identity." In *The American Face of Edgar Allan Poe,* ed. Shawn Rosenheim, and Stephen Rachman, 271–304. Baltimore and London: Johns Hopkins UP, 1995.

McLuhan, H. Marshall. "Edgar Poe's Tradition." *Sewanee Review* 12 (1944): 24–33.

Meisel, Perry. "Introduction: Freud as Literature." In *Freud: A Collection of Critical Essays,* ed. Perry Meisel, 1–35. Englewood Cliffs, NJ: Prentice Hall, 1981.

Merivale, Patricia, and Susan Elizabeth Sweeney, eds. *Detecting Texts: The Metaphysical Detective Story from Poe to Postmodernism.* Philadelphia: U of Pennsylvania P, 1999.

Meyers, Jeffrey. *Edgar A. Poe: His Life and Legacy.* New York: Scribners, 1992.

Miller, Perry. *The Raven and the Whale: The War of Words and Wits in the Era of Poe and Melville.* New York: Harcourt, Brace and World, 1956.

Moldenhauer, Joseph J. "Murder as a Fine Art: Basic Connections between Poe's Aesthetics, Psychology, and Moral Vision." *PMLA* 83 (1968): 284–97.

Mooney, Stephen. "Poe's Gothic Wasteland." *Sewanee Review* 70 (1962): 261–83.

Moore, Charles Leonard. "The American Rejection of Poe." *The Dial* (Jan. 1899): 40–2.

Moran, John J., M. D. *A Defense of Edgar Allan Poe: Life, Character, and Dying Declarations of the Poet.* Washington, DC: William F. Boogher, 1885.

Morrison, Claudia C. *Freud and the Critic: The Early Use of Depth Psychology in Literary Criticism.* Chapel Hill: U of North Carolina P, 1968.

Morrison, Toni. *Playing in the Dark: Whiteness and the Literary Imagination*. Cambridge, MA: Harvard UP, 1992.

Moskowitz, Sam, ed. *The Man Who Called Himself Poe*. Garden City, NY: Doubleday, 1969.

Moss, Sidney P. *Poe's Literary Battles*. 1963. Reprint, Carbondale: Southern Illinois UP, 1969.

Mottram, Eric. "Poe's Pym and the American Social Imagination." In *Artful Thunder: Versions of the Romantic Tradition, in Honor of P. Vincent*, ed. Robert J. DeMott and Sanford E. Marovitz, 25–53. Kent, OH: Kent State UP, 1975.

Muller, John P., and William J. Richardson, eds. *The Purloined Poe: Lacan, Derrida, and Psychoanalytic Reading*. Baltimore and London: Johns Hopkins UP, 1988.

Mumford, Lewis. *The Golden Day: A Study in American Experience and Culture*. New York: Liveright, 1926.

Neimeyer, Mark. "Poe and Popular Culture." In *The Cambridge Companion to Edgar Allan Poe*, ed. Kevin J. Hayes, 205–24. Cambridge and New York: Cambridge UP, 2002.

Nelson, Dana D. *National Manhood: Capitalist Citizenship and the Imagined Fraternity of White Men*. Durham, NC and London: Duke UP, 1998.

———. *The Word in Black and White; Reading "Race" in American Literature, 1638–1867*. New York: Oxford UP, 1992.

Ostrom, John Ward. "Edgar A. Poe: His Income as Literary Entrepreneur." *Poe Studies* 15 (1982): 5.

Page, Thomas Nelson. "Authorship in the South Before the Civil War." *Lippincott's Magazine* 44 (1889): 105–20.

Pahl, Dennis. *Architects of the Abyss: The Indeterminate Fictions of Poe, Hawthorne, and Melville*. Columbia: U of Missouri P, 1989.

Parrington, Vernon Lewis. *Main Currents in American Thought. Vol. 2: The Romantic Revolution in America, 1800–1860*. New York: Harcourt, Brace, 1927.

Pease, Donald E. *Visionary Compacts: American Renaissance Writings in Cultural Context*. Madison: U of Wisconsin P, 1987.

Peeples, Scott. *Edgar Allan Poe Revisited*. New York: Twayne, 1998.

Person, Leland S. *Aesthetic Headaches: Women and a Masculine Poetics in Poe, Melville, and Hawthorne*. Athens and London: U of Georgia P, 1988.

———. "Poe's Philosophy of Amalgamation: Reading Racism in the Tales." In *Romancing the Shadow: Poe and Race,* ed. J. Gerald Kennedy and Liliane Weissberg, 205–224. New York: Oxford UP, 2001.

———. "Poe's Poetics of Desire: 'Th'Expanding Eye to the Loved Object.'" *Poe Studies* 32 (1999): 1–7.

Poe, Edgar Allan. *Collected Works of Edgar Allan Poe.* 3 vols. Ed. Thomas Ollive Mabbott. Cambridge, MA: Harvard UP, 1978.

———. *Essays and Reviews.* Ed. G. R. Thompson. New York: Library of America, 1984.

———. *The Letters of Edgar Allan Poe.* 2 vols. Ed. John Ward Ostrom. New York: Gordion, 1966.

Pollin, Burton. *Images of Poe's Works: A Comprehensive Descriptive Catalogue of Illustrations.* Westport, CT: Greenwood, 1989.

———. "Maria Clemm, Poe's Aunt: His Boon or Bane?" *Mississippi Quarterly* 48 (1995): 211–24.

———. "Poe in Art, Music, Opera, and Dance." In *A Companion to Poe Studies,* ed. Eric W. Carlson, 494–517. Westport, CT: Greenwood, 1996.

———. "A Posthumous Assessment: The 1849–1850 Periodical Press Response to Edgar Allan Poe." *American Periodicals* 2 (1992): 6– 50.

———. "Stoddard's Elegaic Sonnet on Poe." *Poe Studies* 19 (1986): 32–34.

———. "The Temperance Movement and Its Friends Look at Poe." *Costerus: Essays in English and American Language and Literature* 1972: 119–44.

———. "Woodrow Wilson and Julian Hawthorne on Poe: Letters from an Overlooked Scholaraly Resource." *Poe Studies* 12 (1979): 35.

Porte, Joel. *The Romance in America: Studies in Cooper, Poe, Hawthorne, Melville, and James.* Middletown, CT: Wesleyan UP, 1969.

Praz, Mario. "Poe and Psychoanalysis." *Sewanee Review* 68 (1960): 375–89.

Pruette, Lorrine. "A Psychoanalytical Study of Edgar Allan Poe." *American Journal of Psychology* 31 (1920): 370–402.

Quinn, Arthur Hobson. *Edgar Allan Poe: A Critical Biography.* 1941. Reprint, New York: Cooper Square, 1969.

Quinn, Patrick F. *The French Face of Edgar Poe.* Carbondale: Southern Illinois UP, 1957.

Rachman, Stephen. "'Es lässt sich nicht schreiben': Plagiarism and 'The Man of the Crowd.'" In *The American Face of Edgar Allan Poe,* ed. Shawn Rosenheim and Stephen Rachman, 49–87. Baltimore and London: Johns Hopkins UP, 1995.

————. "Poe, Secret Writing, and Magazine Culture: In Search of W. B. Tyler." Paper presented at the Modern Language Association Annual Meeting, New Orleans, LA, 27 Dec. 2001.

Ransom, John Crowe. "Freud and Literature." *Saturday Review of Literature,* 4 October 1924. Reprinted in *Freud: A Collection of Critical Essays,* ed. Perry Meisel, 39–44. Englewood Cliffs, NJ: Prentice Hall, 1981.

Reed, Lou. *The Raven.* Sire/Reprise (Warner Music Group), 2003.

Reilly, John E. "Poe and Imaginative Literature: A Study of American Drama, Fiction, and Poetry Devoted to Edgar Allan Poe or His Works." Ph. D. dissertation. U of Virginia, 1965.

————. "Poe in American Drama: Versions of the Man." In *Poe and Our Times,* ed. Bejamin F. Fisher, 18–31. Baltimore: Edgar Allan Poe Society, 1986.

————. "Poe in Literature and Popular Culture." In *A Companion to Poe Studies,* ed. Eric W. Carlson, 471–93. Westport, CT: Greenwood, 1996.

Renza, Louis A. *Edgar Allan Poe, Wallace Stevens, and the Poetics of American Privacy.* Baton Rouge and London: Louisiana State UP, 2002.

————. "Poe's Secret Autobiography." In *The American Renaissance Reconsidered: Selected Papers from the English Institute, 1982–83,* ed. Walter Benn Michaels and Donald E. Pease, 58–89. Baltimore and London: Johns Hopkins UP, 1985.

Reynolds, David S. *Beneath the American Renaissance: The Subversive Imagination in the Age of Emerson and Melville.* New York: Knopf, 1988.

Ricardou, Jean. "The Singular Character of Water." ("Le Caractère singulaire de cette eau," 1967.) Trans. Frank Towne. *Poe Studies* 9 (1976): 1–6.

Richard, Claude. "Poe and 'Young America.'" *Studies in Bibliography* 21 (1968): 25–58.

Richards, Eliza. "Lyric Telepathy: Women Poets, Spiritualist Poetics, and the 'Phantom Voice' of Poe." *Yale Journal of Criticism* 12 (1999): 269–94.

————. "'The Poetess' and Poe's Performance of the Feminine." *Arizona Quarterly* 55.2 (1999): 1–29.

Riddel, Joseph N. *Purloined Letters: Originality and Repetition in American Literature.* Ed. Mark Bauerlein. Baton Rouge and London: Louisiana State UP, 1995.

Ridgely, J. V. "The Authorship of the 'Paulding-Drayton Review.'" *PSA Newsletter* 20.2 (1992): 1–3, 6.

———. Review of J. Gerald Kennedy and Liliane Weissberg, eds., *Romancing the Shadow: Poe and Race. Edgar Allan Poe Review* 3.1 (2002): 70–72.

Robertson, John W., M.D. *Edgar A. Poe: A Psychopathic Study.* New York and London: Putnam, 1923.

Robinson, Douglas. *American Apocalypses.* Baltimore and London: Johns Hopkins UP, 1985.

Roppolo, Joseph Patrick. "Meaning and 'The Masque of the Red Death.'" *Tulane Studies in English* 13 (1963): 59–69. Reprinted in *Poe: A Collection of Critical Essays,* ed. Robert Regan, 134–44. Englewood Cliffs, NJ: Prentice-Hall, 1967.

Rosebud Graphic Classics, No. 1: Edgar Allan Poe. Mount Horeb, WI: Eureka Productions, 2001.

Rosenheim, Shawn. *The Cryptographic Imagination: From Edgar Poe to the Internet.* Baltimore: Johns Hopkins UP, 1997.

———. "Detective Fiction, Psychoanalysis, and the Analytic Sublime." In *The American Face of Edgar Allan Poe,* ed. Shawn Rosenheim and Stephen Rachman, 153–76. Baltimore and London: Johns Hopkins UP, 1995.

Rosenheim, Shawn, and Stephen Rachman, eds. *The American Face of Edgar Allan Poe.* Baltimore and London: Johns Hopkins UP, 1995.

Rosenthal, Bernard. "Poe, Slavery, and the *Southern Literary Messenger:* A Reexamination." *Poe Studies* 7 (1974): 29–38.

Rowe, John Carlos. *At Emerson's Tomb: The Politics of Classic American Literature.* New York: Columbia UP, 1997.

———. "Edgar Allan Poe's Imperial Fantasy and the American Frontier." In *Romancing the Shadow: Poe and Race,* ed. J. Gerald Kennedy and Liliane Weissberg, 106–126. New York: Oxford UP, 2001.

———. "Poe, Antebellum Slavery, and Modern Criticism." In *Poe's "Pym": Critical Explorations,* ed. Richard Kopley, 117–38. Durham and London: Duke UP, 1992.

———. *Through the Custom-House: Nineteenth-Century American Fiction and Modern Theory.* Baltimore and London: Johns Hopkins UP, 1982.

Rubin, Louis D. *The Edge of the Swamp: A Study in the Literature and Society of the Old South.* Baton Rouge and London: Louisiana State UP, 1989.

Saltz, Laura. "'(Horrible to Relate!)': Recovering the Body of Marie Roget." In *The American Face of Edgar Allan Poe,* ed. Shawn Rosenheim, and Stephen Rachman, 237–67. Baltimore and London: Johns Hopkins UP, 1995.

Sanford, Charles L. "Edgar Allan Poe." *Rives* 18 (1962): 1–9. Reprinted in *The Recognition of Edgar Allan Poe,* ed. Eric W. Carlson, 297–307. Ann Arbor: U of Michigan P, 1966.

[Savoye, Jeffrey.] "Poe's Death." 13 Nov. 1999. *Edgar Allan Poe Society of Baltimore.* Accessed 23 Jan. 2003. http://www.eapoe.org/geninfo/poedeath.htm.

Schecter, Harold. *Nevermore.* New York: Pocket Books, 1999.

Sevastakis, Michael. "A Dangerous Mind: Dario Argento's *Opera* (1987)." *Kinoeye,* 24 June 2002. 28 par. 16 May 2003. http://www.kinoeye.org/02/12/sevastakis12.html.

Shanks, Edward. *Edgar Allan Poe.* New York: Macmillan, 1937.

Silverman, Kenneth. *Edgar A. Poe: Mournful and Never-ending Remembrance.* New York: HarperCollins, 1991.

———. *Houdini!!!* New York: HarperCollins, 1996.

———, ed. *New Essays on Poe's Major Tales.* Cambridge and New York: Cambridge UP, 1993.

Sinclair, David. *Edgar Allan Poe.* Totowa, NJ: Rowman and Littlefield, 1977.

"Slavery." Review of *Slavery in the United States,* by J. K. Paulding; and *The South Vindicated from the Treason and Fanaticism of the Northern Abolitionists. Southern Literary Messenger* April 1836: 336–39.

Smith, C. Alphonso. *Repetition and Parallelism in English Verse.* New York: University, 1894.

Smith, Don G. *The Poe Cinema: A Critical Filmography of Theatrical Releases Based on the Works of Edgar Allan Poe.* Jefferson, NC, and London: McFarland, 1999.

Smith, Ronald L. *Poe in the Media: Screen, Songs, and Spoken Word Recordings.* New York and London: Garland, 1990.

Snell, George. "First of the New Critics." *Quarterly Review of Literature* 2 (1945): 333–40.

Stanard, Mary Newton. *The Dreamer: A Romantic Rendering of the Life-Story of Edgar Allan Poe.* Philadelphia: Lippincott, 1925.

Starrett, Vincent. "In Which an Author and His Character Are Well Met." In *The Man Who Called Himself Poe,* ed. Sam Moskowitz, 67–85. Garden City, NY: Doubleday, 1969.

Staton, Shirley. *Literary Theories in Praxis*. Philadelphia: U of Pennsylvania P, 1987.

Stedman, E. Clarence. "Edgar Allan Poe." *Scribner's* (May 1880): 122.

Stoddard, Richard Henry. "Edgar Allan Poe." *Harper's* (Sept. 1872): 557– 68.

[————.] "A Great Man Self-Wrecked." *The National Magazine* 1 (1852): 365.

————. "Life of Edgar Allan Poe." In *The Select Works of Edgar Allan Poe*. Household Edition, xv–clxxvii. New York: A. C. Armstrong, 1880. Reprinted in *The Works of Edgar Allan Poe*, Vol. 1, 1–200. New York: A. C. Armstrong, 1895.

————. "Memoir of Edgar Allan Poe." In *Poems by Edgar Allan Poe, Complete*, 1–99. New York: W. J. Widdleton, 1875.

Stovall, Floyd. *Edgar Poe the Poet: Essays New and Old on the Man and His Work*. Charlottesville: UP of Virginia, 1969.

Symons, Julian. *The Tell-Tale Heart: The Life and Works of Edgar Allan Poe*. New York: Harper and Row, 1978.

Tate, Allen. "The Angelic Imagination." *Kenyon Review* 14 (1952): 455–75. Reprinted in *The Recognition of Edgar Allan Poe*, ed. Eric W. Carlson, 236– 54. Ann Arbor: U of Michigan P, 1966.

————. "Our Cousin, Mr. Poe." *Partisan Review* 16 (1949): 1207–19. Reprinted in *Collected Essays*. Denver: Swallow, 1959.

Thomas, Dwight, and David K. Jackson. *The Poe Log: A Documentary Life of Edgar Allan Poe*. Boston: G. K. Hall, 1987.

Thompson, G. R. "Edgar Allan Poe and the Writers of the Old South." In *Columbia Literary History of the United States*, ed. Emory Elliott, 262–77. New York: Columbia UP, 1988.

————. *Poe's Fiction: Romantic Irony in the Gothic Tales*. Madison: U of Wisconsin P, 1973.

Three Tales by Poe. Puppetsweat Theater, dir. Robert Bresnick. Presented at International Poe Conference, Goucher College, Towson, MD, 4 Oct. 2002.

Treadwell, Sophie. *Plumes in the Dust*. Typescript. 1936. New York Public Library.

"Treehouse of Horror." *The Simpsons*, dir. Matt Groening. Fox Television, 24 Oct. 1990.

Trent, William P. "The Centenary of Poe." *Edgar Allan Poe: A Centenary Tribute* (1909), ed. Heinrich Ewald Buchholz, 45–54. London: Folcraft Library, 1972.

Van Doren, Carl. "Toward a New Canon." *The Nation* (13 April 1932): 429– 30.

Vines, Lois, ed. *Poe Abroad: Influence, Reputation, Affinities.* Iowa City: U of Iowa P, 1999.

The Voyage of Edgar Allan Poe. Minnesota Public Radio, 16 May 2003. http://music.mpr.org/features/0210_argento/poe_synopsis.shtml.

Walker, Ian. "The Poe Legend." In *A Companion to Poe Studies,* ed. Eric W. Carlson, 19–42. Westport, CT: Greenwood, 1996.

———, ed. *Edgar Allan Poe: The Critical Heritage.* London: Routledge, 1997.

Walsh, John Evangelist. *Midnight Dreary: The Mysterious Death of Edgar Allan Poe.* New Brunswick, NJ, and London: Rutgers UP, 1998.

Warner, Silas L., M. D. "Princess Marie Bonaparte, Edgar Allan Poe, and Psychobiography." *Journal of the American Academy of Psychoanalysis* 19 (1991): 446–61.

Watkins, Mildred Cabell. *American Literature.* New York: American Book, 1894.

Weekes, Karen. "Poe's Feminine Ideal." In *The Cambridge Companion to Edgar Allan Poe,* ed. Kevin J. Hayes, 148–62. Cambridge and New York: Cambridge UP, 2002.

Weiss, Susan Archer Talley. *The Home Life of Edgar Allan Poe.* New York: Broadway, 1907.

———. "Last Days of Edgar Poe." *Scribner's* (Mar. 1878): 707–16.

Wellman, Manly Wade. "When It Was Moonlight." In *The Man Who Called Himself Poe,* ed. Sam Moskowitz, 86–103. Garden City, NY: Doubleday, 1969.

Wendell, Barrett. *Literary History of America.* New York: Scribner's, 1900.

Whalen, Terence. *Edgar Allan Poe and the Masses.* Princeton, NJ: Princeton UP, 1999.

Whitman, Sarah Helen. *Edgar Poe and His Critics.* 1860. New York: Gordian, 1981.

Wilbur, Richard. "The House of Poe." In *The Recognition of Edgar Allan Poe,* ed. Eric W. Carlson, 255–77. Ann Arbor: U of Michigan P, 1966.

———. Introduction. *Poe: Complete Poems.* Laurel Poetry Series. New York: Dell, 1959.

———. *Responses: Prose Pieces, 1953–1976.* Ashland, OR: Story Line Press, 2000.

Wiles, Julian. *Nevermore! Edgar Allan Poe: The Final Mystery.* Woodstock, IL: Dramatic Publishing, 1995.

Williams, Michael J. S. "Poe's Ugly American: 'A Tale of the Ragged Mountains.'" *Poe Studies* 32 (1999): 51–61.

———. *A World of Words: Language and Displacement in the Fiction of Edgar Allan Poe*. Durham, NC, and London: Duke UP, 1988.

Williams, William Carlos. *In the American Grain*. 1925. Reprint, New York: New Directions, 1956.

Willner, Hal. "Producer's Notes." *Closed on Account of Rabies* (CD). Paris/ Mouth Almighty/ Mercury Records, 1997.

Winters, Yvor. "Edgar Allan Poe: A Crisis in the History of American Obscurantism." *American Literature* 8 (1937): 379–401. Reprinted in *The Recognition of Edgar Allan Poe,* ed. Eric W. Carlson, 176–202. Ann Arbor: U of Michigan P, 1966.

Winwar, Frances. *The Haunted Palace: A Life of Edgar Allan Poe*. New York: Harper, 1959.

Woodberry, George E. *America in Literature*. New York: Harper, 1903.

———. *Edgar Allan Poe*. Boston: Houghton, 1885.

———. *The Life of Edgar Allan Poe, Personal and Literary*. Rev. ed. 1909. Reprint, New York: Chelsea House, 1980.

———. *The Torch and Other Lectures and Addresses*. New York: Harcourt, 1920.

Worley, Sam. "*The Narrative of Arthur Gordon Pym* and the Ideology of Slavery." *ESQ* 40 (1994): 219–50.

Young, Philip. "The Earlier Psychologists and Poe." *American Literature* 22 (1951): 442–54.

Zimmerman, Brett. "Allegoria and Clock Architecture in Poe's 'The Masque of the Red Death.'" *Essays in the Arts and Sciences* 29 (Oct. 2000): 1–16.

Index

race, Poe's treatment of, 21, 93–
108, 111–14, 119–20
Rachman, Stephen, 116, 164 n
Ransom, John Crowe, 32
Ravenel, Annabel Lee, 164 n
reader-response criticism, 47–48
Redfield, J. S., 5, 7, 8
Redon, Odilon, 144
Reed, Ishmael, 144
Reed, Lou, 127, 144, 150–51,
154 n
Reilly, John E., 127, 152 n, 153 n,
154 n, 164 n
Renza, Louis, 89–90, 92 n
Reynolds, David S., 116
Reynolds, Jeremiah, 102, 158,
159; as a character in a fictional
work, 160
Ricardou, Jean, 83, 84
Richards, Eliza, 114–15, 116
Richardson, William J., 54, 59
Richmond, Nancy ("Annie"), 31
Riddel, Joseph N, 83, 85
Ridgely, J. V., 97–98, 99
Rilke, Rainer Maria, 51
Ripley, George, 3, 26 n
Robertson, John W., 33, 34
Robinson, Douglas, 85
Rocco, John, 154 n
Romanticism, 76, 77, 78, 83
Roppolo, Joseph Patrick, 81
Rosebud Graphic Classics, 138
Rosenheim, Shawn, 61, 62 n,
92 n, 151–52
Rosenthal, Bernard, 98–99
Rowe, John Carlos, 83, 84–85,
93–94, 97, 98, 99, 101, 103–4,
105, 108, 121 n
Royster, Elmira, 157, 161; as a
character in a fictional work, 133

Rubin, Louis, 20, 27 n, 121 n
Russell's Magazine, 8

Sade, Marquis de, 135
Salinger, J. D., 144
Saltz, Laura, 114
Sanford, Charles L., 91 n
Saturday Visiter, 133
Savoy, Jeffrey, 163 n
Schecter, Harold, 142, 143–44,
154 n
Schlegel, Friedrich, 82
Scott, Winfield, 114
Scribner's, 4, 12, 14, 17
Seawell, Molly Elliot, 20
Sevastakis, Michael, 150, 154 n
Shakespeare Society of New York,
17
Shanks, Edward, 158, 159
Shelton, Elmira Royster.
See Royster, Elmira
Sheridan, Lee, 136
Shew, Marie Louise, 163 n
Silverman, Kenneth, 39, 44, 50,
153–54 n, 163 n
Simms, William Gilmore, 22, 23,
101
Simpsons, The, 66, 126, 150
Sinclair, David, 158, 159
Smith, C. Alphonso, 19, 71, 72,
90, 128
Smith, Don G., 126, 149, 152 n,
153 n
Smith, Ronald, 127
Snell, George, 63, 91 n
Snodgrass, Joseph E., 155
socio-historical criticism, 93–121
Southern Literary Messenger, 2,
94, 98–100, 119, 143, 152
Spiller, Robert E., 71